ABOUT THE AUTHORS

Graeme Codrington is
who has worked with
companies. Together wit
TomorrowToday.biz, he
New Zealand to England
York, helping companie:
economy. He is passion
stand people. The Gener.

works used by TomorrowToday.biz, and one that Graeme is
particularly passionate about.

Graeme is a sought after presenter and consultant and,
together with Sue Grant-Marshall and Louis Fourie, already
has one best-selling book on the market, **Mind Over Money**.

Graeme has four degrees, including a Bachelor of Commerce and a research Masters. His research topics have
included the application of Generational Theory to South
Africa, and to local church environments. He is currently
completing a PhD in Business Administration, with majors in
Future Studies and Leadership.

Graeme has been married to Jane since 1991, and they have
two daughters, Amy and Hannah. They live in Johannesburg,
South Africa.

Graeme can be contacted at graeme@tomorrowtoday.biz.

Sue Grant-Marshall is a multi-award winning journalist who
worked on *The Argus* (Cape Town) and *The Star* (Johannesburg)
newspapers for eighteen years in various senior positions. She
was an assistant editor at a leading South African magazine,
FairLady, for a decade before she began freelancing. She co-
authored the book **Mind Over Money** with Graeme
Codrington and Louis Fourie. She was born and brought up in
the wilds of Botswana by her District Commissioner father,
Peter Cardross Grant and her mother, Mary. She and her
siblings, Jane, John and Annie, had an interesting and unusual
childhood. Sue is married to communications consultant Don
Marshall, and they have a teenage daughter, Amy. They live in
Johannesburg, South Africa.

mind the Gap

Graeme Codrington
and
Sue Grant-Marshall

PENGUIN BOOKS

PENGUIN BOOKS

Published by the Penguin Group
Penguin Books (South Africa) (Pty) Ltd, 24 Sturdee Avenue, Rosebank,
Johannesburg 2196, South Africa
Penguin Books Ltd, 80 Strand, London WC2R 0RL, England
Penguin Group (USA) Inc, 375 Hudson Street, New York, New York 10014, USA
Penguin Group (Canada), 90 Eglinton Avenue East, Suite 700, Toronto, Ontario, M4P
2Y3, Canada (a division of Pearson Penguin Canada Inc.)
Penguin Ireland, 25 St Stephen's Green, Dublin 2, Ireland (a division of Penguin
Books Ltd)
Penguin Group (Australia), 250 Camberwell Road, Camberwell, Victoria 3124,
Australia (a division of Pearson Australia Group Pty Ltd)
Penguin Books India Pvt Ltd, 11 Community Centre, Panchsheel Park, New Delhi
– 110 017, India
Penguin Group (NZ), 67 Apollo Drive, Mairangi Bay, Auckland 1310,
New Zealand (a division of Pearson New Zealand Ltd)

Penguin Books (South Africa) (Pty) Ltd, Registered Offices:
24 Sturdee Avenue, Rosebank, Johannesburg 2196, South Africa

www.penguinbooks.co.za

First published by Penguin Books (South Africa) (Pty) Ltd 2004
Reprinted 2005 (twice), 2006, 2007, 2008, 2010

Copyright © Sue Grant-Marshall & Graeme Codrington 2004

ISBN 978-0-143-02445-3

Typeset in 9.5 on 11pt Stone Serif by Compleat
Cover design: Flame Design, Cape Town
Printed and bound by CTP Book Printers, Cape Town

From Graeme to Jane
For my best friend and wife

From Sue to Don and Amy
For the two darlings who are my whole world

Acknowledgements

Graeme Codrington:

No book is ever written by the authors alone. Those around the writer must make sacrifices, especially during the final few days before the various deadlines approach. My wife Jane deserves the most praise in this regard, managing her life around me yet also helping to keep me in line.

To Amy and Hannah, my beautiful daughters, who remind me every day that I'm not from the young generation anymore.

To my business partners, Keith Coats, Barrie Bramley and Michael Mol, thanks for your encouragement and expert advice. And thanks, too, for taking my research and helping mould it into something world class over these past years. To the rest of the current TomorrowToday.biz team, Raylene, Karyn, Nicky, Lynda, Lezelle and Cherie, thanks for your support and assistance.

To my family, my mom and dad, Jane's parents, my brother and sister, and brothers and sister-in-law, my grandmothers, and other extended family, who represent every generation and have provided me with many reasons to understand the generations, thank you for your involvement in my life.

To the many friends who have encouraged me to write this book.

To Sue Grant-Marshall, my long-suffering Boomer friend and co-author.

Finally, to God, my Father, who continues to give me insight and inspiration.

This book is for all of you.

Sue Grant-Marshall:

This book wouldn't have happened without two people, my (Silent) husband Don Marshall and publisher Alison Lowry. Two books in two years – horrors! Visualise a spindly little bicycle (me) being pushed up a craggy, boulder-strewn rock face, bouncing, crashing but always being picked up, dusted down and enticed on by Don and Alison.

Don, thank you for the big shoulder, for listening at midnight, and for the scrumptious eats. You're the best.

Alison, I don't know why you believe in me but thank goodness you do.

Amy, my (mostly) Millennial daughter, your childhood, your teens and your wisdom inspired me. Maybe one day I will grow up to be like you. My mother, Mary Cardross Grant, Silent in more ways than one due to your stroke, thank you for the supportive sounds and smiles. Hilary Prendini-Toffoli, friends don't come better than you and your wit, intuition and sympathy are in the big league. My brother John, and my friend Bruce Howard, may I one day vindicate your faith in and support of me.

Thank you to all my dear, supportive friends who have 'been there' for me during a tricky time, but particular kisses go to Cherie Jones, Roz Wrottesley, Pauline Cuzen, Cathy Ririe, Tracy Going, Charlene Smith and Tembi Tambo.

Last, but not least to my co-author, the very Xer Graeme Codrington, whose vision this book was from the start. We made it – in spite of our generations!

Preface

Sceptical! That's how I felt when I first saw Graeme Codrington presenting his 'Meet the Generations' way back in May 1999. I'd never heard of Generation Theory or I'd have immediately identified him for what he is: an in-your-face Xer who knows far too much about computers and such stuff. What my (Silent) husband Don and I (Boomer) saw was a tall young man, wearing jeans and sneakers, fiddling with plugs and cords. On a board, set to one side, was a list of the generations: GI, Silent, Boomer, Xer, Millennial. A sentence alongside spelt out the characteristics of each one.

We studied it while Graeme fiddled. I later learnt that he does this on purpose because Silents and Boomers expect speakers to wear suits and stand to attention while they are being formally introduced. He likes to unnerve his audiences. He succeeds with us but not his own generation or the Millennials.

'Well, he's certainly hit the nail on the head with you,' I whispered to Don as I skimmed the Silent list which included: conservative, cautious, careful with money. 'He must have interviewed you for the Boomer list,' countered Don as he read: inquisitive, bossy, stylish.

An hour later the lights came on, revealing an astonished audience who lost no time in pelting Graeme with questions. Many a parent of a child who was at that school, St Mary's School for Girls, Waverley, Johannesburg, had begun to understand why their children behaved the way they did. Better still, they understood their own attitudes towards their kids. And the teachers in the audience gained valuable insight into why there was such a big gap between their world view and that of the youngsters they taught.

When I met Graeme some months later to interview him for a magazine, I arrived in what I soon learnt was typical Boomer gear: a suit and carrying a briefcase. He was wearing his trademark (Xer) jeans and sneakers. I chose the venue: a five star hotel with tinkling waiters and silver platters. 'You know you've chosen a typical Boomer venue, don't you?' he said. 'You love ostentation and attention.'

Then he did an Xer on me. He interviewed me before I could interview him. The way Xers interview their prospective bosses.

He told me he wanted us to write a book together.

The next time we met I chose a coffee bar and rocked up in jeans and sneakers. Since then we have always worked in coffee bars to the dismay of my husband Don. 'How can you concentrate when you're not sitting at a desk?' he asks, because Silents work in offices, at desks.

It's five years since Graeme and I met. We're both pretty typical of our generations. I am talkative, insatiably curious, want to know everything. He's understated, quiet.

He chooses to communicate only by SMS or email. I prefer to hear the tone in a voice.

We're protective of our generations. I fight for Boomers. He sticks up for Xers.

We've had our differences.

One was over which generation should 'own' film star Tom Cruise. Graeme rejected him for Xers. So did I for Boomers. 'He's obviously a Millennial icon,' mediated a journalist friend.

I wonder what *you* are?

Sue Grant-Marshall

Johannesburg, May 2004

Contents

Quick Info Boxes

1

Choose your Generation

Easy Reference Guide

We have decided to use the following dates for the generations:

- GI: Born 1900s to 1920s
- Silent: Born 1920s to 1940s
- Boomer: Born 1940s to 1960s
- Xer: Born 1960s to 1980s
- Millennial: Born 1980s to 2000s

Cuspers are the 'in-betweeners' who are born on the cusp of two generations and exhibit characteristics from both of them (see Chapter 9).

For a detailed explanation of how the generational dates are chosen, turn to the 'What is Generation?' chapter on page 10.

2

Introducing the Generations

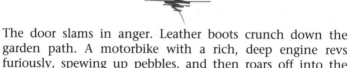

The door slams in anger. Leather boots crunch down the garden path. A motorbike with a rich, deep engine revs furiously, spewing up pebbles, and then roars off into the night. A teenager turns, white faced, to his girlfriend. 'I don't understand,' he says, 'I just suggested that dad would look better without the studs in his jacket and maybe,' he hesitates, 'it's time to cut the little ponytail.'

Across the street a fifty-something father is also staring at a slammed door through which his twenty-something daughter has just exited. He turns blankly to his wife. 'Why is she so cross? I know she's a brilliant accountant. I just suggested her job prospects would improve if she took the ring out of her nose.'

We're talking Boomer dad who won't believe Elvis is dead. We're discussing Xer daughter who says it's her intrinsic qualities that should count in a job market, not her extrinsic appearance. We're dealing with generational differences. This book is for them. If you don't understand why they are behaving in the manner they are, then this book is for you, too.

It's also for the boss who is bewildered and upset when the 25-year-old techno whizz-kid he's just hired wants the corner office, cellphone, company car and expense account *now*. He cannot get his head around the 'young upstart's' injured air of entitlement when his demands are rejected.

And if you've ever wondered why your 40-year-old daughter bought a sports car with the retirement annuity you spent years accumulating, instead of saving it for *her* daughter's education and you wonder what happened to the 'good old days when there were values...' read on. Ah yes, the good old days when values were 'solid' and time meant something. The time, for instance, that you spent in your job. Forty years of work during which you looked forward to retirement. A production manager in a printing company drew up a calendar which he hung on his office wall and spent the last three years of his career crossing off a day first thing each morning. To him it was a ritual but to his amazed staff it was a joke. Increasingly, today's twenty-somethings are surprised if they work for one company for as long as three years in *total*.

Nearly everyone has an attitude, values, expectations that are based on what life was like when they grew up. For you, what was happening then was the norm. Everybody did it. Everybody walked to school barefoot because their parents were too poor to buy shoes. Boys slicked back their hair with Brylcreem and tried to pout like Elvis. Girls curled their hair in 'rollers' sprayed with beer because setting lotion was too expensive. And then they backcombed or 'teased' it into huge, bouffant styles that their daughters crack up laughing at when they page through the yellowing family photograph album. Back then 'everybody' did it, so it wasn't amusing. It was the norm. Back then. When you were young.

Those shared experiences and times have bonded you with your cohorts, your classmates, your generation. As you say to them or your children, 'when we were young... ' or 'in the good old days', what you are actually saying is, 'I wish it was like that now'. It's seldom that anybody says, 'back in the good old days when every fourth child died'.

We often don't realise how much the phrase 'when I was young...' indicates who we are and how much the times in which we grew up influenced us. We are effectively saying 'understand me because... when I grew up... '

Once you gain insight into why your grandmother saves every tiny bit of string and collects old shopping bags (she's from the Silent generation) it won't irritate you so much. When your son bangs his head, and not his body, in time to that 'ghastly' music (he's an Xer), check out his friends' behaviour and you'll understand him better. Next time the young IT boff informs you, her manager, that she worked all night and would therefore like to take the afternoon off, you'll appreciate the reason behind her request. If your mother is never 'there' for you to babysit her grandchildren when you're at work the chances are that her friends behave the same way. They grew up at a certain time with values that have informed their attitude today.

Naturally, not everybody fits into generational 'boxes'. There are 55-year-olds who prefer grunge music to the Beatles. There are thirty-somethings who love wearing suits and ties and enjoy penning letters in longhand to their grandfathers.

The idea behind generational theory is not to pour everybody into a mould. Your age, your generation, is an attitude. The Boomer generation who are, roughly speaking, in their forties and fifties, are running the world right now. They are the presidents, company CEOs, judges, politicians, doctors and so on. The older GI and Silent generations are largely moving out of public life now, and the younger Xers and Millennials have not yet arrived in positions of power.

So, if you want to understand what's going on in the world, learn about the Boomers, however irritating you might find it. They're making laws and running the education system. They're the reason so many advertisements have 1960s tunes to sell cars, beer, greeting cards, financial services. Boomers 'invented' rock 'n' roll, remember, so it makes them feel at home and comfortable when 'their' music is played. And it *is* played, everywhere.

They also 'invented' drugs back in the hippie 60s. Now they're busy banning them, together with alcohol and tobacco. For Boomers sex was recreational. Today sex can mean death. Creating life while facing death. Makes you think.

Boomers are refusing to age. So they are being Botoxed, facelifted and hair-dyed. For them this is 'natural'. If you don't agree then you're the odd one out, not them. When Xer Graeme was twenty-two, he asked a 35-year-old Boomer to mentor him. The Boomer was stunned. He was too young to be a mentor, he stuttered. We all have moments throughout our lives when we realise we've moved on, into a new stage or age category, and that too is what generations is about. We share those moments with others our age and they, loosely speaking, result in us sharing a common mindset.

If we'd been told in the 1970s that today every home would have a computer in it, we'd have laughed, because computers were the size of a home back then. And if at the same time we were told that today we'd be using a little piece of metal and plastic, with no wires, that would enable us to speak to anyone, anywhere, anytime in the world, the reaction would have been incredulity. But Millennial kids have grown up knowing nothing else. They've never known a time when you had to book an international telephone call at a certain time and place and then wait for it to come through.

Technology is obviously a huge driver of change. But there are many other drivers that create change, such as parenting styles, music, movies, medicine and fashion. In this book we take you through some of those changes and reflect on the effect they had on the generations that lived through them. We discuss their implications for us today.

Coping with the Prohibition affected the GIs. Imagine meeting in a pub for your last drink ever! Food rationing and the daily threat of death had its impact on the Silent generation. The rebellious Boomers drank, drugged and made love, not war. The Xers wore jeans half falling down their backsides. The Millennials are turning out to be far more law-abiding than we have been for generations.

BUT these are all generalisations and there will always be exceptions to every 'rule'. So if by the time you get to the end of this book and haven't found the quintessential 'me', just chill and read the conclusion.

We are all unique. All individuals. Some more so than others. Some less so.

Generational theory is just one tool in a boxful that will help you understand how people around you act, and react, to life and events. This is not a 'how to' book. You can't use it as a mechanism to label everybody. It's not mechanistic. It's more like a filter. It will give you the flavour of the people with whom you're living, working, playing.

We'll tell you that Boomers wear their clothing labels, like Armani, Guess or Gap, on the outside of their clothes because they are into status symbols and like showing off. But not all Boomers do. Just enough of them to make it a trend. It's one that characterises a group of people who were born, roughly speaking, during the same twenty years.

Generation theory is not a scientific formula or a rigorously researched model. It is a dipstick into a period of time that produces people who tend, generally speaking, to think and act in a similar manner at certain times.

We have not set out to produce an academic tome on generations. There are masses of those and we suggest you read our bibliography to find books that will encourage you to really get stuck into the theory.

This is a layman's guide. We thought it was time to lift the lid, to create a portal that would allow ordinary people, and not just academics and business consultants, to use generation theory in their everyday lives. We want it to be useful, enlightening, thought provoking, even fun.

We know you won't always agree with us. We'd be disappointed if you did. The reason you're holding this book in your hands right now is that you're curious. People who question and probe aren't fobbed off by easy answers. Why should *you* be!

We have punctuated this book with easy to read lists and summaries that you could bounce off different generations to stimulate discussion. The first of these lists starts on the facing page. We've differentiated the lists to make them easy to distinguish from the rest of the text.

Where were you when... ?

It was glamorous American President John F Kennedy's assassination back in 1963 that froze the world in a moment of time. Most of us will never forget where we were when we heard the shocking news. It was a defining moment for us both as individuals and as members of a generation. Since then the question has been asked, repeatedly, can you remember **where you were when... ?**

GIs:

- Queen Victoria died, 22 January 1901
- The Wright brothers flew at Kitty Hawk, 17 December 1903
- The Titanic sank at 11.40pm, 14 April 1912
- World War I ended, 11 November 1918
- The Panama Canal was opened, 7 January 1914
- Women voted for the first time in a British general election, 14 December 1918

Silents:

- The BBC made its first radio broadcast, 14 November 1922
- Charles Lindbergh made the first solo flight across the Atlantic, 21 May 1927
- The stock market crashed, 29 October 1929
- The Hindenburg exploded, 6 May 1937
- War was declared on Germany, 3 September 1939
- Japan attacked Pearl Harbour, 7 December 1941
- The first atom bomb was dropped on Hiroshima, 6 August 1945
- VE (Victory in Europe) Day, 8 May 1945
- Israel declared itself a nation, 14 May 1948
- Gandhi was assassinated, 30 January 1948

Boomers:
- Mount Everest was conquered by Edmund Hillary and Tenzing Norgay, 29 May 1953
- Roger Bannister broke the four-minute mile, 6 May 1954
- Sixty-nine people were killed in the Sharpeville massacre, 21 March 1960
- Yuri Gagarin became the first human in space, 12 April 1961
- The Cuban Missile Crisis was averted, 27 October 1962
- John F Kennedy was assassinated in Dallas, 22 November 1963
- Robert Kennedy was assassinated, 5 June 1968
- Chris Barnard performed the world's first heart transplant, 3 December 1967
- Martin Luther King Jr was assassinated, 4 April 1968
- Neil Armstrong walked on the moon, 20 July 1969

Xers:
- Terrorists killed 11 Israeli athletes at the Munich Olympics, 5 September 1972
- Nixon resigned from office, 8 August 1974
- The first Concorde took flight, 22 November 1977
- Margaret Thatcher became England's first female prime minister, 3 May 1979
- John Lennon was assassinated, 8 December 1980
- Prince Charles married Lady Diana Spencer, 29 July 1981
- The Challenger space shuttle exploded on take-off, 28 January 1986
- A lone protester stood in front of tanks on Tiananmen Square, 4 June 1989
- The Berlin Wall came down, 9 November 1989

Millennials:

- Nelson Mandela was released from jail, 11 February 1990
- There were riots in Los Angeles after the Rodney King trial verdict, 30 April 1992
- OJ Simpson's not guilty verdict was announced, 3 October 1995
- Princess Diana died, 31 August 1997
- Airplanes flew into the World Trade Center, 11 September 2001
- The Columbia space shuttle exploded on re-entry, 2 February 2003
- The Madrid bombings shocked the world, 11 March 2004

3

What is 'Generation'?

generation: *n. whole body of persons born about the same time*
generation gap: *differences of opinion between those of different generations*
(The Oxford English Dictionary)

Generation cycle: *a four part process of history, spanning roughly 80 years, defined by successive 20 year cohorts of idealist, reactive, civic and adaptive characteristics*
(William Strauss and Neil Howe, *Generations*, 1991)

Why do we bother with generations at all? Throughout history we've had infancy, youth, middle age and old age, and they have adequately described the different stages, the changes, and the value shifts in our lives. So, why don't we leave it at that? The difference now is that time is moving too fast to allow us to do so. Tumultuous, life-changing events are impacting so strongly on a particular generation that it becomes branded or labelled for having lived in that era. The Boomers, for instance, are the Swinging Sixties generation that's defined for ever by rock 'n' roll, 'free love', hippies, peaceniks and landing on the moon. They never forget it. Worse still, they won't let you forget it.

The whole world knew that man had landed on the moon within minutes of Neil Armstrong's 'one small step...' but it took some parts of the world centuries to learn that Jesus Christ had arrived, and died. Likewise with Moses and Allah's prophet, Mohammed. The news of discoveries by explorers such as Christopher Columbus and Sir Francis Drake took months, sometimes years, to get back home.

The difference between *now* and *then* is that although teenagers have been considered wild throughout history, Egyptian and Greek elders could expect them to be wild in much the same manner that they had been. Today we can no longer expect that. We have to accept that our kids will grow up and **not** behave like us.

They will:

- go to schools we consider strange and unusual, studying subjects we've never heard of
- eat 'odd' foods
- sing different songs
- do jobs that didn't exist when we were young
- parent their kids and live in the kind of 'families' that bewilder us
- retire in a way that doesn't sound like retirement at all to us
- live in community structures we cannot begin to imagine

The times, they are a'changing

Historically, we have been hugely influenced by the cultures and the norms of the society in which we grew up. If that was in racy London or in Russia's grand St Petersburg, in a remote village in Cornwall or the vast American Midwest, an ancient Chinese village or a rustic Zulu kraal, we absorbed the thinking and the attitudes of the people amongst whom we lived.

Back in the 'good old days', before the dawn of the twentieth century, there was no need for a formal generational theory in order to get a handle on the mindsets, perceptions, value systems, attitudes and opinions of the era. Time moved slowly, change was measured and almost imperceptible. When a grandparent held her infant grandchild in her arms, she could safely imagine that the life of that child and its future would be much the same as they had been for her. The infant would be reared as she had been and would grow up subject to the same societal norms and restrictions.

While generations have existed since recorded humanity, the differences between each one, because of the slow pace of life, have not been as dramatic and as overt as they are now. It was the advent of the Industrial era, with its factories and production lines, that impacted massively on the pace of life.

In the twentieth century, further industrialisation, a shift to an information economy, and the present transition to an emotion/relationship economy have continued to create change. Rapid advances in technology and media combined with changing social mores have given each generation in the last century its own, unique set of experiences and values. As time and events began accelerating, the concept of generational identity has become more important to describe each new generation.

Today, few people live in a slow, measured manner. Most of us are running the helter-skelter race of our lives, trying to keep aboard the fast moving technology train that's revolutionising our world. No wonder we murmur, as each year draws to a close, 'Where did that one go? Why is time moving so fast?' Even children, who in the past were inured to the passage of time, are exclaiming at the rapid pace of life today.

The global century

Think back to the past, to communities that were virtually islands, living in relative isolation, each with its own dialect that made it almost incomprehensible to others living only 100 miles away. Children in many of them didn't even have their own 'children's clothes'. They were mini-adults and were dressed like little adults regardless of whether they were in rags or velvet. Slowly at first, and then faster and faster, steam trains, ships, trams, cars and airplanes on the one hand, and the telephone, radio, films, television and the Internet on the other, began to create global communities that shared global experiences. Events such as John F Kennedy's assassination, the moon landing, Woodstock, Princess Diana's death and 9/11 affected certain people of the same age and stage across the globe. So did the Wall Street crash, the Great Depression and World War I. Today, people across the world wear generational 'uniforms' such as blue jeans or baseball caps.

We are not saying that everybody who experiences an event thinks and acts in the same way. Every one of us is an individual, with a unique set of attitudes, culture, opinions and personality. All of these combine to give us a unique view of events, and they shape our reactions to circumstances. The way in which we process what is going on around us is known as our 'world view', or value system. It's this part of us that determines what is good or bad, normal or weird, right or wrong. This value system is largely in place by the time we reach our teens. Our behaviour may change in different settings but our underlying values (the reasons for our behaviour) are usually dominant throughout our adult lives.

Our value systems are shaped in our first ten years or so of life by our families, our friends, our communities, significant events and the general era in which we were born. The biggest influence on us is our parents and their parenting style is affected by the mores, standards and culture of the day. Even though we are all individuals, and experience unique influences on our developing value systems as we grow up, those of us reading this book have nonetheless all been exposed to them in the context of the twentieth century.

In that century, global forces were at work in a fashion unlike that of any other century. The extent of these is such that many people throughout the world have had similar experiences or have had to face similar situations at the same time. It's possible, because of this, to identify moments in the history of the twentieth century in different countries and cultures, where similar defining forces were brought to bear on families, communities and societies.

We are also able to generalise about the influence this may have had on the generation of young people who were growing up at the time.

This is why we can explain why many people who are similarly aged, and have been exposed to the same historical and cultural pressure, view the world in, generally speaking, the same way. We can look back at the way in which certain older, and still living generations, have grown up. We can draw conclusions about the shared experiences that have made them react to what's going on around them in a particular way. These are generalisations. But we accept and rely on other, even simpler, ones all the time – such as stereotypical views about men and women. Men are from Mars, women are from Venus. Men lie and women cry. Men fight, women nurture. Men won't ask for directions and women can't read maps. These generalisations don't apply to everybody but they do to many people. And so it is with generational history.

Generational theories

Probably the first person in modern sociology to identify the generational theory was sociologist, anthropologist, explorer and teacher Margaret Mead. She spent most of her life studying and documenting the tribes of New Guinea because she was fascinated by the way they lived their lives according to their ancient history and their ancestors. She was just as intrigued to see the transformation of these people as they came into contact with 'civilisation' for the first time.

She was able to watch, over the course of nearly five decades of direct involvement, as these tribes changed rapidly through the many stages of development (not necessarily 'progress') that had taken others several centuries to attain.

Even though some of her methods have recently been questioned (because she didn't follow strict methodologies) her results have proved to be most valuable in many sociological studies in different parts of the world.

She identified three different cultures or generations in the New Guinea peoples.

The **first** is the one referred to above in which a grandparent could be sure that her past would be the future of her grandchild. The infant would be reared in the same manner that she had been reared.

The **second** culture (or generation) was one in which old and young people alike could assume that it would be 'natural' for the behaviour of each new generation to differ from that of the preceding generation. In this culture, the older generation is still dominant in the sense that they set the style and define the limits within which the younger generation operates. When Margaret Mead studied the sixties society in America, she saw the worst of generation tensions – that between the GI and Silent generations and their highly rebellious, anti-establishment offspring, the Baby Boomers. The latter wore blue jeans, psychedelic socks, smoked pot and wore flowers in their long hair, men and women alike. This was a shock for the older generations who had expected their children to behave according to the same value systems with which they had grown up.

The **third** culture, or generation, that Margaret Mead identified is one where young people set the trends and are expected to differ from any of their elders in behaviour, attitude and value system. This is the current culture evident in most parts of the world today. She wrote, with tremendous foresight, 'nowhere in the world are there elders who know what the children know, no matter how remote and simple the societies are in which the children live. In the past there were always some elders who knew more than any children, in terms of their experience of having grown up within a cultural system. Today there are none.'

While Mead may have been the first person to classify the generation gap, she didn't popularise it. She was an academic sociologist, extremely popular in the sixties and widely read by students and academics at that time. The first to make generations 'pop' was an American, Morris Massey, who became a legend in the seventies with a lecture tour entitled, '*Who you are is what you were when...*' He was trying to help American professors to understand what we today have identified as the Baby Boom generation. The institutions that suffer the most from the generation gap are schools, churches, universities, armies, the workplace – anywhere where there's a big age and attitude difference between the people teaching or giving lessons or orders and those receiving them.

Morris Massey lectured on the generation gap in a manner that turned the academic world on its head because of the funky, brash style he adopted. But, it was still limited to the academic world. It took a book, written by Americans William Strauss and Neil Howe in 1991, called *Generations, The History of America's Future, 1584 to 2069*, to really put generations out there.

The book is a combination of sociology and political history. It is dense, heavy, academic stuff and runs to over 500 pages in small type. It was written as a textbook and as a summary for academics. It would frighten off the average reader and yet, surprisingly, it became a global best-seller.

Strauss and Howe realised they had hit a vital global nerve and followed up with *The Fourth Turning*, which is essentially a non-academic rewrite of *Generations*. In this they review, from a historical perspective, the cultures that have in the past had an idea of generational cycles, going back to Roman culture which talked about the Roman saeculum – a four generational cycle. They also mention ancient Chinese literature which shows the same understanding of a similar cycle in time.

Strauss and Howe look at ancient Jewish history (the Bible), especially the Book of Judges, and see four turns, or phases, in a cycle in which the people worship idols, God punishes them, the people cry out and they are led to freedom. God sends a leader to rescue and restore them. Then the cycle begins again with the people worshipping idols and so on. It's estimated that each of those cycles lasted between forty and eighty years.

It also relates to the rhythm of our four seasons and of the fourth year being a leap year. The cycle is inherent in all of nature and it may be inherent in all of history as well. So the cycles are not new. What is new is that we are noticing them.

Strauss and Howe say that since 1584 the Americans have had four cycles of generations, each with four phases and now they are at the 'turning' of the fourth cycle. They suggest that Generation X is the 13th generation in the fourth cycle, and so they called their third book *13th Gen: Abort, Ignore, Retry, Fail?* Then they moved on to the current 'baby' generation, the Millennials, and wrote their latest book, *Millennials Rising.*

A number of consultancies and companies have climbed aboard the generation gap bandwagon in recent years and have published books on generations, particularly about generations in the workplace. This is a popular field on which to focus as companies try to understand their workforces.

16

Many churches are ahead in generational theory because they realised, early on, what a huge generation gap exists between their young congregants and church leaders. Some progressive schools are also starting to take it seriously.

How to date the generations

Debate, usually academic, rages about the correct dating for the different generations. Sociologists have, sometimes fairly arbitrarily, decided on dates for a generation's beginning and end points because they feel it is so critical to mark these exactly. For instance, bearing in mind that it is cultural events, cataclysmic happenings and so on that affect a generation, you may not understand why 1942 is often referred to as a pivotal year for Americans. After all, it fell in the middle of World War II. But people born before that date were not eligible for the Vietnam draft and it affected them deeply.

American sociologists decided that babies born from 1983 onwards would be called Millennials as they would end their schooling in the new century. As generations are born roughly twenty years apart, that meant the Xers were given 1963 for their birth date because it is a halfway date between 1942 and 1983 and is not significant for anything much more than that. The Xers are defined more for what they are not than by what they are. They are caught between other important dates in American history – and not defined by being born at a significant time.

The world does not need to be dictated to by American dates, of course. Other countries need to work out significant dates and events in their own history. For instance, 1945 was an important year for Europe as World War II ended after seven hellish years and life slowly returned to normal.

The fall of the Berlin Wall in 1989 signalled a massive cultural shift for the divided East and West Germans. The same thing happened in China with the Tiananmen Square massacre in 1989. Maybe you could argue that when the British Labour Party came into power in the early 1990s this signalled a major cultural shift as Margaret Thatcher's rise to power had done two decades earlier. In South Africa, the first democratic elections in that nation's history in 1994 signalled a new era.

Some academics argue, tortuously, about certain dates and years affecting generations, to the extent they will debate endlessly the difference between 1942 and 1943 as cut-off dates, for instance. However, eras do overlap, and move gradually from one to the other. History defines certain times as 'icon moments' but you don't usually find that a date shifts a culture with immediate effect. Some cultures, in any case, change more slowly than others. Countries are not monolithic and it takes time for cultural changes to seep through. China and Africa have massive rural areas which exhibit very different cultures from their cities. America has its Midwest and Southern States which differ greatly from each other, and in turn, they differ from its Eastern seaboard states.

History is sometimes made in a moment, such as a nation walking through the Red Sea by night – but even then it took the Israelites forty years to settle down. What we're emphasising is that generational history is a generalisation and that it is not necessary to become too anxious about one particular date as the be-all and end-all for a generation. In fact, turn now to chapter 9 on Cuspers. You will note that if you fall near the end or the beginning of a generation, you are probably a Cusper and this position gives you a foot in each of those generations.

In conclusion, it is not surprising that America has led the 'generational way', as it does in so many other ways, with different countries following, some up to fifteen years behind it. In general though, as the world has moved into the twenty-first century, the trends that influence and shape generations have increasingly coalesced.

For the purposes of this book we have decided on the following dates for the generations, in order to simplify matters:

- GI: Born 1900s to 1920s
- Silent: Born 1920s to 1940s
- Boomer: Born 1940s to 1960s
- Xer: Born 1960s to 1980s
- Millennial   Born 1980s to 2000s

Cuspers are the 'in-betweeners' who are born on the cusp of two generations, in the 'overlaps' of the dates outlined above, and exhibit characteristics from both of them (see chapter 9).

Generations in different countries:

Note your birth date in the following generational table and use it as a rough guide:

Generation	USA	Europe/ UK	Japan	South Africa
GIs	1900 – 1923	1900 – 1918	1900 – 1925	1900 – 1929
Silents	1923 – 1942	1918 – 1945	1925 – 1945	1930 – 1949
Boomers	1943 – 1962	1946 – 1965	1945 – 1965	1950 – 1969
Xers	1963 – 1983	1966 – 1984	1966 – 1985	1970 – 1989
Millennials	1984 – 2001 …	1985 – 2001 …	1986 – 2001 …	1990 – 2005 …

Inventions of the twentieth century:

Our five generations – GIs, Silents, Boomers, Xers and Millennials – have lived during the fastest moving century the world has ever known. During the past hundred years we walked on the moon, used the atom bomb and discovered the secrets of DNA. Television, the Internet and cellphones turned the planet into a global village.

The following list is based on an idea from the International Express which in 1999 asked Stephen Van Dulken, a curator at the British Library Patents Office, to compile a definitive list of the top hundred inventions of the twentieth century. From the things that shaped the twentieth century, like the airplane and computer, to those that may define the way we live in the next hundred years, they are a fascinating record of what the different generations invented.

1900s
Vacuum cleaner
Meccano
Safety razor
Disc brakes
Vacuum flask
Airplane
Air conditioning
Washing machine
Tea-bag
Teddy bear

1910s
Neon lighting
Formica

Synchronised machine-gun fire from aircraft (to shoot
through turning rotors), which revolutionised aerial combat
Supermarket
Stainless steel
Assembly line
Crossword puzzles

1920s
Traffic lights
Self-winding wristwatch
Television
Synthetic insulin
Theremin, the first electronic musical instrument
Autopilot
Power steering
Rapid freezing of food
Bread slicing machine
Transparent adhesive tape
Aerosol can
Adhesive bandages

1930s
Jet engine
Monopoly
Catseyes
Radar
Parking meter
Polythene
Photocopier
Nylon
Teflon
Electronic hearing aid

1940s
Ballpoint pen
Silly putty

Microwave oven
Tupperware
Computer (ENIAC)
Hologram
Transistor
Bell telephone
Instant photography
Bar codes
Bikini
Nuclear reactor and bomb
Polaroid camera
Frisbee
Scrabble

1950s
Colour television and the remote control
Disposable nappies/diapers
Oral contraceptive (released to the market in 1961)
Velcro
Floatglass, a cheap, high-quality method of
manufacturing glass
Hovercraft
Lego
Microchip
White correction fluid (for typists)
Credit card
Laser

1960s
Pacemaker
Lava lamp
Ring-pull can
Computer mouse
Waterbed
Windsurfer

Kevlar, highly strong substance useful for bulletproof
vests to bridge cables
Baby Buggy
ATM – automated teller machine for banks
VCR – video cassette recorder

1970s
Magnetic resonance imaging, a vital medical diagnostic
tool
CAT Scan (computed tomography scan)
Snowboard
Prozac
Email
Rubik's Cube, the puzzle that swept the world
Smart card
Artificial heart
Personal stereo
Post-it notes
Personal computer
CDs – compact discs

1980s
Wind energy
Walkman
DNA (genetic) fingerprinting
Widget, the secret behind cold beer with a perfect head
straight from the can
Video games
Anti-theft devices for cars
Solar energy
Mobile phones
Laptop computer

1990s
Viagra
Animal cloning technology

Fuel cells, using a combination of hydrogen and oxygen to obtain power.
PDA – personal digital assistant
DVDs – digital video discs
Digital cameras and memory sticks
HTML webpages (www)

2000s
Broadband Internet
Space tourism
Motorised scooter
Camera phone
Quadraphonic cellphones

*Based on an idea from the International Express,
19 September 2000
Also see http://corporate.britannica.com/press/inven-
tions.html*

4

SJ (Hero) Generation: Born 1900s to 1920s

Attitude: We must all agree, all work the same way, and all look the same

Likes: Firm leadership and doing your civic duty

Dislikes: Wimps, whingers and slackers

Heroes: Superman, Biggles

Movie stars: Charlie Chaplin, Katherine Hepburn, Spencer Tracey, Kirk Douglas, Marilyn Monroe

Sports stars: Roger Bannister, Babe Ruth, Juan Manuel Fangio, Don Bradman, Gorgeous Gussie, Jack Dempsey, Arnold Palmer

Music: Classical, opera, camp fire singalongs

Characteristics: Gallantry, civic mindedness

Momentous events:

Marconi sent the first transatlantic radio signal, 12 December 1901

The Wright Brothers became the first to fly an aircraft, 17 December 1903

The unsinkable Titanic sank on its maiden voyage when it hit an iceberg, 14 April 1912

World War I broke out in 1914 and ended four years and nine million dead people later

The Russian Revolution erupted in 1917

Henry Ford gave the world wheels through his mass production of cars

Albert Einstein developed his Special Theory of Relativity and ushered in the atomic age, 1905

Emily Pankhurst went to jail during her fight for women's rights and the vote, 1913

The Panama Canal was opened after twenty-three years of construction, 1914

Childhood

The GIs were born at a time when men were strong and women were fair, and fainted from time to time, probably in between giving birth to families of twelve and more children. During the GI's childhood the average life expectancy of First World countries was only forty-seven years of age, so you can imagine what it was like in less well off countries.

It was the norm in developed countries for birth to take place at home, and it is astonishing to learn today that 90 per cent of all American physicians had no university education. They went to medical schools which were condemned in the press and by the government as 'substandard'. No wonder then that childbirth was a dangerous experience and often resulted in the death of both baby and mother.

Some medical authorities warned that professional seamstresses were apt to become sexually aroused by the steady rhythm, hour after hour, of the sewing machine's foot pedals. They recommended slipping bromide, which was thought to diminish sexual desire, into the women's drinking water.

Most women, back then, only washed their hair once a month, using borax or egg yolks for shampoo.

Antibiotics and insulin hadn't been discovered yet and sticky tape, crossword puzzles and beer in a can hadn't been invented. But cars (just) had, although there were less than 10 000 cars in the United States and the maximum speed was 20 kilometres an hour. There were only 280 kilometres of paved roads for them to travel on. For the rest it was dirt tracks or horses. That didn't bother most people as the automobile, as it was called, was still considered a most hazardous means of travel.

Much of London was lit by gaslight and the tallest structure in the world was the Eiffel Tower.

Most middle class households in Europe, Britain and America had at least one full time servant or domestic worker and the upper classes usually had an army of them... between twenty and forty servants were not unusual.

Marijuana, heroin and morphine were all available over the counter in drugstores or pharmacies. Indeed, one pharmacist of those times said, 'Heroin clears the complexion, gives buoyancy to the mind, regulates the stomach and the bowels, and is, in fact, a perfect guardian of health.' Back then, Coca-Cola contained cocaine instead of caffeine.

In their youth GIs became the world's first 'teenagers', a term that was specifically coined for them. They were also the first Boy Scouts and Girl Guides. New playgrounds were built for them, special 'protective' foods were processed for them and vitamins were popped regularly into their growing bodies. By 1914 almost every state in America had laws that prevented kids below fourteen from working, and this trend spread rapidly around the world. There were significant improvements in schooling and for the first time in history there were more teenagers in school in First World countries than there were out of it.

The prevailing ethos was that good kids 'work hard, play hard and everybody gets rewarded'. The feeling of 'community' was spurred on by GI kids listening to the same radio shows and watching the same early movies and the newsreels that preceded the movie. Prior to this, apart from political rallies and community events, there was not a lot that a whole generation did together, and remembered doing together in later life.

As we discuss in chapter 10 on Parenting, it's the early years in our lives that have the greatest effect on us as adults and, therefore, on a generation's characteristics as it grows up. The GIs were taught, as a pampered, cherished generation, that the harder you worked, the more you were rewarded. The classic GI examples of leaders who adopted this attitude are legends such as Nelson Mandela, John F Kennedy, Martin Luther King, Margaret Thatcher and Ronald Reagan.

Adulthood

The dominant characteristic of the GI generation is their civic mindedness. This stems from their fairly protected youth, the result of their parents seeing the ill effects of leaving children to their own devices on the 'lost' generation that preceded the GIs. Society determined that this new generation of youth would grow up clever and cooperative.

The GIs have been given their name by generational American gurus William Strauss and Neil Howe because it is indicative of the 'general issue' or 'government issue' clothes that became synonymous with the soldiers of both World Wars. It also sums up, nicely, their attitude of community and regularity.

The GIs formed the manpower component of the engine that beat the combined crisis of World War II and the Great Depression. It was their ability to work as a team, to fight together as a unit and obey hierarchical chains of command, which enabled them to overcome those devastating events that tore apart the world as they knew it, and their lives. No wonder they believe that it's 'good' and 'normal' for people to all agree, to work the same and even to all look the same.

Many of the twentieth century's most powerful politicians came from this generation. They include Nelson Mandela, Margaret Thatcher, Ronald Reagan and John F Kennedy. The last described his generation in his inaugural address as 'born in this century', because he was the first American president to be born in the twentieth century. GI presidents dominated the White House for most of it.

It was the GIs who built gleaming new suburbs in the aftermath of World War II as they encouraged people to move out of crowded city centre tenements and bring up their families in houses with gardens. GIs invented miracle vaccines that kept alive thousands of people who had previously died from their ailments. Edmund Hillary and Tenzing Norgay scaled Mount Everest, the Russians achieved their vision of getting into space with their sputniks and launched Yuri Gagarin, the first man in space. The Americans launched moon rockets and achieved the ultimate dream of landing a man, Neil Armstrong, on the moon.

Those were stirring times, visionary times, and although they were marred by the assassinations of President John F Kennedy, his brother Robert, and black civil rights leader Martin Luther King Jr, this does not detract from the extraordinary energy and determination that this generation displayed.

Who they are today

GIs are concerned that they dress appropriately and behave well. Their gentlemanly approach to life sees this generation even putting on a suit and tie to pop down to the local store to buy the Sunday papers... well, at least a jacket. Women wear neat frocks with tidy hair and try to behave with becoming decorum at all times.

There are many of this generation who are spry and fit, taking long walks to keep themselves that way and living in retirement homes where they play bowls, bridge and have music hall song and dance evenings.

They have not forgotten that back in their young days, women might not have had the vote but they had fun. Pin-up pictures taken in 1916 of Gypsy Rose Lee, one of the first dancers to make the leap into mainstream theatre in sequinned, feathery outfits that leave little to the imagination, easily outshine Britney Spears or Madonna.

Now, in the latter days of their lives, some legendary GIs are still going strong. John Glenn, the first person to man an American orbital mission, became the oldest person in space at seventy-seven when he embarked on a nine day space shuttle mission in 1998. Former heads of state Nelson Mandela and Jimmy Carter are well into their eighties but continue to give of themselves as they help the less fortunate of the world.

It is interesting that the GI generation, fussed over in their youth, are the richest ever generation to reach the age they have. Of course there are many sick, frail and poor elderly people. But as a generation that has worked hard, saved hard and lived fairly frugal lives, they are better off than the generations that preceded them. They have been able to pocket most of the retirement benefits they earned, which is a great deal more than their grandchildren will be able to do.

5

Silent Generation: Born 1920s to 1940s

Attitude:	Pay your dues, work hard
Likes:	Security, stability
Dislikes:	Debt, borrowing, upstart young people
Heroes:	Winston Churchill, Nelson Mandela, Mahatma Gandhi
Movie stars:	Clark Gable, Vivien Leigh, Ava Gardner, Ginger Rogers
Sports stars:	Gary Sobers, Gary Player, Jack Nicklaus, Joe Namath
Music:	Big bands, Frank Sinatra, Glenn Miller
Characteristics:	Reserved, stoic, clean living, gentlemanly

Momentous events:

Alexander Fleming discovers penicillin, 1928

Start of the Great Depression on Black Tuesday, 29 October 1929 in New York

President FD Roosevelt launches the 'New Deal' to combat the Depression, 1933

Crash of the Hindenburg (the German Zeppelin), 6 May 1937

Television gets its first public outing at New York World's Fair, 1939

The start of World War II, September 1939

The Blitz: fifty-seven consecutive nights of German planes bombing London, from 7 September 1940

Japan bombs Pearl Harbour, forcing America into World War II, 7 December 1941

D-Day Invasion of Normandy, 6 June 1944

First atomic bombs dropped on Hiroshima and Nagasaki in Japan, August 1945

VE (Victory in Europe) Day on 8 May 1945
Horrors of the Nazi concentration camps are exposed, 1945
United Nations and International Monetary Fund formed to govern
global affairs, 24 October 1945
Publication of The Common Sense Book of Baby and Child
Care, *by Dr B Spock, 14 July 1946*

Childhood

The Silent generation arrived on earth during some of its
darkest ever hours – World War II and the Great Depression.
They lived through times that were so depressing that it is
hard for their materialistic Boomer children and spoilt, cushy-
living Xer and Millennial grandchildren to imagine what they
endured in their childhoods and teens.

A trip to the Imperial War Museum in London is a good place
to start for anyone who wants to catch a glimpse of their
difficult start to life. There you will see posters exhorting the
war-weary Brits to save every scrap of food for making stews.
'Better pot luck with Churchill today than humble pie with
Hitler tomorrow,' they urged. Everything was saved, no jacket
was too old to mend, no dress too dull to wear, and women's
magazines were full of tips to brighten up drab outfits. You
could learn to be a dab hand at putting patches on trousers
and the worn elbows on coats. Imagine *Harper's Bazaar* or
Cosmopolitan carrying fashion features like that today!

And even when you did manage to save up enough ration
coupons to go shopping, there were signs everywhere
declaring: 'Don't take the squander bug when you go
shopping'.

Indeed, the word 'squander' (to waste) is so outdated and
unused that it's virtually disappeared from our vocabulary.
That tells a story in itself. People everywhere were encouraged
to grow their own food. Posters depicting women with shovels
urged Britain to 'Dig for Victory'.

Imagine walking to work today and seeing posters of women
in factories, blaring 'These women are doing their bit. Learn to
make ammunitions'. Depending on your generation, that's
what your mother or grandmother might have been doing if

she grew up in Britain, Europe or America. In the latter country, posters of 'Rosie the Riveter' in a factory urged women to join her. It conjures up a very different picture in your mind from the white haired, quaint old lady you now know.

Silents were raised by serious and pragmatic parents during World War II and the Depression because they wanted to ensure the safety of their children during these terrible crises. In Britain and many parts of Europe city children were separated from their parents and evacuated to the safer countryside. Many of them will never forget milling around railway stations with placards around their necks bearing their names and that of their schools.

These sad children had to accept all this, toe the line, and welcome stability and consistency, and so they tended to be withdrawn, cautious, unimaginative and unadventurous. And it helps you to understand why the Silent generation is indeed so 'silent'. They grew up in a time when children 'should be seen and not heard'.

As they grew up, they saw banks and businesses failing in the aftermath of the Great Depression which began on Black Tuesday, 29 October 1929 in New York, and so they learnt not to trust others for their security. To this day they are self-reliant, something they regard as a virtue, and find it difficult to spend money, whether it is buying themselves a new outfit or financing large business projects, because they are fearful of getting into debt. They also believe that it's 'good' and 'normal' to work hard. In fact, they believe they can achieve anything by sheer hard work. They are suspicious of those who make money by luck or by gambling. Not surprisingly, they imbibed along with mother's milk that it's not much good complaining about 'one's lot in life' and accepted that the 'right thing to do' was to knuckle down and just get on with it.

Their early lives were not filled with earthly pleasures but they do have deep romantic streaks as people living in times of war and conflict often do. This romanticism, mixed with a feeling of duty to work, continues to define this generation. It has always felt a little overlooked and 'missing out' because it was too young to make any real contribution during World War II, and it was too old for Vietnam or the Falklands wars. Too young to be World War heroes and too old to be the swinging, flower power hippies.

They were caught between the thirty-something returning war heroes and the coddled, post-war Baby Boomers.

Adulthood

In the 1950s and 60s, the Silent young adults entered a world of rising prosperity and tremendous job opportunities that had not existed for their parents. They attended university in unprecedented numbers, emerging with more degrees than any other generation on earth ever had. Only the Boomers have yet managed to exceed this. Then they moved into the gleaming suburbs that their GI elders were building and raised their families in houses with gardens and dogs.

Wives who might have, if they were old enough, worked in ammunition factories, or been Allied spies, or had mothers who had been, were exhorted by *Good Housekeeping* magazine to follow 'The Good Wife's Guide'. Here are some of the tips, taken from their 13 May 1955 issue:

- Greet your husband with a warm smile and show sincerity in your desire to please him.
- Listen to him. Let him talk first. Remember his topics of conversation are more important than yours.
- Make the evening his. Never complain if he comes home late or goes out to dinner, or other places of entertainment without you, or even if he stays out all night. Count this as minor compared with what he might have gone through that day. Instead, try to understand his world of strain and pressure and his very real need to be at home and relax.
- Prepare the children, wash their hands and faces and change their clothes. They are little treasures and he would like to see them playing the part.
- At the time of his arrival, eliminate all noise of the washer, dryer or vacuum cleaner. Try to encourage the children to be quiet.
- A good wife always knows her place.

In the seventies, the Silent generation produced talk shows like Phil Donahue's one, which allowed people to communicate with each other at an 'ordinary' level (although we're certainly not talking Jerry Springer yet!). Those shows led on to a generation of therapists who counselled Boomer and Xer kids to 'open up' and vent their feelings.

Who they are today

Now the Silent generation is entering its elderhood with unprecedented affluence, a 'hip' and friendly style towards younger generations that enables them to stay in touch with young people. They do so in a way that the GI generation has not been able to, tucked away as so many of them have opted to be in their protected sunshine villages and clubs.

Silents are the most affluent elderly in recorded history although they will, in time, be outdone by the Boomers. In America over 80 per cent of them are homeowners, they have 43 per cent of all discretionary income, 75 per cent of America's wealth and they own 80 per cent of savings and loan deposits and a large proportion of the equities.

They continue to work hard, even in retirement, are frugal and save every cent they can. The Silent generation father of a friend of Sue's had millions in the bank but refused to buy himself a new pair of spectacles. He simply taped the broken ones together. He wouldn't buy himself a new car although his old one had so many dents that it resembled a war zone and when a crack appeared across the windscreen – that's where it stayed. One of his keenest joys in life after his devoted wife died was a whisky, but he bought the cheapest he could. Weeks before his death, his Boomer son begged his bedridden father to allow him to buy him a more expensive whisky. He grudgingly coughed up a few cents more for one brand better – but not the best. He went to his grave happy that he had saved those few extra cents.

Sue's Silent generation mother served her GI husband tinned pilchards and packet mashed potato, never ever threw away scraps of food, re-sewed Sue's 20-year-old curtains to fit her cottage and wore the same blue jeans for at least ten years. She cut her own hair and that of the entire family for years. It's not surprising to learn that she grew up in war-torn London.

Frugal the Silent generation may be, but that does not mean they're not having fun. As they've reached retirement many have mellowed. Indeed, as they've aged, having survived those early rough, tough years, and worked hard all their lives, some of them are, at last, learning to relax. They're taking world cruises, hiking along mountain and sea trails, playing tennis and bowls, going on cycling and barge holidays through Europe. And why not? They are the healthiest ageing generation the world has seen. They are financially comfortable with adult children finally capable of looking after themselves.

In fact, many a thirty-something mom and dad, struggling to hold down jobs, care for their babies and toddlers and lead a balanced life, wishes their carefree parents would stop cycling, hiking and cruising and just stay home for a while to babysit. But the days of sweet old ladies who knit in their rocking chairs and doddery granddads who smoke pipes in leather-elbowed jackets while they play tiddlywinks with toddlers have almost been relegated to a bygone era. Today's Silents are out having the time of their lives. They deserve it.

6

Baby Boomer Generation: Born 1940s to 1960s

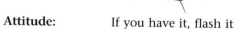

Attitude:	If you have it, flash it
Likes:	Shopping, ostentation, winning, leading, vision
Dislikes:	Paying off debts, ageing
Heroes:	Neil Armstrong, Richard Branson, Princess Diana, Betty Friedan
Movie stars:	Robert Redford, Paul Newman, Meryl Streep, Susan Sarandon, Roger Moore, Harrison Ford, Arnold Schwarzenegger
Sports stars:	John McEnroe, Billie Jean King, Michael Jordan, Michael Schumacher, Muhammad Ali, Martina Navratilova, Chris Evert Lloyd, Mark Spitz, Lance Armstrong, Dan Marino, Steve Redgrave
Music:	Rock 'n' Roll, Elvis, The Beatles, The Rolling Stones, Bob Dylan, Cliff Richard, Abba, Queen, Cilla Black, Janis Joplin, Buddy Holly
Characteristics:	Talkative, bossy, inquisitive, stylish, competitive

Momentous events:

Mau Mau Revolt, Kenya, October 1952

Coronation of Queen Elizabeth II of England, 2 June 1953

Edmund Hillary and Tenzing Norgay are the first to summit Mount Everest, 29 May 1953

Rosa Parks refuses to give up her seat to a white person, 1 December 1955

Russia launches the first satellite, Sputnik, 4 October 1957

The female contraceptive Pill is launched in 1960, changing the world forever

Russian cosmonaut Yuri Gagarin becomes the first man in space, 12 April 1961

Russia blinked first in the Cuban Missile Crisis, November 1962

Bay of Pigs, Cuba, starting on 17 April 1961

Assassination of John F Kennedy, in Dallas, Texas, 22 November 1963

Nelson Mandela was sentenced to life for high treason on 12 June 1964

The Beatles took America by storm with 73 million watching them on TV, 9 February 1964

The world's first heart transplant by South African Christiaan Barnard, 3 December 1967

Martin Luther King assassinated, 4 April 1968

Robert Kennedy assassinated, 5 June 1968

Neil Armstrong became the first man to land on the moon, 20 July 1969

The war in Vietnam raged from 1965 to 1975

The 16 June 1976 Soweto riots in South Africa spelt the beginning of the end of apartheid

Childhood

Imagine, or remember, the supersonic b-o-o-o-o-m of Concorde, that graceful, gleaming icon of the Baby Boom generation and you will have some idea of the impact and the power of the largest ever generation to touch down on our globe. Nobody could ignore Concorde, for wherever it landed, people rushed to glimpse its silver sleekness. The Boomers' arrival had much the same impact as they were born at the end of World War II, in numbers that the world struggled to handle. Hospitals ran out of labour wards, nappy manufacturers were depleted of stock, and schools couldn't build classrooms fast enough to cater for the waves of children that surfed into their playgrounds.

They arrived with a bang and have been noisy, attention-demanding (and receiving) ever since. Every single stage of their life has been era-defining and trendsetting. When

Boomers decide to do something, they do it big. Nobody can afford not to notice them, both literally and figuratively.

They were born into boom times when the dreariness of the war-rationed years was fading and the world scrubbed its collective bruised and battle-scarred face. As soldiers marched home, determined to put the horror of 50 million dead, the bomb-devastated cities and towns, and shell-shocked families and communities behind them, what better way to do it than through new life?

And so the lusty infants grew into kids who tore into the 1950s and 60s, indulged by their parents. They declared to their offspring, 'We want you to have all the things that we never had.' Although much of that was materialistic, it was also freedom. A freedom that children hadn't experienced before and haven't really enjoyed since, in our crime-ridden, sexually abused, drug-crazed and permanently anxious society.

Back then, infant cots were covered with lead-based paint and had no padded sides to stop heads getting stuck between the slats. Kids drank water from the garden hosepipe, ate worms, licked mud pies and chomped raw carrots they pulled from the family vegetable patch. They slept on their backs, their sides or their stomachs and lived to see the sun rise. They would leave home in the morning and play all day, returning dirty, mud-caked and sunburnt, escaping a hiding as long as they made it back before dusk.

They rode on the open back of a lorry or light delivery van without suntan lotion or hats. There were no childproof lids on medicine bottles, doors or cabinets and kids rode their bikes without helmets. They broke bones falling out of trees and slashed open their arms and legs when they tumbled off go-carts. Sue's brother shot his twin sister in the leg, at the age of six, with the cop next-door's rifle. The policeman had moved into a house with two metre high grass, riddled with snakes. When John saw the rifle protruding from underneath the truck seat, he whispered to his sister Annie to stay behind as the rest moved into the house. The cheeky little boy was lucky he didn't kill his sister. But there were no lawsuits from this and other accidents, because that is what they were: accidents.

Kids drank litres of creamy milk without needing grommets for mucous-plugged ears, ate cakes and ice cream and didn't suffer from obesity because they never stopped running, biking, climbing and swimming. They were told to 'eat up – remember the starving in China'. Today China is thriving and we eat too much.

The idea of a parent bailing children out if they broke the law was unheard of. Some parents dragged their kids along to the police station by the scruff of their necks and reported them for misdemeanours. It wasn't unheard of for a strict father to leave his son in jail overnight – sometimes by arrangement with the cops.

Boomer children are famous, or notorious, for being raised on what has been described as Dr Benjamin Spock's 'permissiveness'. He advocated a common sense approach to child care, urging parents to put away the canes and studded belts with which they, self-righteously, hit their children. It was probably only the younger Boomers who gained from this transition in parenting style. But the impact of Dr Spock's influence was felt fully when Boomers themselves became parents and thoroughly embraced his less restrictive attitude.

The heady combination of such 'permissiveness', laced with the arrival of the Pill, led to what some describe as THE decade of the twentieth century, the Swinging Sixties, famous for drugs, sex and rock 'n' roll. Society had been softened up a little in the fifties with Bill Haley and the Comets, Buddy Holly, angel-faced Pat Boone and Cliff Richard and, of course, the wildly sexy, hip-gyrating Elvis Presley who had maidens and matrons alike in a swoon.

The Beatles, The Rolling Stones, Joan Baez, Cilla Black, Dusty Springfield, Bob Dylan and Abba, amongst others, became the world's first massive entertainment superstars, influencing culture and creating the cult of the celebrity.

The Pill, an invention that some consider is on a par with that of the steam train or the telephone, changed society for ever. It created a sexual revolution with sociological consequences – free love but fewer babies – that we're experiencing the effects of today as populations in developed nations shrink and threaten the very fabric of society (see chapters 13, Generations @ Work, and 19, Re-tyreing). But back then, few anticipated that freeing women of the bondage of having baby after baby could so dramatically affect life on earth, and promiscuity reigned at Woodstock and many other rock festivals where long-haired hippies flung off their robes and made love amongst the flowers.

The hippie movement was a fringe one but its ethos of 'make love, not war' and its anti-establishment, anti-authority stance became increasingly prevalent, especially on university campuses and in the streets of cities across the world as they rioted against conscription in general and the war in Vietnam in particular. Their war cry, 'don't trust anybody over thirty', sounded like a clarion call to a rebellious youth that was challenging just about every societal convention it could, from men growing their anti-establishment, anti-military long hair, to women sleeping with whomsoever they wanted as they overturned thousands of years of sexual bondage.

Adulthood

These events combined in the fifties and sixties to create an extraordinary time that saw the birth of the most powerful group of people born in a century. As they matured, they created a society that has taken the world economy by the scruff of its neck and produced one of the strongest, longest and most sustained growth spurts in history.

Globally, GDP (gross domestic product) growth hovered around ten per cent, or even higher, in many countries. The purchasing power of money was about as good as it ever got in the twentieth century and the prospects for the future had never seemed brighter. It was an age when the future held limitless possibilities.

Visionaries like John F Kennedy promised to fly men to the moon – and did so. He, and others, vowed to end racial discrimination in their vast country, to ensure that the Free World did not succumb to Russia during the Cold War, and faced, bravely, the many challenges that came their way. When Kennedy was shot the world, newly exposed to mass media via television, cried along with his beautiful widow, Jacqueline

Kennedy, and his two pretty children. And when his handsome brother Robert, and the visionary black leader Martin Luther King Jr also died at the hands of assassins, some thought the end of the world was near.

The 1960s and 70s were a turbulent time as young adult Boomers went to university and into the workplace, rebelling against the GI and Silent generation dominated institutions they found there. Their moralistic outlook spurred them on to activism against the establishment, although their rebellion was not aimed so much at toppling the system per se but rather at removing the perceived corruption within the system.

Boomers are happy with the system of authority as long as they are in authority themselves. This they soon were, with one of the youngest ever American presidents, Bill Clinton, and young British prime minister, Tony Blair, taking office. Leaders like Gerhard Schroeder, Vladimir Putin, Junichiro Koizumi, John Howard and Luiz Inácio 'Lula' da Silva have brought Boomer pizzaz to their countries' top leadership positions.

As Boomers grew into their thirties and forties they became moralistic, principled and domineering and in the 1980s they began to transform themselves from the flower-power hippie generation into a solid, middle class, materialistic, self-absorbed set of midlifers.

Although the Yuppie (Young Upwardly Mobile Professional) is a small percentage of all Boomers (like hippies were), their attitude of materialism, self-satisfaction and self-immersion came to define Boomers no matter what their economic status was.

Who they are today

Today Boomers occupy the political, governmental and big business hot seats of the world. Ironically, these anti-establishment rebels are now seeking to uphold all the rules they were so intent on breaking in their youth.

They are legislating against drugs, smoking (suing tobacco companies in the process) and trying to curb sexual promiscuity and pornography. For these fiery leaders, many of whom believe their leadership is God given, there is no compromise and no room for grey in a world of black and white, especially when it comes to the next generation of youngsters coming up behind them. American satirist and journalist PJ O'Rourke has called this the 'new seriousness'.

They have no difficulty legislating against the excesses of their own youth and their rallying cry is a greater sense of morality and social standards. Their inner-directed approach, so typical of the 'Me Generation', lends itself well to their style of leadership which does not consult much with other generations.

The Xers, who increasingly rub up against the domineering, 'know-it-all' attitude of the team-focused, 'let's make sure we're all on the same page' Boomers, accuse them of being moralistic and hypocritical. It irks the Xers in particular that these free-spending, self-indulgent Boomers still seem to be having the time of their lives precisely because they are still bucking the system. They are refusing to age quietly and gracefully. They're challenging convention, once again, as they lead the wrinkly rebellion and zoom into their midlife years.

They've moved the goal posts for old age. It used to be sixties and seventies. Now they're calling that middle age. And middle age they have renamed as 'middle youth'. They are deluding themselves that 'old age' will never come as they Botox away their wrinkles and have facelifts.

Men dye their hair nearly as often as women and both sexes pound away in the ever increasing numbers of gyms built to cater for their age-defying exercise classes. Fact is they're younger and fitter than any generation before them and more than one Xer has drooped over his computer as he writes despairingly of his parents' refusal to age. As Grainger David (23) wrote of his father, Doug David (53) in *Fortune* a few years back, 'It looks as though you're trying to become the first fully reconstructed generation in history... with bionic knees, implanted hearing aids, regenerated hair, negative cholesterol and vacuum-cleaned colons, you're starting to sound like a technology instead of a group of people.'

The 'silver surfers', as they call the wrinklies who hog the Internet (because they have more leisure time now than their progeny), were working mothers and are now working grandmothers, to the despair of their Xer children who want stay-at-home babysitters. As British Boomer and *International Express* journalist Jan Etherington wrote, 'We are a generation of "second-agers" rich not just in money, but in skills. For us, it's a time, not of reflection and complacent retirement but of new beginnings, of new horizons, a new hair colour and sometimes a new partner. We're not afraid of new challenges. We're not afraid, full stop. We're not refusing to grow old – we merely refuse to give up our opinions, passions and curiosity for life. When we travel, we're more likely to trek through the Nepalese foothills or dive with whale sharks than sit meekly in a coach, being patronised by a teenage tour guide who organises singalongs and herds us off at "comfort-stops". We always knew how to have a good time and just because we happen to be over fifty doesn't mean that we're going to slip quietly into middle age, clutching a mug of Ovaltine.'

The biggest shock to the Boomer system was the economic downturn at the end of the 1990s which saw millions of them being kicked out of jobs they thought they were secure in for life. Many a Boomer has now grown used to having no long-term job security and often rocky pension schemes. But if they're still working, which most of them are in one way or another, it is often not just because they need the money but because they **can** work and **want** to work.

One such 'worker' who clearly doesn't know when to stop is the Rolling Stones' Mick Jagger who is still reeling in some of the biggest rock 'n' roll concert crowds ever seen as he struts the stage at sixty. He's also reeling in the bucks, even though he's worth a one hundred and seventy-five million pound fortune and could conceivably take a rest. But why do that when, as *Fortune* magazine wrote, the Stones have pioneered and perfected the modern rock tour operation. The group has been around for more than forty years, yet in 2002 it could claim the second highest grossing North American tour of all time. And the highest grossing tour? That too went to the Rolling Stones (who have a collective age of about 240 years) for their Voodoo Lounge world tour in 1994/95.

Many an Xer and Millennial child quietly despairs of their ageing fathers ever cutting off their greasy ponytails, ditching the Gucci leather jacket or hanging up the keys to their age-defying youth symbol, their Harley-Davidson. They coped with, and now even admire, the way their mothers raised them by introducing them to reincarnation and teaching them about all the religions of the world, even though they got marked down in school essays that challenged Christianity's morality throughout the ages.

Life's still a challenge for Boomers who, optimistic as ever, compare their lives to the glass of half full (not half empty) water, and believe that they are only half done, with the greater and better half of their years still to come. What the Boomers won't realise is that this attitude poses an ever greater challenge for the coming generations than it does for them.

They're not going to be put out to pasture before their time, as their icon, the sleek silver Concorde has been, towed up river on a barge in December 2003 to its final resting place in a museum called Intrepid. They intend, in years to come, to morph into revered silver heads, who will lead their nations through dangers to a better world beyond, as a result of their principled, optimistic outlook on life.

Boomers – what a difference thirty years makes:

| 1970 | long hair |
| 2000 | longing for hair |

| 1970 | the perfect high |
| 2000 | the perfect high yield mutual fund |

| 1970 | acid Rock |
| 2000 | acid reflux |

| 1970 | moving to California because it's cool |
| 2000 | moving to California because it's hot |

| 1970 | growing pot |
| 2000 | growing pot belly |

| 1970 | watching John Glenn's first historic flight with your parents |
| 2000 | watching John Glenn's last historic flight with your children |

| 1970 | trying to look like Marlon Brando or Elizabeth Taylor |
| 2000 | trying NOT to look like Marlon Brando or Elizabeth Taylor |

| 1970 | killer weed |
| 2000 | weedkiller |

| 1970 | getting out to a new, hip joint |
| 2000 | getting a new hip joint |

| 1970 | Rolling Stones |
| 2000 | kidney stones |

| 1970 | take acid |
| 2000 | take antacid |

| 1970 | passing your driver's test |
| 2000 | passing your vision test |

Boomers – first (again!) to...

The Boomer generation, which has led the way in so many fields, was the first to experience the following:

- See photographs of the earth from space whilst they were young kids.
- Motor, regularly, at speeds in excess of 50 miles per hour.
- Be part of a global majority middle class.
- Travel to virtually any destination in the world.
- Live in an age where so many have seen our planet from the air.
- Witness, as children, human beings blasted into space.
- Consider supersonic flight normal.
- Be part of a world where more than half of them have completed their schooling.
- Live in developed countries where more than half their generation has tertiary qualifications.
- View world events, in their living rooms, in full colour news broadcasts.
- Have a dedicated telephone in nearly every private home.
- See how 'other people' live, in reality (documentaries), showbiz and simulated 'reality TV'.
- See the rise AND fall of a political ideology (communism) in one lifetime.
- Divorce, and marry, repeatedly.
- Have full colour photographs of their childhood.

7

Xer Generation: Born 1960s to 1980s

Attitude:	'Whatever...', enigmatic
Likes:	Sharing, chilling, being individualistic, being with friends, change
Dislikes:	Bossiness, corporate culture
Heroes:	Mark Shuttleworth, Linus Torvalds, Bill Clinton, Richard Branson, Steve Jobs and Steve Wozniak
Movie stars:	John Cusack, Macaulay Culkin, Julia Roberts, Cameron Diaz, Lucy Liu, Mike Meyers, Halle Berry, Keanu Reeves, River Phoenix, Brad Pitt
Sports stars:	Dennis Rodman, Shane Warne, Andre Agassi, Juan Pablo Montoya, Mike Tyson, David Beckham, the Williams sisters, Wayne Gretzky, Karch Kiraly, Maradona, Carl Lewis
Music:	Grunge, Hip Hop, Rap, Bono, Alice Cooper, Marilyn Manson, Kurt Cobain, Sheryl Crow, Alanis Morrisette, Jimmy Cliff, Peter Gabriel
Characteristics:	Pragmatic, individualistic, arrogant, risk-taking

Momentous events:
Launch of the computer on a chip, the microchip, 15 November 1971
Watergate break-in, 17 June 1972
Women get the right to choose abortion in Roe vs Wade case, 22 January 1973

America pulls out of Vietnam, evacuating troops from Saigon, 30 April 1975

Steve Jobs and Steve Wozniak create the first Apple computer, 1 April 1976

Soweto schoolchildren riot, 16 June 1976

The world's first test-tube baby, Louise Brown, is born, 25 July 1978

Margaret Thatcher becomes Britain's first woman prime minister, 3 May 1979

Prince Charles marries Lady Diana Spencer, 29 July 1981

Mikhail Gorbachev becomes prime minister of Russia, 11 March 1985

AIDS is given a name, Acquired Immune Deficiency Syndrome, 27 July 1982

Zola Budd accidentally trips Mary Decker at the Los Angeles Olympic Games, 1984

Challenger shuttle explodes, on 28 January 1986

The Berlin Wall comes down, 9 November 1989

Nelson Mandela, the world's most famous prisoner, is released on 11 February 1990

Childhood

If the Baby Boomers arrived with a bang, then the Xers made their entrance with a whimper. This misunderstood, grungy, loner generation, defined more by what it is not than by what it is, had the extraordinary misfortune to time its appearance just as the economic boom years were flattening and the high-spirited revelry of the 1960s began to unravel in the 70s.

They are described as 'whiners' in stark contrast to the 'winner' Boomers. This 'lost generation' wears their baggy jeans slung low down on their hips and slaps baseball caps, backwards, onto their often shaved heads. They can't get out of bed in the morning and struggle to find work, or life, exciting and challenging. They were in the dot-com boom and are now the dot.bomb bust generation except for a lucky, sensible few who made their multiple millions and got out before Silicon Valley crashed. No wonder they've been branded the 'thirty nothings'. They are without a doubt the (micro) chip generation but often that chip is worn on the shoulder as they bewail the tough times they've grown up in.

'Few of my generation were alive, much less remember, the assassination of John F Kennedy, but the oldest of us, even at the age of two, could sense something had gone wrong. For the rest of our childhood, things seemed to go that way,' wrote an American Xer, Bret Ellis, in an article in the *New York Times* in 1993. (American Xers are often defined as being born from the early 1960s. See page 19 for a table of dates for different countries.)

The 'going wrong' haunted them through adolescence and into early adulthood. They grew up in an 'anti-child' era as their Boomer (and a few Silent) generation parents focused more on their own personal needs. They quoted Dr Benjamin Spock, saying that the best gift you could give your children was a happy parent. To achieve this status, you had to focus on doing your own thing.

Boomers, remembering the stifling control that was imposed on them by their own Silent/GI parents, went to the opposite extreme, and allowed young Xers inordinate freedom. Indeed, so lavish were they with their freedom that it often bordered on neglect.

The neglect, however, wasn't always deliberate. Often it was the result of the circumstances they found themselves in, for during the 1960s and 1970s the divorce rate rocketed throughout the western world. By the mid 1970s, nearly 40 per cent of all couples living in major cities were getting divorced, or had been. In America the number of children involved in divorces increased by 300 per cent in the forty year period from 1940 to 1980.

The divorce boom meant that many an Xer spent every second weekend at their other parent's home, and saw a profusion of different family relationships, such as 'dad's girlfriend', 'mom's previous ex-husband', 'my second step-father', or 'my stepsister's half-brother's mother'. No wonder that Xers are sceptical about relationships, yet feel a need to fill the void with something else. That 'else' has turned out to be surrogate families made up of friends and peers who are chosen for their closeness, loyalty and dependable relationships. The result is that Xers often have long-lasting, dedicated friendships that can elude other generations.

As young adults, manoeuvring through a sexual minefield of AIDS and blighted courtship rituals, as the legacy of the 1960s revolution and feminism lives on, and remembering, with pain, their Silent generation parents' failed marriages, they date and marry cautiously.

Xers complain that they are defined by what they are not, and yet they are not pleased if you try to define them at all, protesting that they will not be boxed or labelled. Not surprisingly, as has happened throughout history, they are compared with the generation ahead of them, the Boomers.

When the latter were kids, in the 1960s, life stayed much the same on a day to day basis. They watched the same TV shows, listened to the same news broadcasts and followed the same sports teams. Muhammad Ali was The Greatest.

In the 70s and 80s, when the Xers were growing up, hardly anything stayed the same as professionalism hit sport, and TV shows proliferated. Compare the message that Mike Tyson has given this generation with that of the wholesome Muhammad Ali. Sociologists comment on the strong parental roles in 60s TV shows like *Leave it to Beaver*, *Little House on the Prairie* and *Bonanza*, but question what lasting and positive messages were gained from the 90s shows *South Park*, *Married with Children* and *The Simpsons*. Bart Simpson is the Xer's most famous cartoon character, irreverent, self-reliant and he doesn't care what adults think about him. He's often in trouble but always lands on his feet and usually fixes up the messes of his father – all Xer characteristics. The upside of this, of course, is that Xers are pragmatic, they get things done and don't get bogged down in discussions about discussions. They 'Just Do It', as their Nike apparel often proclaims.

Xers were expected to grow up quickly, and they did so, in schools that were miniatures of adult communities with drugs, violence, sex and even murder. Today, children's issues have become political issues and, increasingly, new laws are enacted to protect them. The Xers had no such care lavished on them and would have laughed at the very thought of metal detectors and body searches to stop guns and knives in the classroom.

Xer music was grungy and dark. Nirvana, Snoop Doggy Dog, Marilyn Manson and Alice Cooper (the latter two are men) topped the Xer charts and some of the music had to have warning labels on the albums. Boomers, who are still rocking to Elvis, The Rolling Stones and The Beatles, wonder if Xers will still remember their grunge music and want to dance to it when they're in their fifties.

Adulthood

As Xers have moved into young adulthood, they've been seen as arrogant and lost and very little hope has been pinned on them by older adults. They buck the system by being non-traditional in their approach and also by forging new employment opportunities that are often overlooked by established businesses. One of their outstanding character-istics is the courage to take enormous risks. But some complain bitterly that this made them perfect 'cannon fodder' for the Boomer bosses who headed the IT companies during the technology boom, then took the money and ran when the bubble burst, leaving the Xers high and dry.

The burst dot-com bubble left many former Internet million-aires in mountains of debt and turned the older Xers into the 'thirty nothings'. One such Xer was Jennifer Jeffrey, who was the multimillionaire owner of a Californian dot-com company, during the heyday of the Internet phenomenon. She told the London *Sunday Times*, 'The whole way of life was excessive. Champagne wasn't enough. It had to be vintage champagne. Caviare had to be flown in. If you didn't drive a top-of-the-range European car you weren't taken seriously. And the hours were ludicrous.' Today she rents a one bedroom apartment.

Others can't even afford that. At the age of thirty-one they are moving back home with their parents as their own homes and cars are repossessed. As one 'repo' man said, 'A kid whose car I towed was in tears. He loved his Lotus Esprit, said it went from 0 to 100 in 10 seconds. That's the same amount of time it took me to hitch it to my towing wagon.'

No wonder the book *What Should I do With My Life?* by American Xer author Po Bronson is a best-seller on both sides of the Atlantic.

Despite writing two best-selling novels, being named 'sexiest writer alive' by *People* magazine in 1999 and having a happy family life, Bronson felt directionless. Other Xers confirmed they felt the same way. So Bronson interviewed 900 of them and then distilled his collection to fifty for his book. The bottom line is that Xers do not work for the money. They work to fund the kind of lifestyle they want, usually a non-materialistic one, and they need to enjoy the work they're doing.

As Warren G Bennis and Robert J Thomas wrote in *Geeks and Geezers*, they want much greater financial reward at an early age, yet they are convinced that this money requires them to have an acute social conscience. They give freely to charities and become personally involved in worthy causes.

They're sceptical of corporations, realising that long-term commitment is unlikely to pay the dividends it did to their parents and grandparents. They are, therefore, opposed to paying their dues the way their Silent grandparents did and they look for quick, short-term rewards, are prepared to embrace risks and work hard for themselves.

This entrepreneurial, selfish and individualistic attitude is often mistaken for the rebelliousness displayed by Boomers and many of the older generation simply ignore it, believing that Xers will soon grow up and move out of this phase. However, Xers are not rebelling against authority the way Boomers did (and still are in some cases). They're simply asserting their individuality, one of their defining characteristics. They're just not prepared to sell their soul to the company and will be the first American generation who can expect to earn less in real terms than their parents. In fact, economically, Xers are amongst the poorest people in America.

Generation Xer expert Douglas Coupland sums up their situation and the kind of jobs they are working in as 'McJobs', which are, he says, 'low pay, low prestige, low benefit, no-future jobs in the service sector. It's those kind of jobs, combined with the fact that many people working in them are doing so to repay student loans, which see many a twenty-something moving back home, something no self-respecting Boomer or Silent generation would have done.'

Who they are today

It's not all doom and gloom for the Xers. Their value systems, honed in their tough childhoods, will see them end up with a far better work/life balance than their parents and grand-parents had. Indeed, they are already the subject of envy by older generations. In the post-9/11 world, many people have seriously reassessed their priorities. Boomers are resigning from their top jobs and moving from city to country to try and regain balance and make up for lost time with their fragile families.

Xers won't have to move in such an earth shattering way, because they've never stopped moving all their lives as their divorced parents have moved from bed to bed. Xers are used to having the rug pulled from under them. True, the suicide rate amongst them is high, but, against all the odds, many of them do land on their feet when other generations, faced with similar situations, might have despaired.

Xers wear suits but have a solid silver stud in their lower lip, or a gold earring, to set them apart from Boomers. Those who choose to work hellish long hours are hiring others to peel the potatoes, as they have gourmet meals delivered to their homes. They hire 'lifestyle managers' who sort out everyday tasks such as cleaning, travel arrangements, laundry and so on, according to UK market analyst Datamonitor. The study of workers in seven European countries predicted that 16 per cent of households would employ cleaners by 2006 compared with ten per cent in 2001.

When they are not working, which is fairly often in their work/home/leisure balanced lives, they are risk-taking chal-lenge-lovers for this is the generation that invented extreme sports such as bungee jumping. They've turned outdoor pursuits such as canyoning, river rafting, downhill mountain biking, rollerblading and the like into mainstream activities. Xers' drugs of choice are not the high-inducing, spiritually based hallucinogens of their Swinging Sixties Boomer brothers and sisters. Xers prefer cocaine, speed and ecstasy, energy-boosting drugs that allow dancers to rave on all night, and high-flying entrepreneurs to sustain 120+ hour working weeks.

As Generation Xer professional fitness trainer Derek Archer says, 'We have too much information in our lives. We're overloaded and bombarded with the stuff. We work so fast and absorb so much that life ends up being boring for us if we can't keep up that pace, which is why some Xers go for the drugs, the bungee jumping. We're also incredibly stressed and so we need the "highs" of dangerous biking and mountaineering to get us down again.'

Indeed, to older generations Xers often seem impatient for answers, always demanding information, asking questions and pursuing multiple lines of enquiry simultaneously. This is often taken for a lack of attention span, whereas it is, in fact, a style of interacting with information which comes naturally to these children of the information revolution.

Today's young people think in 'sound bites', 'big pictures', and concepts, with an incredible capacity for information gathering. They want to be able to communicate 24/7 (twenty-four hours a day, seven days a week) anywhere in the world. If it's not on the Internet, it doesn't count for Xers.

To sum up the Xers (at the risk of upsetting them): relation-ships matter the most to them; they are risk-taking challenge lovers; sex is expected yet confusing and, because of AIDS, is dangerous. They live with change and embrace it yet they are stressed and organised to death. The levels of pain and anger are rising. They want rules but from the right authorities only. Their 'now' matters more than their future. They don't want to know 'Is it true?'; they want to know 'Does it work?' They are spiritual seekers who believe in the supernatural. Music is huge in their lives. It is the 'window on their soul' and the language they use to express themselves.

An Internet emailer sums up today's Xer lifestyle:

- Your reason for not staying in touch with your family is because they do not have email addresses.
- You have a list of fifteen phone numbers to reach your family of three.
- Your grandmother asks you to send a JPEG file of your newborn so she can create a screen saver.
- You pull up in your own driveway and use your cellphone to see if anyone is at home.
- Nearly every commercial on TV has a website address at the bottom of the screen.
- You buy a computer and six months later it's out of date and sells for half the price you paid for it.
- Leaving the house without your cellphone is a cause for panic and you turn back immediately.
- You've just tried to enter your password on the microwave oven.
- Courier services that don't do same-day delivery are too slow.
- You hear most of your jokes via email instead of in person.
- When you disconnect from the Internet, you are left with the sensation of having pulled the plug on a loved one.
- You get up in the morning and go online before getting your coffee.
- You wake up at 2am to go to the toilet and check your email on the way back to bed.
- You have started tilting your head sideways to smile :-)
- You are reading this... and even worse... you are going to forward it to somebody else.

8

Millennial Generation: Born 1980s to 2000s

Attitude:	Let's make the world a better place
Likes:	Shopping, labels, family, friends, the environment, technology
Dislikes:	Dishonesty, unbalanced lifestyles, ostentation
Heroes:	Nelson Mandela, Princess Diana, the Dalai Lama, Bono, Harry Potter, Barney
Movie stars:	Jennifer Aniston, Nicole Kidman, Natalie Portman, Anna Paquin, Hayley Joel Osment, Leonardo di Caprio, Hugh Grant, Drew Barrymore, Tom Cruise
Sports stars:	Tiger Woods, Anna Kournikova, David Beckham, Jonny Wilkinson, Michael Johnson, Andy Roddick, Skyler Siljeg
Music:	Britney Spears, Christina Aguilera, Enrique Iglesias, Avril Lavigne, Westlife, Blue, Beyoncé Knowles, Eminem, Boyz II Men
Characteristics:	Tolerant, caring, honest, balanced, independent, optimistic, clean-cut

Momentous events:
AIDS sweeps the world in the 1990s
Nelson Mandela released from twenty-seven years of imprisonment on 11 February 1990
Oklahoma City bombing, 19 April 1995
Princess Diana dies in a car crash, 31 August 1997
Dolly the sheep is cloned on 5 July 1996, and presented to the world in early 1997
Viagra is launched, 27 March 1998

Anti-globalists protest at the World Trade Organisation meeting,
Seattle, on 29 November 1999
SMS (short message service) takes the world by storm in 2000
The World Trade Center is hit on 9/11 in 2001
Britain's Queen Elizabeth, the Queen Mother, dies 30 March 2002,
aged over a hundred
George W Bush attacks the 'axis of evil' on 29 January 2002
America and Britain invade Iraq, 20 March 2003
Email spam increases at a horrifying pace, 2003
The Madrid bombings shocked the world 11 March 2004

Childhood

The 'Baby on Board' car stickers warning surrounding motorists that the most precious cargo on earth is being transported says it all about societal attitudes towards children in the Millennial era. The contrast between the Xer 'latchkey kids' who let themselves into empty homes after school and were left to their own devices in the afternoon while their parents worked, and the fussed over, cuddled and cosseted Millennials, could not be greater. It serves as yet another stark example of the generational swing – what happens in one generation is often vehemently rejected by the next one.

Madonna, who reinvents herself on an ongoing basis, epitomises this in her child-rearing approach. She vaunted her naked body, lasciviously, in books, posters and magazines for years before becoming a Millennial mother. Now she brings up her children strictly, with tough bedtime and behaviour rules that she would have scorned in her youth.

Babies and kids were an irritant to workaholic Boomer moms and dads. But all that changed as the 1990s drew on with babies suddenly becoming status symbols. Models clutched them for glossy magazine photo shoots, Demi Moore posed, heavily pregnant and naked, on the cover of *Vanity Fair*, British prime minister Tony Blair and Cherie had their fourth baby in a blaze of pro-baby publicity, and sports stars like South Africa's brilliant golfer Ernie Els are seen holding their trophies in one hand and baby in the other on newspaper front pages.

What's going on? Is it just a generational backlash?

Part of it is indeed a reaction to the neglect and negativism that the Xers endured as kids. But it's also changing societal and demographic trends. For a start, the developed world is now seriously threatened by falling population figures (see chapter 19, Re-tyreing) with many countries showing ZPG (zero population growth). The serious implications of this led futurist author and management expert Peter Drucker to predict that the 'demographic challenge, the shrinking of the young population, will be the basic disturbance of the twenty-first century.' So, alarm bells are ringing for governments.

At the same time young Millennials have experienced abortion and divorce rates ebbing, with popular culture beginning to stigmatise hands-off parenting and to recast babies as special. Marriage is even beginning to become more popular, with figures rising in some countries. Conversely, increasing numbers are choosing to have babies without marriage, so that would account, in an age where unmarried motherhood and 'illegitimate' babies are no longer the taboo they once were, for the falling abortion and divorce figures.

But babies are best. The new status symbol of an up and coming family is to have a stay-at-home mother or, increasingly, father. Our high-tech world offers greater numbers of parents the opportunity to work from home. SoHos (Small Office, Home Office), combined with flexi working hours, telecommuting and the rapid trend to independent/contract workers, are changing both parenting and working.

That's how Graeme works as he runs his TomorrowToday.biz company from his home in Johannesburg, South Africa. When his computer skills trainer wife Jane is out working, he's working too but keeping an eye on their two girls, both aged under five. It's how Sue has worked ever since her teenage daughter was born, holding down a full-time office job as a journalist but working flexi hours at home, at night, so she could be with her daughter during the day. And, they both choose to work this way because children and family come first in their lives. Sue, a Boomer, was ahead of the game. Graeme is doing the GenXer bit now.

It's a world trend to downsize your living standards, to move out of town to more child friendly little towns and villages and to improve your quality of life even though the Joneses might sniff at your 'vintage' car and unfashionable address. Could we be coming full (generational) circle from the civic GI generation who moved out of towns and tenement buildings and built the gleaming new suburbs of post World War II?

The current reappraisal of family values began in the early 1990s when American trends analyst Faith Popcorn's 'cocooning' took off massively and some Boomer parents began to mend their wild, workaholic ways by staying home more with their kids. As they did so, they revised their hands-off approach to child raising.

'The 60s generation, once high on drugs, warns its children,' headlined *The Wall Street Journal* in 1990. And, 'Do as I say, not as I did,' echoed *The New York Times* about Boomer parents who (polls confirmed) did not want their own children to have the same freedom with drugs, alcohol and sex that they had once enjoyed.

Parenting books are leading (or reflecting) the change in parenting style. When Boomers were children their strictly raised GI and Silent parents were advised by Dr Spock to be more relaxed and less rule-bound with their offspring. Now the wild Boomers are being advised in a plethora of childcare books to tame that indulgence and practise a stricter approach. Xer parents don't need to be told that – they're not going to let their children run free and neglected.

Indeed, as Millennials replace Xers in the puberty age bracket, the adult message in practically every medium is becoming more prescriptive and less equivocal. In tot-TV, *Barney and Friends*, with its happy teamwork and emphasis on what all kids share in common, stole the limelight from Sesame Street with its more nuanced story lines and stress on what makes each child different, write William Strauss and Neil Howe in their *Millennials Rising* book.

Bill Clinton really got stuck into the childcare trend, making political hay out of his child focused speeches. America's youngest ever ex-president is working hard to bring more morality, less violence, less sex and swearing to Hollywood.

Today, many politicians define adult issues, such as tax cuts, in terms of their effect on children. The Nelson Mandela Children's Fund is aimed solely at Millennial generation kids, with nothing set aside for the 'lost' Xers.

Naturally, Hollywood has come to the party by replacing the Xer type cinematic child devils and lost children (remember *Rosemary's Baby*, *The Exorcist* and *Taxi Driver*) with child angels and heroes in *Home Alone*, *Little Man Tate*, *Power Rangers*, *Matilda* and *Kundun*. Steven Spielberg (now a father) says that if he could remake *Close Encounters of the Third Kind*, he wouldn't have let the father in it abandon his family and go off with the aliens.

Strauss and Howe predict that new pop culture trends will be big, bland and friendly. 'In film, young stars will be linked with positive themes, display more modesty in sex and language and link new civic purpose to screen violence. In sports, players will become more coachable, more loyal to teams and fans and less drawn to trash talk, in your face drunk and end-zone taunts. In pop music, Millennials will resurrect the old ritual of happy group singing, from old campfire favourites to new tunes with simple melodies and upbeat lyrics. Whether in film, sport or music, the first Millennial celebrities will win praise as good role models for children,' they write in *Millennials Rising*.

If this all sounds too good to be true, well, much of it IS true but there's a darker side too.

Growing up fast

Children are growing up quickly today as the world spins faster and faster to the high-tech tune. Marketers and advertisers have their sights set firmly on them before they're even ten years old. They're wearing adult clothes, high heels and lipstick by the age of eleven. Swear words their Boomer and Xer parents haven't heard in years pop out of gum-chewing mouths. They surf the Internet, sometimes stumbling onto porn sites, where older men lie in wait to trap them. The recent rash of young British girls running off with ageing men met in Internet chat rooms is a huge social concern, leading Microsoft to shut down its MSN chat sites in 2003.

Kids are body conscious by the age of four when out of the mouths of babes come words such as, 'I've got fat thighs, Mummy,' and they insist on wearing trousers to hide them. By ten some are anorexic as they drown in the wave of advertisements from hundreds of metres high billboards and TV sets urging them to look like Barbie or Britney. Their mothers swallow diet shakes instead of eating vegetables, and have breast enhancements, while their fathers dye their hair and eyebrows and have fat suctioned out of their thighs. Just listen to the message those kids are receiving!

We know it happens in nearly every generation but the newspaper headlines are again screaming, 'What's happened to the Age of Innocence?' as London's *Daily Mail* did recently. The pictures of raunchy Kylie Minogue and Christina Aguilera with bulging breasts and barely disguised pubic patches made the head of a British teachers' association exclaim, 'It looks as though they've forgotten to get dressed. Kylie might be a great singer but you see more of her bottom than you hear of her voice.'

Adults worry that such images put too much pressure on little girls to grow up too fast because they want to copy people who are seen to be succeeding. When soccer idol David Beckham changes his five-thousand-pounds-a-month hair style, many in the Millennial male world do too.

Indeed, the Millennials are sorely lacking when it comes to traditional heroes. Instead, they have celebrities who are famous for being famous, and sports stars whose claim to fame is popularity instead of heroic acts of intrinsic value. Many a celebrity will actively follow a destructive lifestyle and then warn youngsters not to follow his or her example. We all know the corollary to that one as the celebs hit the headlines for the wrong reasons and gain the admiration of our youth. In a postmodern world pop stars and catwalk models have become the new societal role models who tell us how to dress and behave.

In addition to an overactive entertainment industry, today's schoolchildren are growing up immersed in a world of computers and other information technologies. They play video games and listen to music on digital MP3 players.

Heaven help the family who hasn't got a Millennial to programme the computerised controls of videocassette and DVD players. Our Millennials have on their desks and at their fingertips access to more information of every sort than any human beings have ever had in the whole of history. They have in their homes more raw data processing power than most nations have ever had.

Take the example of a birthday card that plays happy birthday when it's opened. When you toss the card into your bin, you're casually throwing away more computer power than existed on the entire planet in 1950.

Millenials' spending power, in terms of the way they are able to influence their parents in such big ticket items as cars and houses, is awesome (see chapter 14, Advertising). The latest stats show that American Millennial kids spend about $120 billion of their own money and influence a further $250 billion each year.

They also have more money in their pockets than any other generation has ever had at a similar age. No wonder they are such a target market.

The future

Millennials are entering the workplace at a much earlier age than their predecessors. Many work a few years before studying, or start their work careers as teenage part-timers. In America, where Millennials are older, there has been a 25 per cent increase in managers between the ages of twenty to twenty-four in the last ten years. Service and retail jobs, which are traditionally 'first formal employers' of teens, are expected to grow 15 per cent in the next five years. Turnover of workers is at an all-time high amongst young people, with 54 per cent of 20 to 24-year-olds spending less than twelve months in a job.

Eric Chester, in *Employing Generation Why?*, writes that the Millennials have, more than any other young generation, an ability to 'filter out every command, every request and every instruction that is not bundled with acceptable rationale...

they demand reasons and rationale, so the traditional "because I said so" isn't going to cut it (with them).'

This confuses and irritates older generations, especially GIs and Silents, who think, 'We did what we were told and so should they, without a whole list of reasons.'

Millennials are already declaring their intention to have work/ life balance. Indeed, it is the next 'big thing' in Human Resources and Corporate Leadership and companies are already gearing themselves up for the generation that expects flexibility, freedom and balance as a right.

The strong positive signal already emerging from this generation is that they are as wise, if not wiser, than any other generation at the same age. They are reading and questioning more than the Xers did. They are doing their best to resist the overwhelming pressure of their parents and society to perform better and higher than anyone before them, one example of which is the 'homework wars'. Even parents are beginning to fight the system that sees Millennial seven-year-olds doing two hours of homework when their Boomer parents were out climbing trees and making mud pies at the same age.

And while it's obviously too soon to identify definitive Millennial traits and characteristics, some are emerging that show they are confident and energetic, passionately tolerant, and are extremely concerned about community and the environment.

Eric Chester suggests twelve words to define this generation: impatient, desensitised, disengaged, sceptical, disrespectful, bluntly expressive, adaptable, innovative, efficient, resilient, tolerant and committed. He says, 'They have an underlying desire to do the right thing, to know the truth of a situation, to have a job that means more than a pay cheque and to live a life that matters.'

Philosopher Hannah Arendt writes, 'If you ask a member of this generation two simple questions: "how do you want the world to be in fifty years?" and "what do you want your life to be like five years from now?" the answers are often preceded by, "provided there is still a world" and "provided I am still alive".'

There is such a world of wisdom, concern and understanding about what previous generations have done to their planet coming out of the mouths of our youngsters that it is both sad and exhilarating to contemplate it.

You know you're a Millennial when you:

- Have only known one pope in your lifetime.
- Think Michael Jackson has always been white.
- Have never owned a record player.
- Have always had an answering machine.
- Don't know there was a Cold War.
- Can't believe babies' nappies were once made of cloth.
- Don't care who shot JR (actually, you've never heard of JR).
- Don't remember the Space Shuttle blowing up.
- Have never thought of Jaws while you were swimming in the sea.
- Think the Vietnam War is as ancient a war as World Wars I and II.
- Can't imagine what hard contact lenses are.
- Have only known a world with AIDS.
- Can understand 'c u b4 2nite'.

Some words that defined the generations...

Words first used by each generation:

1900s
Anorexic
Airliner
Bomb
Suffragette
Electronic
Undies
Teenagers

1910s
Babe
Birth control
Come off it
Jazz
Prenuptial agreement
Posh
Sex objects
Sex discrimination

1920s
Bimbo
Cold turkey
Jive
Perm
Penicillin
Foreplay
Greenhouse effect

1930s
Barbecue
Gay
Jingle
Loch Ness Monster
Peanuts – the cartoon
Pizza
Filofax
Durex

1940s
Bikini
Doodlebug
Hologram
Alien
Genocide
Quiz
Computer
Cleavage
Apartheid

1950s
Hi-fi
Go-kart
Rock 'n' roll
Sliced bread
Y-fronts
Hippies
Holocaust

1960s
Meltdown
Laser
Barbie doll
Disco
Miniskirt
Mini (car)

1970s
Streaker
Supermodel
Pig out
Networking
Politically correct
AIDS
Sloane Rangers
Supermodels
Global warming

1980s
Break-dancing
Out of order
Road rage
Yuppie
Designer stubble
Fantasy football
Internet
Girl power
Laptop computing
Glasnost and Perestroika

1990s
Cool Britannia
Ball tampering
Cybercafé
Docu-soap
Heroin chic
New lad
World Wide Web
Biotechnology

2000s
Metrosexual
SARS
Weapons of mass destruction
9/11

(Based on an idea from the International Express, 24 August 1999)

9

If you don't fit in...
you could be a 'Cusper'

If you have arrived at this chapter, having read all about the five generations we are profiling in this book, you might feel that you don't fall into any of our descriptions. You may be feeling really left out, even perhaps a bit irritated? Well, apart from the reasons we give in the introductory chapter about generational theory – that it is a generalisation, that there are no hard and fast rules about if, and where, people fit into the generations – you may be one of those people who fall in between generations.

Sociologists have decided to call you 'Cuspers'. A cusp is the point at which two parts of a curve meet. You have fallen into the overlap between two generations. You were born either early in a generation and so have taken on some of the characteristics of the generation that preceded yours, or you were born late in your generation and have adopted some of the characteristics of the generation born after you.

Also, you may be the young child of older parents, or the old child of young parents, and not have the classic gap of one to one and a half generations between you and your parents.

It means that you were born in a time between eras and you have been influenced by both. Each of these transition moments between generations has its own character and influence but there are no generic cusper characteristics as such. It is just that you straddle generations and eras, with the result that you, more so than those born right in the middle of a generation or era, feel that you don't fit in.

Interestingly, most Cuspers tend to choose characteristics of the one generation they want to adopt rather than exhibit characteristics of both generations they straddle. This can occur when you marry someone of a particular generation and find you are taking on their quirks and way of thinking. You might choose a career that puts you on a certain generational path. Or, you may simply wish to differentiate yourself from your parents or your peers. You may, for instance, sympathise with another generation to the extent that you dress like a Boomer, but you may have a strong sense of the Silent generation within you. This may enable you to play a mediating role between Silent and Boomer generations because you can identify with them both.

GI/Silent Cuspers

You may have been born just before the 1920s and that means you were sandwiched between the late GIs and the early Silent generation. The era was the time after World War I and you may have experienced the sad after-effects of that but enjoyed the early Roaring Twenties with the fun of the Flappers, the Charleston and early silent movies. You may have taken on some of the visionary aspects of the GIs or may have become more stoic and quiet like the Silents.

As more and more Silents move into the ranks of the elderly, this set of cuspers is becoming less distinctive, and is required to play less of a mediating role between GIs and Silents as may have been necessary a few decades ago.

Silent/Boomer Cuspers

This group which straddles the Silent and Boomer generations was born too late to remember World War II but has played a very important role in history. They have been the 'glue' between older Silents and younger Boomers over the past two decades. These Cuspers are extraordinary negotiators, able to find win-win solutions between conservative Silents and visionary Boomers and have helped many an organisation to navigate the choppy seas of change.

Graeme's father was born late in the Silent generation with a conservative approach to life. This meant that Graeme and his siblings were brought up in a reasonably authoritarian home where, for instance, they were not allowed to swim on a Sunday or watch more than an hour or two of TV a week. He was not an overly affectionate father, as was the case with so many Silents, but he has many Boomer characteristics in him, including being a visionary workaholic and seeking status and success. As he grows older, these have become more evident. He has had a major role to play in many organisations, helping them to move forward while keeping everyone on board.

The South African president, Thabo Mbeki, is a Cusper who has both Silent and Boomer generation characteristics. He has the Boomer tendency for grand visions, such as his dream of an African Renaissance and Nepad (New Partnership for African Development), but he is shocking at handling the media – something at which any self-respecting Boomer excels. His approach to the political regime in Zimbabwe has been typically Silent generation. It has been 'silent' with 'quiet diplomacy' and the attendant attitude that fellow Africans do not air their dirty linen in public.

Compare this approach with that of Boomer president George W Bush and Donald Rumsfeld, the American Defence Secretary. The latter was even less 'silent' than his boss often is, exemplified by his quote on hearing of American soldiers dying in Iraq, that 'you get good and bad days in war'. It was almost as if he was saying, yes, well, that explains why scores got killed today... a bad day at the office, you know. Other generations are irritated by the brashness of Boomers. The Silent/Boomer Cusper, while understanding the Boomer's attitude and motivation, can do a much better job of presenting these thoughts to an older, more conservative and reserved Silent generation.

The Boomer/Silent Cuspers have a unique position in linking an outdated conservative world to the go-getter world of the Boomers. They can help be a bridge between the two generations and would make good negotiators, understanding both generations as they do. Because of this, these Cuspers tend to make better managers than leaders.

Boomer/Xer Cuspers

Birth in the late 1960s and early 70s meant that the Vietnam War was raging and these Cuspers would have heard their parents discussing it. They can remember getting their first computers. They were the 'trenchmen' of the IT generation. They didn't make a fortune out of IT as the Boomers did, but they have IT skills and the correct attitude for working in the industry and are the ones who are really changing the workplace as a result.

They are the unfortunate ones who got burnt in the dot-com boom, the 'troops' who made and lost fortunes in the early days of the boom. But they learnt a great deal at the same time. Now these Cuspers are able to fit into the Boomer world. They know when to wear a suit and tie and have a sense of how to behave appropriately so they don't irritate Boomers in the way that full-on Xers do.

They know it's necessary to 'play the game' by attending the office party so that they are seen there even though they don't enjoy it. An inordinate number of these Boomer/Xer Cuspers are stockbrokers, analysts, bankers and actuaries and they will don the pinstriped suit for the office.

But when they get home off comes the suit and ripped jeans are pulled on. They put their earrings back in and spike up their hair. These Cuspers have hair that can be slicked down or gelled up. They wear beaded necklaces under their collar and tie, bracelets under their shirts and tattoos where nobody can see them.

So don't be fooled by that quiet accountant in your bank from Monday to Friday because at the weekend he's mountain biking, or abseiling impossible peaks or skateboarding his heart out. He's straddling both worlds and getting the best out of them.

Graeme, co-author of this book, is one such Cusper. He chooses to be an Xer, to be able to dress and think in a 'grungy' manner. He has chosen to be contactable only via email as those who ring his cellphone find out. He says that he is brash, 'in your face' and sceptical. These are all good Xer attributes but he knows when to wear a suit. He understands and can talk to Boomers, which often surprises them because they don't anticipate this. Boomer/Xer Cuspers will probably be at the centre of the future workplace revolution on how people should be treated in business.

Xer/Millennial Cuspers

They have inherited the healthy aspect of the Xer scepticism and savvy but they also have the Millennial attitude of 'we can change the world'. You won't find these Cuspers flopping down on a couch, from which they struggle to rise, reacting with a 'Whatever' to every question they are asked. They've not swallowed so much scepticism that they cannot act.

At school, for instance, they will take on the system and challenge the idiot teacher, maybe even start a campaign to get him fired, or at least make him so uncomfortable that he will resign or retire.

The full-on Millennials who follow these Cuspers may be slightly more naïve than their predecessors.

Summary

The lesson for Cuspers appears to be that you have the best of two worlds, which is wonderful. Cuspers also make great generational mediators and may not feel the discomfort that people who are really typical of one generation experience with another. This makes you extremely valuable in multi-generational workplaces.

We suggest to Cuspers that, as you peruse this book, read both the generations that you fall between. Take the best from both of them and use it to make your contribution to the world.

10

Parenting the Generations

The attitude of each generation towards its parents:

GIs: My parents were Victorian and aloof.

Silents: Hard working, wise, but not there for me; out of touch emotionally.

Boomers: Too strict, I couldn't breathe, I had to rebel.

Xers: They were absent parents, worked too hard, and were too permissive.

Millennials: They need all the help I can give them. Fairly harmless as parents.

And as parents themselves – what is their parenting style?

GIs: Victorian, aloof and cold.

Silents: Authoritarian, dictatorial, controlling.

Boomers: Permissive, detached, freeing, warm.

Xers: Concerned, protective, deliberate.

Millennials: We predict it will be relaxed and confident, and not smothering.

In no area of our lives is the generational cycle more evident, and arguably more important, than it is in parenting. The way we were parented usually affects us for the rest of our lives, and in turn determines the manner in which we choose to parent. There's no other human endeavour that affects us quite as much. No other human beings are as influential in our lives as our parents, even if they are absent. Indeed, particularly when they are absent. When we look at the forces that have shaped our lives, our parents come first. Some of us spend a lifetime trying to 'get over' our parents and our childhoods.

So, understanding how we were brought up, why our parents treated us the way they did and how our childhoods and families still affect the way we work, play and relate to others is hugely important.

This chapter is critical to your understanding of generational theory.

Our values are formed in the era in which we were born and they will, largely, depend on the manner in which we were parented. Our parents bring us up in the style that is fashionable or current at the time. For instance, Silent generation parents left their infants to cry, sometimes for hours on end in a separate room. Boomers reacted to this when they became parents by breastfeeding on demand and putting their babies in their beds with them. That's because each generation tends to go to the opposite extreme of what they perceive to have been their parents' failures.

The children of alcoholics often tend not to drink at all, and their children, rebelling against the 'no liquor under my roof' dictum, can hit the bottle big time. Parents who seldom allowed their children to watch cartoons or videos can expect their grandchildren to be glued to the TV day and night.

The Boomers' permissive style of parenting left their children, the Xers, so much to their own devices that Xers are labelled the lonely, latchkey generation, who let themselves into empty homes after school. Now Xers in their turn are making extraordinary efforts to create a balance between work and home so that they can be with their families. Maybe the Millennials will, conversely, give their kids more space because they feel smothered by all the attention. And so the generational cycle goes!

Parenting styles are also heavily dependent on the times in which those parents lived. We have explained this in the introductory chapter and the chapter on leadership, chapter 15. When you're living through the Depression (the 1930s) or a war (1940s) or an economic boom (the 1960s), you, the parent, are having demands made on you that will hugely affect the way you bring up your children.

Boomers who are now the parents in power, such as British prime minister Tony Blair and American president George W Bush, are horrified at what they perceive to be the weakness of the family structure today. They, and many other leaders, believe the family as a unit is disintegrating. There are many reasons for this, including the rising number of couples who have babies, stay together as a unit, but do not get married. Tony Blair's former spin doctor Alastair Campbell, for example, has three children, the eldest of whom is into her teens, and while, at the time of writing this book, they all live together as a family, he and their mother have not married.

There have been some extraordinary changes in family structures over the past hundred years. Let's take a look at the different generations and how they were parented and then how they, in their turn, raised their kids. The chances are you will recognise yourself, your family, and your friends' and relations' families, to a lesser or greater extent. We want to remind you, yet again, that putting the generational matrix over society is a generalisation and while bells may ring for you here, they will not ring for everybody.

GIs (born 1900s to 1920s)
Childhood

Back in the childhood of the GI generation, the family was such a powerful institution that everybody took it for granted. When the GIs came marching home from war, marrying and having children was what was expected of them. Those who didn't do so were the exceptions to the norm. They were called bachelors and spinsters – terms not often used in their true sense any longer today.

Roles were clearly defined. Dad went out to work. Mom stayed at home with the kids. Both of them were supported by societal institutions ranging from schools to universities, the police, doctors and the church. That changed during the Boomer's and Xer's childhoods.

GIs arrived in a world still greatly influenced by Victorian values and ethics, so not surprisingly the parenting style they experienced was a Victorian one with all the overtones that

that denotes. You didn't wear your heart on your sleeve back then, especially if you'd been brought up in the British Empire or its colonies. Parents were formal, to the extent that some were even addressed by their children as 'sir' and 'ma'am'. Kids were seen and not heard. They remember their parents as remote, distant, authoritarian, even cold. That was the parenting style, but in spite of this, the GIs were a more 'coddled' generation than the two preceding it.

GIs were, from the start, regarded as a special generation by society as it worked hard to ensure that this generation of youth grew up clever and cooperative, unlike the 'lost' generation that went before it. They were the first to eat 'processed' protective foods and vitamins, and new play-grounds were built for them.

When GIs were small, there was an upper and a lower class but not much of a middle class. There was city and there was country but suburbs, as we know them today, hadn't been invented yet. Children were seen as a blessing, not only from an emotional perspective but in the sense that this meant more helping hands on the farm and in family businesses.

In America there were significant improvements in public schooling and for the first time in that country's history there were more teenagers in school than there were out of it. When they weren't at school, there was summer camp, which was invented for the GI kids to get them out of the 'unhealthy' city and into the wholesome countryside.

So GI kids grew up feeling special and cared for even though parenting was strict, formal and stern. The kind of childhood they enjoyed encouraged them to be team workers who got things done by organising themselves into clubs, groups and unions to wield more clout. They were keen to make the world a better place so they put the needs of others before their own; pleasure took second place to duty and if that meant they had to delay gratification, they did so. What a far cry from our present day instant gratification society.

At the end of World War II, the special care that society afforded this generation kicked in once more with the GI Bill in America. University and vocational training was heavily subsidised by the government, which meant that GIs were able to obtain the sort of education that their parents could not afford. Between 1944 and 1956 nearly eight million people took advantage of it. In addition, the government also helped GIs to own their homes. The Veterans Administration subsidised one in five home loans in terms of the 1944 GI Bill. No wonder that today between 70 and 75 per cent of all older men and women own the homes they live in and that three quarters of them are completely paid off. They were, as young adults, the richest generation that had ever existed.

Helped to this extent, it's no surprise that after the war it was the visionary GIs who put a man on the moon, built modern suburbs and were in power longer than any other generation in history has been ... so far. GI presidents sat in the White House for a record thirty-two years.

GIs as parents

As parents, GIs continued in the tradition their parents had passed down, with an emotional divide between adults and children. Although GIs were more physically demonstrative than their parents had been towards them, they were still fairly aloof and distant from their children. This situation was exacerbated by circumstances prevailing in the early years of their parenting – the Depression and World War II.

Tips for GIs

- GIs are increasingly great-grandparents and, in this global world, are often living in different towns and on different continents from their grandchildren. Keeping in touch with them will enrich both your lives and theirs. So write that letter, and if you think there's nothing much for you to say about your life today, talk about past events and family. One day it will form an invaluable record of a bygone era that your children and great-grandchildren will marvel at and treasure.

- Some people in their eighties are even learning to email, which is the fastest way to an Xer's or Millennial's heart. But if you can't face that, dictate a letter to your son or daughter who can input it for you.

- The bottom line is that the more you keep in touch with young people, the longer you remain in tune with the world.

Silents (born 1920s to 1940s)

Childhood

The childhood of most Silent generation folk was a nightmare that those of us born in the aftermath of World War II shudder at as we read books about the war such as *Charlotte Gray* or *The Grapes of Wrath*, and see films ranging from *Saving Private Ryan* to *Schindler's List* and the miniseries *Band of Brothers*.

No wonder the Silents felt their childhood was one of removed parents, particularly in Britain and Europe. Father was off fighting the war, mother was nursing or was 'Rosie the Riveter' working in factories, or making ammunition or military uniforms. Children were evacuated to the country-side, wearing placards bearing their names around their necks, to live with strangers who had often reluctantly opened their homes to them. Some of them have not, even today, come to terms with the pain of separation from home and parents and the constipating effect it had on their ability to both give and receive love.

Food rationing was fierce and clothing even worse. The average British woman bought only one new outfit of clothes a year and magazines were filled with tips on how to patch their clothes.

Given this background, it is hardly surprising that the Silent's GI parents were focused, both during and after the war, on solving the problems of the world and building new societies. Parents told their children to get on with their lives on their own, so being a child back then was hardly a great emotional experience and there was little parent-child bonding. They too sometimes called their parents 'sir' and 'ma'am' and were closer to their nannies, dogs and teddy bears.

Fifty million people died during World War II, nearly fifty times more than were killed by the Black Death. In many a home when a death of a loved one was announced, the children were told almost in the same breath that 'life continues and you must get ready for school now'.

Almost as bad for some of them during the Great Depression years was the realisation that their parents were fallible. They could not get jobs. They did not have the means to feed and clothe them. Life was uncertain. Life was downright scary.

Given this background of uncertainty, no wonder they believe it is 'good' and 'normal' to work hard, to 'pay your way', and 'earn your dues'. A day off work, no matter how ill you are, is 'slacking'. It is the 'right thing to do' to knuckle down and get on with the job – and life. No point in complaining, they say.

Silents as parents

They were determined that their children, the Boomers, should not suffer as they had. 'You will have everything we never had', is their war cry, but woe betide the Boomer who loses it, breaks it, or doesn't 'make it'.

As parents they showed little emotion and they didn't 'worry the children' with the issues of the adult world. They were strict and structured parents. Sketches and portraits of family life in the 1950s showing father arriving home to a beautifully dressed wife with perfectly turned out children, cat and dog in tow, were true depictions of many a family scene back then.

Tips for Silents

As you become the healthiest and most active grandparents the world has ever yet known, many of you have a sense of loss as you think back on your somewhat distant parenting style. You sometimes wish you could turn back the clock, so you could show more affection to your children, put less pressure on them to achieve and support them more in their endeavours.

Sometimes too much water has flowed under the bridge for that to happen now and you may, sadly, never enjoy the close and affectionate relationship with your children of which you dream. But the wonderful thing about being a grandparent is that you get a second chance. Use it.

- Be affectionate with your grandchildren.

- Make time for them. Cancel the bridge, the bingo and the golf, once in a while.

- Let them teach you how to SMS, how to programme the video machine and play computer games.

- Don't judge your children's parenting style and don't undermine them with snide criticism when you have their children in your home.

Boomers (born 1940s to 1960s)

Childhood

This is almost a 'born with a silver spoon in your mouth' generation. They arrived post war, post famine, post Depression, as a shattered world gathered itself and tried to fit the pieces of torn apart countries together again. Their English and European parents were still struggling with the last vestiges of rationing, as were, to a much lesser extent, some of their colonies throughout the world.

In America, GI war veterans and some older members of the Silent generation were tapping into the government's tertiary education and housing help. The trickle out of the cities with their street-fronted tenement housing became a torrent as suburbs became 'the thing'. They were safer, cleaner and brighter, and boasted garages and gardens. 'Rosie the Riveter' had been sent back home, and nurses retired as men at the Front didn't need nursing, and ammunitions factories scaled back production.

Motherhood was now a 24-hour job while fathers worked 9 to 5 days in big, womb to tomb, nanny corporations. They tramped wearily home to be met by sparkling wives in spick and span houses, immortalised in the 1950s Pete Seeger song *Little Boxes* and in the movie *The Stepford Wives*.

Children were born, and born and born, almost as if the world was trying to make up for the 50 million dead as soldiers returned to the arms of their eager wives and girlfriends. And the world was caught with its pants down in more ways than one, particularly in America, as the baby boom wave swallowed up everything in its path.

In the early 1950s, American hospitals couldn't cope and women gave birth in corridors as labour wards overflowed. There wasn't enough baby food and there weren't enough diapers, and American department stores began running out of toys. Next under siege were schools. They had, quite extraordinarily, not anticipated the tidal wave of Boomers beginning to pour through their classrooms, and new ones, even prefabricated ones, were hastily built to cope with the demand. The collaborative tendencies of the Boomers, team-work but also competition, probably started in these over-crowded, under-resourced schoolrooms. When they got to university the same thing happened there all over again. Nobody, it seems, could handle the huge Boomer wave.

As Boomers swept into the world, so the world gathered them up in its collective arms, spoiling them rotten as their GI and Silent parents set out to give them 'everything we never had'. Soon the American dream of a house in the suburbs with two garages, a washing machine, swimming pool and front and back gardens became a worldwide aspiration. Countries like Australia and New Zealand have taken this middle class society ideal to new levels.

The Silent generation mothers of Boomers, marooned in their lonely but lovely suburban homes, often without their own mothers and grandparents to turn to for childrearing advice, read Dr Spock instead. And they liked what they read. He advocated a more indulgent, gentler approach to bringing up junior than they'd received at the often stick and belt-wielding hands of their own parents. The slightly gentler approach had its materialistic side too as a generation that had had so little in its youth, gave its children toys they had only sighed about.

Soon hula hoops, radios, rock 'n' roll, LPs and Singles took markets by storm and clever marketers leapt onto the bandwagon with one of the most successful marketing campaigns and products of all time – blue jeans. Blue jeans were worn by Marlon Brando in the movie *The Wild One* and by baby faced heart-throb, James Dean in *Rebel Without a Cause*. Jeans became a Boomer uniform worldwide. They were banned in American schools, sold for sky high prices in London and Paris and were smuggled into Russia. Boomers still insist on wearing jeans today no matter their age or shape. It's an age-defying symbol of their youth, as are the greasy little ponytails worn by sagging Boomer men as they ride their equally age-defying Harley-Davidsons.

Boomers, not surprisingly in a new, more carefree era, rebelled against the strict 'save it, don't waste it', and 'do what I say without questioning me' approach of the GIs and Silent parents. The material goods didn't make up for the hugs and kisses all kids want, but that their war-battered, unemotional, stiff-upper lip parents were incapable of giving.

'Give me space, give me air, I'm growing my hair,' was the rebellious, rallying Boomer cry. It was an incredibly potent anti-parent weapon, every bit as devastating as an automatic rifle as it mowed down parental authority. Until World War I men had worn their hair long as an indication of rank, but trench warfare with its attendant horrors of months spent in close quarters with rats, lice, mud and incessant rain necessitated a change for hygiene reasons. By World War II, short hair had become synonymous with being in the military and all that it stood for in terms of hierarchical structures, centralised control, obedience without questioning – in short, all the values that the Silent generation held dear.

As Boomers hit their teens and swung into full rebellion mode, what better symbol of authority to attack than hair. And so they grew 'long, beautiful hair, shining, gleaming' as they chanted in *Hair*, the wildly popular musical that keeps returning for more and more reruns to satisfy Boomer demand. In addition, hippies wore long flowing kaftans, twisted flowers in their hair, wafted incense and strolled about barefooted. It was as far removed from army uniforms as it was possible to go.

They gyrated to Elvis and Cliff Richard, which was about as much as their parents were able to stomach. But in the eyes of many a GI and Silent parent, the Beatles' 'yeah, yeah, yeah' was the beginning of a downhill slide into Mick Jagger's moans about his lack of 'satisfaction'. His urging in the era of drugs (marijuana) and free love, thanks to the newly arrived Pill, to 'spend the night together', was for many a mother a pill too big to swallow.

Boomer rebellion, anti-authority, anti-establishment, anti-elitist, soon burst into the streets of world capitals and on to university campuses as students protested against the atomic bomb and the Vietnam War. Some of them died.

But the youthful Boomers were undeterred. Their moralistic outlook spurred them on to activism against just about every institution they entered. Their rebellion was aimed not so much at toppling the system per se, but at removing what they perceived to be corruption within the system. They regarded themselves as being young, free and in charge.

Their rebelliousness was challenged when GI heroes who symbolised their questioning stance were mown down in heart-stopping events that will be remembered long after the Boomers are gone. John F Kennedy, his brother Robert and Martin Luther King Jr died in a hail of bullets. As Bob Dylan wailed 'the times they are a-changing', and as the Boomers learnt of the injustices of racial prejudice and the horrors of the Vietnam War, some turned on their parents' generation, blaming them for the world's social problems.

They also took up the cause of women's rights and gay rights. In 1963 Betty Friedan's book *The Feminine Mystique* kickstarted the women's movement and was taken up by Germaine Greer and Gloria Steinem. In June 1969 a cross-dresser in a Greenwich Village, New York, bar returned a cop's blow and swept away the, until then, submissive approach of most gays and lesbians.

But all the outward social change could not revolutionise the internal workings of many a Boomer's heart and psyche. Their rule-bound, doing it only one way, 'the right way', Silent generation parents imposed their dreams and expectations on their Boomer children. Regarding them as blessed with opportunities they wished they had been given, they wanted them to be successful with a capital S. And, yes, we're repeating it, because it was the Silent generation parent's battle cry: 'I want to give you everything that I never had'.

Many a 40 and 50-year-old Boomer sits in a therapist's office today trying to come to terms with a life spent never 'shaping up' in their parents' eyes. As they emerged from their hippie and rock 'n' roll teens, they settled down into serious life which meant acquiring all the materialistic trappings of smart addresses, swish cars, yachts, holiday homes and private schools for their kids. Add one more item to the shopping list: parental approval.

For many, this was the most elusive of all. One Boomer who'd experienced many a false start, finally cracked it with his own accountancy firm in his early forties. He was living in London, his father in South Africa. On the day he finally made it to millionaire status, he made that international call. 'Hi, dad, James here. Thought you'd like to know that as from today you will be calling a millionaire when you, finally, pick up that phone to me.' He clicked off and burst into tears. When he'd graduated from university and was leaving home, his father had said, 'I have given you every single thing I possibly could to help you succeed and you have wasted it all. Son, you will never amount to anything. Goodbye.'

Boomers as parents

As hippies graduated into Yuppies, and fast-forwarded into parenthood, their selfish, materialistic values soon labelled them the 'Me Generation'. They set about changing the workplace, once again breaking the rules so beloved by their Silent bosses and parents. Boomer women who'd begun working in unprecedented numbers decided they weren't going home when the baby hit the delivery table. They stayed on in the workplace, demanding flexible working hours and on-site crèches and nurseries.

And, as Boomer men decided it was time to regain some balance in their lives too, so they have downscaled, refusing promotion, declining to move cities, earning less in order to spend more time with their families.

Some Boomer women who were fast climbing the career ladder suddenly checked their biological clocks, realised in horror that their baby-making time was fast drawing to a close, and raced into action. When that failed, they turned to IVF (in vitro fertilisation) as they swallowed hormones and submitted to the fairly degrading fertility procedures.

Some women were working and playing so hard when they hit their forties they forgot to find a partner or a husband so they went solo, going to sperm banks and raising their children alone. Indeed, it may soon be possible for a woman to create a child without a man, by fertilising eggs from any part of the body and not just from sperm. No prizes for guessing that it'll be the 'last ditcher' Boomers lining up when the time comes to take that futuristic and challenging step. They have broken, changed and made new rules all their lives so why should they stop now!

But where they have become trapped juggling too many balls is in the 'Sandwich generation'. They are sandwiched between the needs of their ageing GI and Silent generation parents, for whom they are, increasingly, providing elder care, and the demands of their own Xer and Millennial children whom they are still busy bringing up and educating. Take a look at this aspect of generational history in chapter 19, Re-tyreing.

Torn between the demands of old and young, working harder than any generation before them, many workaholic Boomers set themselves up to be poor 'parenters'. Besides being absent, they are also the most divorced generation of all time. Boomers have placed hefty responsibility onto schools to impose discipline on their children, yet shout if teachers carry this to its logical conclusion. Many a teacher feels that today's school problems are more about delinquent parents than they are about delinquent children.

Even when Boomer parents were at home, they tended to have a 'hands-off' approach as a direct consequence of the overly strict and protective line taken by their own parents. To avoid being as dominating or controlling as their parents had been, they swung the pendulum and became permissive, putting too few boundaries in place for their children.

If they stood up to their Xer children, insisting they eat certain foods or do homework at defined times, they feared 'repressing their personalities'. And that, to the rule-defying Boomers, was anathema. But their (lack of) action had its consequences.

Tips for Boomers

- It's probably too late for you to have quality time with your children. After the age of fifteen it's the kids who initiate quality time, on the whole, with their parents. Accept that it's too late, at this stage, to impose your will on your children. The best thing now is to build bridges that bring you together.

- Many a Boomer parent, attempting to make up for lost time, lost years and opportunities to be with their children, is trying too hard. Most Xers who have parents trying to do this find it irritating. Parents: chill. The Xers want to be left alone.

- You can't recreate the past by suddenly treating your kids with the kind of love and respect you should have done years ago. Set out instead to create a new relationship based on mutual respect and dignity.

- It's never too late to show considerate, unconditional love and respect.

Generation X (born 1960s to 1980s)
Childhood

The 'cut me some slack' Xers began making their appearance on planet earth just a few years after the Pill was invented. It was to have a dramatic impact on this generation's lives for not only were far less of them born, but it liberated their mothers with far-reaching consequences for their kids. Fewer children meant they could decide when to have them, and increasingly Boomer mothers chose later rather than earlier. And having fewer children allowed this 'Me Generation', the indulged, spoilt Boomer generation of mums and dads, to follow their own hearts as they 'discovered' themselves, their needs, wants and desires as no other generation had been able to do before them.

There had to be a consequence to this and there was. Xers are the 'most different' of all the generations and the most misunderstood by the others. This has a great deal to do with their parenting and the era in which they grew up.

The euphoria and boom time of the 1960s in America began to fade as the full impact of the Vietnam War hit home, literally and figuratively, in the United States. They weren't used to seeing young men coming home in body bags in the full glare of instant TV news. The rise of Castro in Cuba, the Bay of Pigs debacle, the showdown between John F Kennedy and Khrushchev and the closing of the border between East and West Berlin, all added to a sense of gloom. Although few Xers were alive when the Kennedy brothers were assassinated, or when Nelson Mandela was sentenced to a lifetime in jail, the oldest of them could sense that something had changed profoundly in their parents' lives.

In South Africa, Xers are those who are old enough to remember apartheid and to be judged by history as having been a part of it, yet not quite old enough to have been involved in any form of struggle, whether that was to uphold the apartheid state, or to fight against it. White Xers just missed out on national service and young black Xers would not have been old enough to join the Boomer schoolchildren of 1976 who demanded 'liberation before education'. Yet they have all grown up in the shadow of these events. History is beginning to view Xers as having been culpable and part of the problem, even though this may not necessarily be the case.

The approach to parenting had changed for Boomer and some Silent generation parents who had children later in life. When Boomers were children, child rearing gurus like Benjamin Spock assumed families were strict and gently urged more indulgence. When Xers were young kids this trend had swung completely with a laissez-faire attitude to child rearing. Indeed, some childcare manuals advised parents to 'consider yourself' ahead of a child's needs. They celebrated the mutual independence of parent and child in something they called 'detachment parenting'. It's interesting that many a 1970s childcare manual was dedicated to friends, lovers and spouses of the writers whereas the 90s books are usually dedicated to their children.

So, the flower power, pot-smoking hippies who believed in free love, peace and the right of everybody to express themselves, bolstered by such advice, influenced by feminism and affected by rising divorce rates, were hardly going to strait-lace their kids into life.

But as we now know, too much freedom can be a dangerous thing. True life stories of children abandoned for days, even weeks on end, while their criminally neglectful and selfish parents went on holiday without them, horrified the world.

Those are extreme cases but they highlight the times that young Xers lived through in terms of society's permissive and hands-off approach to child rearing. An American magazine, *Atlantic Monthly*, described their childhood as 'the most virulently anti-child period in American history ... the age of the latchkey child, the boomerang child and the throwaway child'. Pretty devastating stuff. This is the 'divorced' generation that has a profusion of different family relationships such as 'dad's girlfriend, mom's previous ex-husband, my second stepfather or my stepbrother's father's ex-wife'. No wonder Xers grew up sceptical about relationships. In their need to fill the family void with something else they turned to friends and peers who became surrogate families. Today Xers value highly a small, tightly knit band of friends who fill in for family.

Xers remember, with pain, that their parents were not there for them, not at prizegiving, nor swimming galas, sports matches or the school play. They accuse their parents, with justification, of trying to make up for their absence with toys, games, clothes and electronic equipment.

'We were never in direct conflict with our parents because we always got anything, and everything, we wanted,' says a thirty-something Xer. They're not slow to go back home when the money runs out, even in their thirties, so that mum can do their washing and ironing once more and they can feed from the ever-full fridge and swipe dad's beer.

And when they're short of cash, mom reaches for her wallet.

For the above reasons, Xers have poor skills in the following:
- anger management
- negotiation
- conflict management
- money management

Xers were the first generation to be raised on TV. As Warren G Bennis and Robert J Thomas write in their book *Geeks and Geezers* (their terms for Xer and Silent generations): 'People born and raised after the introduction of television in the 1950s are marked forever by their ease in processing a tsunami of visual information at breakneck speed. Today's ordinary American is exposed to more novel visual images in a single day than the average Victorian experienced in a lifetime.'

You only need to look at how differently the generations learnt fundamentals. As children, Xers didn't learn the alphabet in a measured singsong, as did virtually everybody over fifty today. They shouted it out, one letter chasing another, as they learnt to do on *Sesame Street*. They never slogged through grammar lessons of heartbreaking tedium. Instead, 'Conjunction Junction' and the other upbeat lessons of Schoolhouse Rock were set to jazz riffs, tunes still sung aloud on social occasions in Silicon Valley and other capitals of the New Economy.

So, as Xer kids grew up, feeling like castaways, avoided by their parents who were more interested in discovering themselves, the general public was indifferent, on the whole, to the dangers posed to a divorce-battered, crime-exposed, sexually transmitted, disease-affected generation. Xers are such a diverse generation that they are not easily labelled. Indeed, the 'X' stands for a generation that marketers did not know how to define. They sometimes apologise for or even deny the existence of their own generation.

As the Xers moved into their teens, they were, and still are, left to fend for themselves. It's interesting that Xers were, in fact, only 'discovered' as a generation around 1980 when they began to take over youth culture. Their music was rap, rave, and MTV. Films about them were hardly inspiring and uplifting; rather they were dark themed ones such as *Rosemary's Baby*, *The*

Exorcist, Taxi Driver and *The Omen.* Their hero was Bart Simpson who didn't give a damn, the archetypal anti-hero. In spite of this he's the one who usually put things right for his parents when they screwed up.

They are a worried generation. They worry there aren't any good jobs available for them as the world downsizes, worry they won't keep them when they get them and worry about ever falling in love. Sex is expected yet confusing, and downright dangerous due to AIDS. They also worry about marrying. And unlike previous generations, they can't turn to their parents for much guidance. Their parents are often as lost as they are in this chaotic world.

The last worry on the above list has not prevented marriage and children but, and it is a big BUT, many of them are choosing to have the children without marriage.

In Britain, in 1952, three and a half per cent of babies were born outside marriage. In the year 2000 this had risen to 40 per cent. In 1952 only five per cent of partners in first marriages lived together beforehand. This number rose to 70 per cent in 2000. (Figs from *TIME* magazine, 3rd June, 2002.)

They are cynical about love and marriage which is hardly surprising given their parents' high divorce rate and their own troubled childhoods.

Xers as parents

They are pioneering a different form of marriage or committed partnership, in which couples don't necessarily both concentrate on their careers, full-time, as their workaholic Boomer parents still do. One spouse or partner will concentrate on his/her career while the other studies, or takes on a lower paying job for a while.

Xer women are pouring into universities and colleges with, in many cases, half the student body being comprised of women. Not surprisingly, they can move into high paying jobs while their partners may continue studying. And then, they swap roles, with the women doing postgraduate studies while their partners move into the workforce.

The oldest Xers now have children just beginning to toddle off to school and they watch with the pride born of being truly hands-on parents. As a result, the parenting 'industry' is booming. From antenatal classes to child psychologists, baby stores, and parenting books the demand is such that it's hard to keep up. Most Xer parents have been on at least one parenting course. They don't like taking advice from their parents and are the first generation that has, en masse, not gone running back to mother at some stage in the first year of their child's life. They prefer parent-support groups.

They share parenting roles with their partners far more equitably than any other generation before them has ever done.

They have forced governments to grant paternity leave and extended maternity leave as basic rights. They have encouraged shopping centres to create nappy change facilities, and made their workplaces start daycare facilities and breastfeeding rooms. They demand more flexibility to enable them to collect their children from school in working hours and make up for it by working at home, at night, when their kids are asleep.

As their children grow up and reach their teens, Xers will probably interact well with them. They don't feel as out of touch with technology as many Boomers do so most Xers will be able to stay ahead, or at least on a par with their children technologically. Xers are used to constant change, and if they apply that to their relationships with their children, they should be able to make the necessary adjustments when the teen years arrive. Their shortcoming is likely to be that of overprotection. They will need to learn to let go, and allow their precious Millennial babes to grow up, bump their heads and find out about life for themselves.

Tips for Xers

- Teach your children the skill of delayed gratification. For example, if they watch TV now, they will only get one sweet after supper. If they do their homework first and then watch TV, they will get four sweets.

- Help them to put their own wishes second and to consider the needs of others as more important than their own needs.

- Explain that learning, accepting instructions, is the clever way to go.

- Don't settle for less than the optimum – you can have the best of both worlds and be both a good employee and a great parent.

- You may disappoint your boss and your friends but don't disappoint your kids. It's you they need – not your money.

Millennials (born 1980s to 2000s)

Childhood

The contrast between the Xer and Millennial generations in their childhoods is so stark that, at first glance, it seems like a total backlash against just about everything the much maligned Xers have come to stand for. It **is** a backlash. It's the generational cycle coming full circle, and that is what generational history is all about. The Millennials, so-called because all of them will finish school in the new millennium, are the equivalent generation of the GI generation.

It's predicted that the Millennial kids, like the GIs, will be civic minded, determined to help their communities, will (and already do) care for each other, volunteer more, be prepared to be conscripted if the cause is just, and are increasingly wearing uniforms to school in countries where this has not been the norm.

Why has there been such a dramatic change in the Millennial generation compared with the slacker, can't-get-out-of-bed Xers, the selfish, status-symbol-obsessed Boomers and the cautious, slightly depressed Silent generation?

It's the generational story, the era in which they are being born, plus the parenting they are receiving and the attitude of society towards them.

The arrival of the first Millennial babes in the 1980s marked a dramatic societal shift from the latchkey kids. If the key on a string around their necks symbolised the Xers, then the 'Baby on Board' car stickers mark a new era in which babies were not only seen and heard but actually became status symbols.

Suddenly pregnancy and infants are hot stuff. Take a look at the highly glossy, celebrity obsessed magazines *Hello!* and *OK*. Hardly an issue goes by without some 'schleb' ranging from Madonna to Posh and Becks, Victoria Spencer and Elizabeth Hurley, appearing with their newborn infants.

There is no way that a Boomer celeb would have done this. Boomers didn't flaunt babies, they flaunted status symbols. Xers flaunt their pregnancies, wandering around shopping malls exposing their huge, bare bellies with pride to the world.

Millennials arrived already adored, desired, demanded and cosseted before they uttered their first cry. They've had music played to them in the womb, stories read to them, powerful and positive thoughts relayed to them. In fact, the new status symbol is a stay-at-home mom.

Part of the reason for this new child centred world is that many of their (late) Boomer and (early) Xer mothers struggled to fall pregnant. Working too hard and too long, they suddenly woke up and began panicking, turning to fertility treatment, surrogate mothers, rent-a-womb mothers and adoption in order to land the much wanted infant on planet earth.

No wonder the first trip the babes make is in a vehicle plastered with the not so subtle 'watch out for me, here I come with a "Baby On Board" car sticker'. It's the equivalent of 'Dynamite' or 'Poisonous snakes' with a skull and crossbones. Substitute the latter with a cherub and its golden halo, and you're getting the picture.

As Xers began having babies, so they reacted against their lonely, unprotected upbringing. They do so in a completely natural, instinctive manner, unlike the Boomers who set out to discover 'family values' as a conscious and deliberate lifestyle choice. *TIME* magazine ran a feature in which they described the Generation Xer as 'Gen Nester'.

If you've seen a baby in transit today, you'll know why. The logistics and the paraphernalia involved in the exercise are mind-boggling compared with what existed in previous generations. The padded pram cum pushchair, the safety harness, the month-by-month, age appropriate, stimulating toys hanging from every possible nook and cranny of the pram, the nappies, wet wipes, bibs, and aerodynamically designed milk bottles would have stunned a Silent generation mother. Babies are handed over to aunts and grandmothers today with a list of instructions as long as a babycare website address.

As these adored darlings have grown from toddlers into teens, their every step and utterance (not forgetting the actual birth) have been recorded on video and digital camera and instantly downloaded by their worldwide families and friends. The world has changed to accommodate them.

Changes include: lead free paint on cots, child safe medicine bottles, safety plugs in electric sockets, baby seats in cars, bicycle helmets and hard hats for horse riding. Society's rules have changed dramatically too.

There are new crimes – in America one spouse cannot hit the other in front of the children. If you have a gun in your house and a child finds it, the parent can go to jail. In some American states the same happens if a child is not in a safety harness in the car. The British 'name and shame' approach to paedophiles is another example of societal concern.

Schools in many a Western country are now virtual fortresses, access to which is denied unless you have a security sticker on your vehicle. Children can only go home with friends if they have a parental letter giving permission for this. In 1998 a *Newsweek* headline shouted, 'It's 4pm. Do You Know Where Your Children Are?' Too sure they do in this new, 'we're in love with children' era. It's also the working parents' era and they know EXACTLY where their children are nearly every minute, nay, every second of the day. Cellphones, satellite tracking with GPS and webcams all assist in this process.

Workplaces are having to come to the party as well. If they can't provide on-site childcare, locating crèches, nurseries and playrooms in buildings nearby, they are virtually required to provide 24-hour CCTV (closed circuit television) coverage so that anxious parents can watch their kids.

We have the child caring trend in addition to the safety aspect of child rearing today. Some restaurants not only welcome kids but they provide high chairs, plastic bibs, crayons and colouring-in books. Airlines provide special fun kits for kids, while some even have videos and in-flight games for them. Shopping malls increasingly provide rooms where you can breastfeed and change nappies; there are playrooms and in Switzerland some high-tech trains have carriages with mini playgrounds on them where toddlers climb jungle gyms and slip down dinosaur-shaped slides.

Xers take their child rearing very seriously as we can see from the flood of books on the market, guiding them through every single aspect of their child's development. It's interesting to note that these manuals are advocating a somewhat stricter approach than the swinging Boomers were handed down. They want hands-on rules as opposed to the hands-off approach of the Boomer parenting style and the 'detachment' parenting Boomers practised has given way to 'attachment' style which means babies in your bed as well as 'on board'. Taking toddlers, and children generally, to work is also suggested so they know where parents are and don't have to worry about them.

The latter is a huge Millennial trait. The older Millennial kids look after their 'scatty' Boomer parents, checking they have their seat belts on, warning them about crossing the road and calling attention to the changing-to-red traffic lights. The British TV show *Absolutely Fabulous* personified this approach with mum Eddie constantly being rebuked by her serious, spectacle wearing, neatly dressed, non-drug taking, celibate daughter about her wild and erratic behaviour and unseemly attire. When Eddie absent-mindedly sells her daughter to slave traffickers in a Moroccan market place, many a Boomer mum, silently, understands her actions.

In their youth, Millennials have experienced abortion and divorce rates ebbing.

And while the single parent family is on the rise, it is no longer regarded as a 'fragile' family.

The following figures from the US Bureau of the Census 2000 show how single parent demographics have changed over the years. Among children who live with a single mother, only two per cent in 1950 had a 'never-married' (as opposed to divorced or widowed) mother. In 1980 that figure rose to 15 per cent and in 1998 it soared to 40 per cent.

Yet as Neil Howe and William Strauss point out in their book *Millennials Rising*, 'Today's Millennial children of never-married moms present an entirely novel situation, whose impact – especially to a child's eye – is not the same as divorce. In these families there seldom hangs the shadow of life-shattering betrayal because no child-centred family ever existed in the first place. Many of these households have a real or putative father who is still present from time to time. An estimated 80 per cent of the biological fathers are romantically involved with never-married mothers at the time of childbirth and half of them have lived together. Whether they are present or not, life in a family with a near-married mom is all their kids have ever known, it's all many of their friends have ever known, and it's simply a fact of life in their child's world. It's not ideal but it's not divorce either.'

World and societal changes have played a huge role in the Millennial kid's upbringing, as they have in all generations' lives. In America, Bill Clinton's emphasis on what was right for children was obvious in his speeches which covered subjects ranging from food (not chips) to smoking, drugs, uniforms, even curfews.

In Britain, Tony and Cherie Blair blazed the way for later-in-life babies with the arrival of their son Leo when Cherie was in her late forties. Tony, ever mindful of a good publicity shot, was pictured with Leo in his arms on the cover of the new *Dad* magazine which, as the title suggests, focuses on the role that fathers are playing in today's society. Tell a GI that and he'll choke with surprise.

In South Africa the Nelson Mandela's Children's Fund is aimed solely at Millennial generation kids. There is free medical care for children under six and pregnant mothers are cared for by the State in a way hitherto unknown.

In nearly every poll taken of the Millennial generation, the common indicators used to assess a generation are all moving for the better.

Millennials as parents

They're likely to be as focused and committed as their Xer parents but unlike them they will take advice from their (Xer and Boomer) parents. They will probably get married at a younger age than their parents did and will start having children when they are younger.

Full-time parenting will be shared between mom and dad and flexibility in the workplace will allow for much more parent/child time. They will give their children more space and freedom than they are presently enjoying, in reaction to their Xer parents whom they will probably accuse of 'being around us too much'.

Generational theory predicts that a crisis will emerge sometime early in the parenting stage of the Millennials. This crisis will be largely precipitated by the insular focus of the current Boomer-led generation. The crisis, at present, appears to be related to a world that's increasingly threatened by terrorism. The civic minded Millennials will focus energy on solving the crisis and may miss out on being hands-on parents. This may well be their biggest challenge as parents – to get the balance right.

Tips for Millennials

- Look at the homes you are growing up in now – and if you don't like what you see, ensure you don't repeat the mistakes your parents are making.

- Understand that your parents are only human and are trying their best.

General parenting tip:

It became very 'hip' during the Swinging Sixties for Boomers to call their GI and Silent generation parents by their first names, no doubt because it irritated parents so much. When Xer kids arrived, some emulated their Boomer parents. Wise Xer and Millennial parents will know better than to try and be their children's 'friends'. We have many friends in life but only one set of parents. They are special. Let's keep them that way.

When you get to the end of the book, ask yourself:

Have I forgiven my parents for my childhood, for the way they brought me up?

If so, have you told them so? Then you could ask yourself, 'Is 'forgiveness "the appropriate word?"' because what they were doing was appropriate for their era. Their parenting style was, on the whole, based on the common sense, the wisdoms and the culture of the times. If we'd been parents in their particular era, we'd probably have done the same. Maybe 'release' is a better word than 'forgiveness'. Maybe the time has come to release your parents, and yourself, from your childhood.

Before sex:

GIs:	Get going – not a topic for discussion
Silents:	Get married
Boomers:	Get high
Xers:	Get protection
Millennials:	Get tested

Dress:

GIs: Dressed their kids like little adults.

Silents: Followed their parents' example but did so curtailed by rationing. Boys wore ties to play soccer.

Boomers: The first to make a huge distinction between youth and adult clothing. Jeans arrived with a bang. They wore labels on the outside with the rationale that there's no point wearing Armani if nobody knows that it's Armani.

Xers: Had to fight their parents for their own distinctive jeans look and wore them dirty, torn, grungy and hanging down their backsides.

Millennials: Have gone back to wearing what their parents do – only now it's jeans and T-shirts. Don't mind looking like their parents.

Structures of families in the past one hundred years:

GIs: Mother, father and seven children, a couple of whom might not have survived into their teens. Dogs, cats, horses, servants, gardeners.

Silents: Mother, father, five children, two servants, three dogs, grandparents live close by and are involved.

Boomers: Ma, pa (if he survived World War II), four children, a maid, two dogs, and grandparents who often lived in the country.

Xers: Pa, ma, 2.47 kids, four bedroom, three-bathroom home with double garage, a dog. Parents divorced by the time you were fifteen. Then it was mom and your new pop; dad, his girlfriend and her two kids.

Millennials: Mom and dad and 1.67 kids. Or... any possible combination of mom and mom; dad and dad; or mom and sperm donor; or mom and partner who IS dad even though they're not married. Cluster home, apartment. Goldfish and budgie.

Madonna:

Madonna has managed to invent, and reinvent, herself in so many different guises, so often, that she has come to be all things to all generations. This is, of course, the aim of all those who wish to be an ongoing commercial success, to never have to reach the dreaded 'sell-by' date. Here's how she's done it.

Madonna is, to the following generations:

GIs and Silents:	Evita
Boomers:	Material Girl
Xers:	Weird sex lady, with cone bras
Millennials:	American Pie and children's book author

Dating and courtship rituals:

GIs:	Rituals were formal and took place at the family home after asking permission of the father to be there. This was the last generation to have dance cards, where men booked women for dances and then swept up at the appropriate moment to lead them onto the dance floor.
Silents:	They were not as formal but were still stylised. There were rules and procedures. Boys always asked girls out. Boys asked girls to dance and those who weren't asked were called 'wallflowers'.

Boomers:	Think of the film *Grease* and it will sum up the Boomers who pioneered the concept of a date with cars that had massive back seats, were parked in drive-in movies, and drew up at roadhouses. Boys without cars suffered. It was still boys who asked girls out. Girls who did the asking were considered 'fast'.
Xers:	Girls ask boys to go out with them. They ask boys to dance with them and if the answer's 'no' they dance on their own anyway, with everybody else on the floor. Dating lost what was left of its 'innocence' as date rape and date rape drugs arrived. Xers began using the Internet for dating purposes.
Millennials:	They will have virtual dates where a couple will watch a movie at the same time on different continents. They will be 'intimate' over the Internet using video link-ups.

11

Educating the Generations

Attitude to education:

GI:	Serious stuff for serious students.
Silent:	Lucky to have one – we'll do our very best.
Boomer:	It's my RIGHT to attend school and university.
Xer:	I'll listen but I can teach myself.
Millennial:	There's more to school than (boring) memorising.

When George Bernard Shaw said that his education had been interrupted by having to attend school, he could not have realised how prophetic his words were. During his childhood, children sat in rigid rows of wooden desks, in dark, cold classrooms with small, high-up windows. They memorised facts from the blackboard and regurgitated them. Overall the classroom atmosphere was boring and exhausting and most children were thrilled to leave school, glad they had 'got their education over with'.

Today, education, as George Bernard Shaw visualised, is a lifelong learning process. School, increasingly, teaches you *how* to learn. Many children, and their parents, realise school is just the first step – there will be a great many more education 'portals' along the way. Chapter 12, on Training, will deal specifically with the different teaching and training techniques and environments preferred by each generation. This chapter is concerned with the history, and future, of education as a whole.

Education has become a massive and hotly competitive industry, and educational institutions are having to change rapidly to keep up with new trends. Many schools are developing into campuses with a variety of amenities on offer. Classrooms are often brightly painted and have sliding glass doors on to pretty gardens.

No wonder that grandparents and great-grandparents cannot understand the casual approach their grandchildren have towards school today and the manner in which they learn. This approach puzzles them because they realise these children have far greater pressure exerted on them to achieve and are much brighter, on the whole, than they were at that age.

The sight of a Millennial learner, lying on her stomach, in her school tracksuit, listening to her walkman or MP3 player as she does her maths stuns her grandmother. The school kid is equally surprised to discover that education 'in the old days' was associated with pain (the cane, the belt) and suffering. It wasn't meant to be easily, or cheerfully, attained and severe-looking teachers ensured that this was the case.

Now a successful teacher will impart knowledge and expertise in a manner that best enables the student to absorb it. The easy way out for a teacher is to teach in the manner in which they were taught. Then the effort of learning a new approach isn't required. But good teachers acquire the skills that best help their students to learn. They ignore, at their peril, the fact that today's generation learns differently from those that preceded it.

This means that teachers should track generational changes more keenly than many other professions do.

When GIs, Silents and Boomers were children they were tested only on their linguistic and mathematical abilities. Today we realise there are at least thirteen different intelligences which range from musical, artistic and spatial intelligence to physical, spiritual and emotional intelligence. A wise teacher knows that when she's got Millennials in her class she needs to take into account their different intelligences and adapt her teaching methods and communication accordingly.

Not every change is new, though. Many a GI grandparent (now in their eighties and nineties) was educated at home with tutors or governesses. Today, the home school is one of the fastest growing forms of education throughout the world. There are nearly 400 000 home scholars in America and about 50 000 in South Africa, according to the Home School Associations in those countries.

And so the generational cycle comes full circle, with Millennials echoing GIs.

What schools were like when the generations were scholars

GIs (born 1900s to 1920s)

Schools were built of heavy stone blocks in the English 'cathedral school' style, around quadrangles. They were often set in spacious grounds with lovely old trees. The wood fittings in classrooms were usually dark and heavy, probably made from mahogany, and desks were the single unit type that you see in movies, with flip up seats. They were fitted with porcelain inkwells that had real ink into which the GIs dipped their pens made from wood with a nib at the end of them. The naughty ones flicked ink on to their friends' starched, white shirts.

Status was everything. Prefects ruled through the fag system in which little boys sat on their toilet seats on chilly mornings to warm them up, made them toast and carried out errands.

Teachers often wore academic gowns or some sort of apparel that served as a 'uniform', and in convents the nuns were heavily swathed in black cloth from top to toe. The approach was to be as far removed from the pupils as possible, and stern, unsmiling faces were what their pupils saw. Children were reminded, constantly, that they were to be seen and not heard. The teacher was the absolute authority and questioning her was not wise practice.

Notices were erected in some schools that proclaimed, 'Parents! This far and no further'. A huge brass bell on a heavy rope proclaimed the commencement and end of classes. There were no heaters in the classrooms.

In the colonies, many a school had a balcony, often built above the main entrance, for when the British Monarch came to visit.

Silents (born 1920s to 1940s)

They followed in their predecessors' footsteps in most aspects of school life. When new schools were built, an effort was made to emulate the grand style of the GIs but generally they did not have the resources to do so. The architecture was heavy and oppressive but a less expensive stone and wood were used. The approach was functional rather than stylish, reflecting the Depression and the uncertain times in which they grew up. Much-needed renovations were put on hold due to financial constraints, and peeling paint, broken light fittings and rickety desks are etched in the memories of the Silent generation when they remember their schooldays.

Windows were small and placed high up the walls in order to prevent pupils being distracted by activity outside the classroom.

The Silents were the last generation to go to school in the Industrial era. They could not have known, as they sat at their hard wooden desks, that the world for which they were being prepared would soon no longer exist as the Information era waited in the wings.

Boomers (born 1940s to 1960s)

This was the first generation to grow up in the suburbs that were created after the end of World War II. To save parents from commuting to a town or city centre, new schools were built in the suburbs and they mushroomed in order to cope with the baby boom that followed the war. Such growth put a strain on resources, so the grand stone buildings of the two preceding generations gave way to brickwork. The buildings tended to be highly functional, utilitarian, even drab, and often all looked the same with an administration block and two to three multi-storey blocks of classrooms. Some looked like today's battery chicken farms as they were hastily erected to keep pace with the growing population.

Boomers were the first generation to consistently share resources, such as books and stationery, at school. Consequently, they had to learn to work together and were judged and rated on their ability to do so, with the result that today, one of the main Boomer characteristics is their determined approach to teamwork.

The old 'GI' desks were still there, but fountain pens had arrived so the inkwells weren't used and secretive scribblings were pushed into them to avoid the gaze of still stern teachers. They were, by and large, professional teachers now (graduates from teacher training colleges and not direct from universities) and so the academic gowns gave way to suits and formal frocks.

Titles were still much in evidence with 'doctor' and 'professor' being insisted upon by many a teacher. Pupils filed neatly into their classrooms, stood quietly at their desks and spoke when spoken to.

'Greenboards' replaced the old classroom blackboards and cork poster boards lined the walls. Some classrooms had heaters installed. Scholars took sandwiches and fruit juice to school, although in many countries the State subsidised free food and milk on a daily basis for school children.

Generation X (born 1960s to 1980s)

New school buildings were often a far cry from those of the GI generation. The Xers inherited the prefabricated classrooms that went up in the grounds of grand buildings to accommodate late-born Boomers. The once spacious school grounds were being squeezed. Windows got bigger as the environment was allowed to step inside the classroom and some teachers even talked about the outside world during lessons.

Many schools had extra resources and were able to upgrade their facilities. But inside the classrooms old desks coexisted with new in schools where finances didn't allow for a complete refit.

Many more classrooms had heating, and the whirring noise of fan heaters added to the much noisier atmosphere that existed in them than had been the case when the Boomers were school children. Xers asked questions and demanded answers.

Ballpoint pens were in common usage whereas most Boomers had been banned from using them as it was feared their writing would be ruined. Overhead projectors became more common and blackboards made way for white screens, which teachers never seemed to be able to pull down, and then keep down.

Academic gowns were reserved for prizegiving and some young (Boomer) teachers wore hippie clothes. A teacher at Graeme's old school, Parktown Boys' High School, Johannesburg, even wore flowers in her hair and skipped barefoot around the classroom, describing which drugs gave the best high and terrifying some of the teenage boys as she did so.

Teachers were allowed some latitude in giving their classrooms an individual feel and could paint them the colours of their choice. One teacher encouraged his pupils to paint the ceiling with the proviso that they didn't spend all lesson gazing at it.

Not having the time, or the energy, to make a packed lunch for school, working Boomer mothers welcomed the lifeline that tuck shops threw them and thankfully pressed coins into their kids' hands.

Millennials (born 1980s to 2000s)

Schools that have been built during the past few years have brought the environment into the classroom, with massive glass windows and huge sliding glass doors that open on to attractive gardens. Old established schools have put in bigger windows and glass doors. Some schools have atriums, filled with greenery and flowers, between each classroom.

White, light plaster lends an airy feel to campuses that are more like modern office parks, and teachers try to emphasise the individualistic approach. One teacher pinned up posters of rugby heroes next to Albert Einstein in her maths class.

The approach now is to create a school campus with many more facilities than used to exist back in twentieth century schooldays. State of the art science laboratories are being built, particularly in girls' schools that have not traditionally emphasised this subject. Design and technology classrooms are also high on many a developing school's agenda, as are art studios and music centres as schools embrace the concept of balancing left and right brain development. Computer and media centres replacing old 'books only' libraries are a necessity.

In the Boomer's school years, the most basic of tuck shops were just beginning to make an appearance. Now, some big new schools have fast food and pizza shops on their grounds while chips, sweets, coffee and hot chocolate are dispensed from state of the art vendor machines or brand name carts.

Where to from here?

There are many SoHo entrepreneurs today whom schools, with their underutilised facilities, could target by renting conference venues and meeting rooms to them and, in the process, generate some extra income. They could even offer fax, email and secretarial services.

Learning style

In each generation a specific style of teaching and learning has predominated. It is important to recognise these styles, as they have influenced not only *how* we *learn* but also how we *teach**.

GIs and Silents

Teachers imparted facts in a linear, modular, progressive format. Pupils memorised them by rote and regurgitated them in their exercise books. Learning was largely considered to be the accumulating and memorising of facts. It was a brave teacher who departed from the straight and narrow and encouraged students to interpret facts in their own way. When he had finished the lesson, he returned to the staff room, satisfied that he had completed his task.

Boomers

It was a tough time to be at school. In a world that was questioning everything and where the boundaries were being pushed in just about every sphere from sex to music, drugs and science, Boomers were seldom allowed to question anything

* *You'll find a more detailed look at specific training and teaching techniques for the different generations in chapter 12.*

inside the classroom. Lateral thinking was just arriving, thanks to Edward de Bono. Some Boomers remember lining up alongside their desks and chanting passages from their history books. For the Latin pupils the chant was 'amo, amas, amat'. The approach, on the whole, was still linear and modular and you spewed onto the exam pad, in fountain pen ink, what you had learnt from teachers and textbooks. The emphasis was on learning the facts stipulated in a curriculum. But things were changing, and a new deductive style of learning started to emerge. Today Boomers are strong supporters of deductive analysis and brainstorming.

Xers

Connecting points A and B with only one straight line was out. You could connect point A to point B via any route you chose. It was not linear, not logical and not progressive. At least, that's what the best of the new breed of, mainly Boomer, teachers were saying to the Xers. The emphasis was moving away from simply memorising a curriculum to guiding pupils towards the ability to interpret and analyse information. But only the good teachers really got it right. It was the start of considerable polarisation in education, where you had real professionals doing an outstanding job, while many others were teachers simply because they were unable to do anything else. The result was an educational standard that ranged from superb to appalling, even in one school.

Xers prefer learning by doing. They don't like to be told the answers, preferring to find things out for themselves, and using inductive learning techniques.

Millennials

Teaching today is probably tougher than it's ever been, with the emphasis on different intelligences ranging from spatial to music and emotional. It's not for the faint-hearted, since everything will be challenged, the classroom will be noisy, and teachers have to come to terms with the fact that often their pupils know more than they do. It has required a HUGE paradigm shift, which only the best teachers have succeeded in making successfully. Teachers must pose questions and throw problems at their pupils, using multiple means of communication and whole brain intelligence. Silent and Boomer teachers ask, 'But how **do** today's children learn?' The answer is that in a class of thirty children there may be five or six different learning styles, compounded by multiple personality traits. Teachers are increasingly challenged by their students. Gone are the days when the teacher was the 'know-it-all'. Today, some youngsters have travelled to three different continents by the time they're four years old, have enjoyed sledge rides in the Alaskan snow and seen the volcanoes of Hawaii. Tricky for the teacher who's told, 'But it didn't look like that, Miss. I've been there.'

Nowadays the emphasis has shifted from learning a set curriculum. Today pupils need to be taught how to learn (in their own individual style) and how to love the process of learning, because that's what they are going to spend the rest of their lives doing... learning!

Teaching tools that generations remember from their schooldays:

GIs: Books. Teachers stood up front with books in their hands.

Silents: Blackboards were black and chalk was chalk.

Boomers: Blackboards were green and chalk was multicoloured graphite.

Xers: Overhead projectors.

Millennials: The computer.

Boarding school

GIs

They had to board because there were no neighbourhood schools. Many lived on farms or in the country. In some European countries, summer holidays are more than a month long and in most parts of America they are still three months. The reason for this harks back to a time when farm kids were needed at home during the busy summer season to work on the family farm.

Silents

Farming was still a predominant occupation and so there was no option but to board.

Boomers

In spite of schools moving into the suburbs, many children were still sent to board because it was tradition – their parents had done so. Many parents packed their children off because families were still big and they wanted space and time out from their kids. Some sent their kids to boarding school because it was seen as a character building exercise.

Xers

They were sent to boarding school if it was 'right' for the child. Many parents sent their problem children to be sorted out, and single parent families in the wake of the Boomer's divorce era sent their children off in search of role models.

Millennials

With far fewer children being born today, parents are reluctant to let them go, and boarding is usually an option only when strictly necessary. There has been a huge drop in boarders in the Millennial generation and many boarding schools are battling to keep going.

Classroom vibe

GIs

From the moment they walked through the school gates, life was different, rarefied, not the world outside.

Silents

The outside world reached into the classroom as World War II necessitated the evacuation of children to the countryside in England. Millions of children were displaced in Europe; and in many parts of the world others worried about their dads at the Front. In America the Depression years saw thousands of families wandering the land searching for jobs and food. Many of this generation did not finish their schooling.

Boomers

There was a sense of rebellion and revolution in the air brought on by the swinging, hippie sixties. In America students began to elect student representative councils and to write school newspapers. There was an increasing sense that they were 'little adults'. In South Africa, the school-children of Soweto took to the streets on 16 June 1976 in open rebellion against the education authorities. The world had entered the classroom.

Xers

School became a place where you could feel scared. Danger came to school in the form of guns and knives. Sometimes the guns were fired. Think of the Columbine school shootings. The schools featured in Hollywood movies about urban, dangerous schools were Xer generation. In some American schools, the kids weren't allowed knives at mealtimes and walls were erected around schools. In South Africa as the fight against apartheid intensified, schools increasingly received bomb threats. Evacuation drill and bomb disposal practice became the norm.

Millennials

Some have never known schools without high walls and security guards. Drug dealers, of all ages and both sexes, operate both in and outside schools. Teens take fruit juice laced with gin and vodka to drink at break time. Pupils are given frequent lectures on drug, sex and alcohol abuse. Even the youngest know and understand about HIV/AIDS. The distinction between student and teacher, adult and child, in school and out of school, has become blurred. The Millennials are both naïve (due to protective parents) and street smart by the age of eleven. These civic minded children plan to return the world to a time of stability and peace, as it was in the life and times of the GIs. And so the generational cycle comes full circle.

Respect

GIs and Silents: Respected teachers and the schooling system.

Boomers: Openly rebellious. Teachers beat them into order.

Xers: Ignored authority, but quietly. Beatings had little effect. A more sophisticated approach was required.

Millennials: More respect for teachers but cynical about 'the system'. Want an honest, open-minded approach to education.

So, who likes a uniform?

The answer is – not many of us, because pettiness and infinite attention to the tiniest detail usually accompany it. For instance, in many a girls' school ankle socks were only allowed to be rolled over once. Twice was once too much. Girls had to kneel on the ground so that hems could be measured from the knee upwards. During nail inspection you held your hands up, palms towards you, and if the prefect saw the smallest bit of nail peeping over the top, zap! it had to be cut. Boys' hair was measured with a ruler from their eyebrows and was not allowed to cover their ears. Former colonies like

South Africa, Australia and New Zealand sweated in uniforms created for northern climes. Long grey flannels and heavy black blazers were worn even on the hottest day. Now some schools are giving their pupils the option to wear shorts or longs, golf shirts and no ties, and some even allow open sandals in the summer. Some younger, modern schools have created a new trend, giving students the flexibility to wear casual but school-appropriate clothing that reflects their individuality. It has a clear school ID as a badge.

Awards

GIs

A really understated approach to medals, awards and certificates. They tend not to hang them on walls or frame them at all. One GI who was awarded the MBE (Member of the British Empire) and the OBE (Order of the British Empire) simply lost them.

Silents

Would only show off a cup or hang a framed certificate if it was really meaningful to them and they felt they really deserved it.

Boomers

Frame everything they can, even their Labrador's training certificate, or a certificate to prove they've simply attended a company training conference.

Xers

Might attempt to get awards abandoned altogether – not their scene.

Millennials

Won't let the Xers kill awards.

Universities

These are, by definition, radical places, because students are in a radically different phase of their lives. They are questioning, demanding, rebelling and determined to establish a new order. Let's take a look at when generations were students.

GIs

They were radical about Prohibition. It was an adrenalin rush to have bootleg whisky and a Model T Ford going at 30km an hour on a dust road on a Saturday night.

Silents

They were educated under the GI Bill which gave free tertiary education to all returning soldiers. Back then, not surprisingly, they were the most degreed generation in history (as has been the case with each subsequent generation).

Education represented a gift to Silents, it was their ticket to success. For this reason, they felt they couldn't have a wild, rebellious student time. They needed to 'pay back' and for this reason they subsequently felt they had missed out a bit in life.

Boomers

They saw university as a riot. If there wasn't one, then they created it. Boomers marched for any cause – they marched because they liked protesting per se. They put daisies in soldiers' guns in Paris in the late sixties and rioted against the atomic bomb. They have, as lecturers and professors, created the most extraordinary degrees at some universities. At some US universities there are degrees in surfing and honours in motor mechanics. There's hot competition for lecturers to get students to sign up for their classes as they are paid on their student numbers. Some even give their students easy 'As' to get them into their classes.

Xers

They set out to grow up at university. Interesting things happened along the way because they deliberately sought experiences that would help them achieve their goal. For them university is about getting a degree so that the world will accept them. They regard it as a serious stage in their lives. Today, university is too expensive to allow Xers to mess around as the Boomers did. Most Xers graduate with huge student loans that they need to pay off. For most of them the world is too competitive not to graduate and to graduate well.

Millennials

They will be very directed about university, clear about their goals and passions. They won't go to university just because 'it's the right thing to do'. They will attend one if there's a good reason to do so and they'll take it seriously. When they get there, they will have fun, anyway.

Another Millennial trend, however, will be the move away from university-based tertiary education. Today's young people see the market for skills, not degrees, and many corporates agree with them, ignoring qualifications on a CV and focusing instead on proprietary psychographic and skills tests as entrance criteria for job interviews. Millennials will make much more use of part-time courses, technikons, colleges and short, skills based courses, and will expect formal training and qualifications to be accredited to them for all on-the-job training they complete.

Boomers as professional teachers:

For the first time in many decades, teachers are consciously aware that they are preparing young people for a world that they, the teachers, know nothing about, and are struggling to understand. Parents are in a similar position. This is not as disheartening as it might seem as awareness is a step in the right direction.

Compare this with the situation that existed in most countries in the 1960s and 70s when studying to become a teacher was easy. Governments provided full bursaries for most teacher candidates and there were few barriers to entry. There was a saying back then, that 'those who can, do; those who can't, teach'. Many such teachers have worked over the past two to three decades without being properly equipped as professional educators and schools are now reaping the consequences.

But radical change has been occurring in the classroom, firstly with Xers, and now with Millennials. Realisation is sinking in that it takes a committed and fully professional educator to ensure that today's young people are properly educated and prepared for their challenging futures. Such educators will, thankfully, have the confidence with their professional approach to assert themselves with children, parents, other teachers and the world at large.

What the future holds for education

Let's take a glimpse into the past to understand just how far we've come ... and where we are going.

GIs and Silents

For a start, they worked in quiet and disciplined classrooms. The students who achieved were often those who established how 'the system' worked. They figured out what teachers regarded as important and then delivered it. They were good at memorising and employed good exam techniques. They were cool and didn't panic.

Boomers

They were brought up in the same education system but rebelled against the stylised, rote form of learning. Boomers now sit in the seats of power in education throughout the world and they have popularised new ways of learning, such as the Montessori, the Rudolf Steiner and the Waldorf schools approaches. OBE (Outcomes Based Education) is their brain-child. Boomers are into 'vision, purpose and core competencies', to quote their jargon, in a big way and they've overlaid the education system with it. They have improved it but it's basically only a tweaking of the old, not a radical new system.

Xers

They were taught in the old system but technology was arriving faster than teachers could keep up and it made them nervous. On the whole, teachers were slow off the mark when it came to learning how to operate computers, and how to adapt to new computer requirements. When things broke or didn't work, teachers often had to ask their pupils to fix them. 'Open book' exams became more common and calculators were allowed into science and maths exams. Slide rules disappeared.

Millennials

Cellphones arrived in a big way and new rules for new technologies were introduced. No cellphones were permitted to ring in class. No SMSing was allowed either and cellphones in some schools had to be handed in before an exam. Schools will introduce new 'sports' such as skateboarding, videogames and extreme sports.

The education system will change hugely while they are at school. Today they are not asked 'what do you remember?' but 'what did you learn?' Subjects will not be rigidly differentiated as they have been until now. In future, for instance, children might be given an assignment on dolphins and during it they will:

- do research about them for biology
- make the research read like an English essay
- translate that into another language
- compile data for maths

We will move away from a 'pass or fail' system that often aimed to catch you out and it will be replaced by a progressive system of evaluation that aims to educate. Collaboration will no longer be viewed as cheating. Computers will be used during exams.

In the future students might be required to pass with 100 per cent in the way that pilots have to do. They don't learn to land a plane on a 50 per cent pass. Imagine if a pilot could take off successfully but not land properly because he had only passed the take-off section of the exam? Doctors, on the other hand, can pass their medical exams with a 50 per cent pass and we hope that your vicious tummy bug isn't part of the 50 per cent they didn't crack.

Passing with 100 per cent will require a drastic change in our current approach to teaching. This would mean that students would need to progress at their own rate of learning, not en masse with the class. In that way, as they master a section, they will move on to the next one. As in life, so in school.

In future, we may see parents volunteering to teach at schools. Xers are great volunteers as long as the process is professionally managed. They would be especially keen if it provided personal stimulation while allowing them more time with their children. Imagine if an accounting firm made it a requirement for articles that one had to teach accounting or maths in a school one morning a week. Wouldn't it be great if a big oil company made scientists available to teach science? The spin-off for both schools and the company could be vast. But not just anyone will be able to volunteer as a teacher. It takes a real professional to teach in today's chaotic Millennial classroom, so volunteers will need to be excellent at teaching.

The education race

'Brainware' is what the world wants now. Global competition is resulting in clever people being headhunted across countries and continents. Parents are acutely aware of this and pressure to get their pre-schoolers into the top schools is a worldwide phenomenon. There are international stories of parents 'buying' school heads with houses and yachts, anything to get their little tot into the right school. And increasingly Xer parents are doing their bit in a way that GI,

Silent and Boomer parents would have been amazed to see when their kids were young. Today children can read and are computer literate by the age of five. They have computer toys and games and many a home with toddlers is filled with education videos, DVDs and software. Parents end up fighting just to get 10 minutes at the computer.

Our message to parents:

The definition of learning for Millennial children is self-development and NOT memorising facts. You need to help them to love learning. As most GIs, Silents and Boomers weren't educated with this approach many of them have a problem relating to the manner in which their children and grandchildren study. But it's never too late to start a life of lifelong learning. Inspire your children and start studying again. Oscar-winning film director Steven Spielberg did just that by obtaining a Bachelor degree in Film recently, as an example to his children.

How the generations communicate:

GIs:

They wrote letters in ink, by hand, that were often hand delivered. Posted letters, depending on the country, and its size, could be delivered within days or weeks. Letters to other countries went by sea and took weeks, if not months, to arrive. Offices had typewriters with flick-out pins. If you wanted copies, you slipped carbon sheets between the paper. Telegrams were popular, although expensive because you paid for each word. They were used almost exclusively for urgent news such as births or deaths, and for birthday messages. You wrote short sentences with the word 'stop' at the end of each one and you even paid for 'stop'. The fortunate few who had telephones used them sparingly due to their expense, and the early ones had a detachable ear piece that you lifted off a hook and held to your ear.

Silents:
They were the first to take advantage of a burgeoning airmail system but it was relatively expensive and many people used airmail lettergrams that lessened the price. Telephones became more popular but many people, especially those in country areas, could not dial direct and had to go through a manually operated telephone exchange. Alternatively, party lines were used where you responded to a set number of rings, for example, short, short, long, and gossipers had a field day listening in to others' conversations.

Boomers:
They soon became accustomed to fairly fast local postal delivery with a lot more access to international airmail delivery. Boomers invented the courier service in order to get packages across the world as the pace of commerce quickened. 'Overnight delivery' is a Boomer innovation. Telephones still had the round dial on the front and some people found it hard to hold the phone and dial at the same time. International calls were made with increasing frequency and you always knew you were receiving one because of the crackle on the line and the long delay after one person had spoken. Offices used telexes to transmit letters and documents. The golfball typewriter improved typing speeds, and self-correcting strips saved many a secretary from having to start her boss's letters again. Electronic typewriters that allowed Boomers four lines of text with corrections before you had to print, were the forerunners of computers.

Xers:

Personal computers arrived on office desks at about the same time Xers pitched up to work. Few Xers have used a manual typewriter or heard a telex machine rat-a-tat-tatting in the background. Computers took care of all that and Xers took full advantage of them in the 1980s for word processing and communicating, both in and outside the office. Touch dial telephones became the norm and few have known an office without a fax machine. The Internet, email and web pages have become commonplace during their lives. Today Xers cannot remember a time before cellphones (mobiles) but it's only in the last few years that 24-hour, non-stop usage of them has become the norm.

Millennials:

They cannot believe there was ever a time when the world existed without email, the Internet, the World Wide Web and being able to SMS on a cellphone. Computer controlled voice recognition has already arrived for some. This enables you to talk into a computer that seamlessly converts your words into written documents for editing. The converse, where written communication is converted into digital voice and then sent around the world via the Internet at a reasonable cost, if not free, is almost here. Who knows how long it will take for built-in microchips to pick up our brainwaves and convert them into emails that we can send just by thinking about them!

12

Training the Generations

Attitude to training:

GIs:	Been there, done that.
Silents:	Keep it serious, do it 'properly'.
Boomers:	Challenge us.
Xers:	Make it fun.
Millennials:	Must entertain me and enable me to do meaningful things with it.

Few trainers, teachers, facilitators and presenters are fortunate enough to walk into a session with only one generation facing them. At the start of this new century, it's increasingly likely that participants on a course are a more age-diverse group than ever before because the hierarchical systems in the workplace that once kept generations separate are breaking down. Talent and merit have overtaken length of service and experience as the key factors in career advancement.

The tough part for trainers, as you will appreciate from having read this far in the book, is that each generation has a unique perspective on the world. They also have highly different ways of absorbing, organising and applying information and skills.

But knowing how members of each generation prefer information to be organised, the type of teacher or trainer that appeals to each, which activities they respond best to, and learning formats that appeal to them will give you the edge as a multi-generational presenter, trainer, teacher and/or facilitator.

GIs (born 1900s to 1920s)

There are increasing numbers of people in their eighties and nineties who are surprisingly lively and determined to continue working. We know of several who still drive themselves to the office or to their own businesses. It's not that uncommon to hear of people in their eighties going to university to study for a degree they always wanted to have. They are miffed by friends' suggestions that they are too old to work, and should go fishing, birdwatching or play bowls instead.

Those who are still working for corporations are unlikely to be interested in formal training at this stage but if the occasional one is, then ensure that training is adapted to the formal, classroom style they appreciate.

They enjoy learning or they wouldn't have reached the venerable age they have and yet continue to work. Some of them want to learn how to operate computers, are keen to learn how to email and SMS, so welcome them into a training environment and take care not to humiliate them for their lack of twenty-first century technical knowledge.

It's a sensible organisation that holds on to the wisdom gained by someone who has stayed on board the bumpy ride that constitutes a business or industry, operating over scores of years.

Silents (born 1920s to 1940s)

Learning environment

The Silents tend to enjoy conformity, consistency, logic and discipline. They don't like taking risks and they want a clearly understood structure established from the moment they walk in. They like a classroom style layout for training sessions and prefer conservative trainers who establish the ground rules early on – and then stick to them. It's a good idea to send Silents a list of books and any other reading matter prior to the course. If you give them an agenda, stick to it because they are used to people doing what they say they'll do.

Ideal trainer

This would be a knowledgeable expert, because Silents believe in authority figures and want to respect their trainer. Dress formally and structure the course in a manner that will suit their conformist habits. Younger trainers have to establish credibility quickly, either by including a detailed CV in the course notes or by being introduced by someone who spells out their qualifications for that particular session. Trainers can also establish rapport by acknowledging their participants' experience and listening carefully and with respect when they speak. If all else fails, dye your hair grey.

Likes

Silents prefer training on a one-on-one basis, especially when it's related to technology.

They appreciate the classical, straightforward presentation of information. They are really motivated by training that is linked to the overall good of the company.

Dislikes

Trainers who are informal and too familiar won't crack the ice with this generation. They are irritated by overly casual dress and manner of speaking. Don't use slang and avoid anything that could be construed as rude or offensive such as risqué jokes, swearing and even bad use of grammar. Many Silents are turned off by personal anecdotes, examples and stories – they want their information left brained and logical. Don't rush them – they prefer their training slightly slower than some of their wired younger colleagues.

Training materials

Print out the course notes. They will require handouts. They don't want electronic notes or a list of websites. Avoid small font sizes and funky font styles. Get that grammar and spelling perfect.

Boomers (born 1940s to 1960s)
Learning environment

Boomers have more degrees among them than any other generation so some tend to believe they can rely solely on these formal studies and don't really require further 'educating'.

Training them is a challenge. However, Boomers were brought up on a diet of collaborative learning in their large classrooms and busy schools so they enjoy opportunities for interaction, networking and teamwork. They're not intimidated by physical contact and interaction and really excel at working in small teams. They are turned off by an authoritarian approach. Although they appreciate predictability, they also respond to brainstorming, lateral thinking and want to provide their own input.

Ideal trainer

Boomers like someone who comes across as a knowledgeable 'friend', whom they feel is an equal or a colleague, even vulnerable and personal. But the trainer must have recognised qualifications. He needs to come across as a facilitator who helps participants to learn rather than a teacher who imparts information.

Likes

They love solving problems, and no wonder, for they tend to be optimistic, motivated and self-driven. It was Boomers who invented the 'motivational guru' and self-help industry. They enjoy spectacle and appreciate showmanship. They challenge everything and are keen to right anything they perceive to be wrong. So it's good to focus on personal challenges with them, instead of just giving them generic examples or 'canned' case studies. The recent rise of 'on the job' MBA (Master of Business Administration) courses proves that Boomers want training that's relevant to their lives.

Dislikes

Role playing, acting out or interactive industrial theatre. Boomers tend to intellectualise and are often not aware that while they may have the knowledge, it doesn't mean they have the skills. In general, their strengths are strategic thinking and vision, down-the-track stuff, rather than short term implementation and action. So you will have to encourage them to practise newly acquired skills but ensure they don't feel foolish as they do so. Watch out for the 'know-it-all' Boomer with a chip on his shoulder. He may indeed know a lot but he hasn't the faintest idea how to apply it.

Training materials

Ensure that any information is readily accessible. For instance, a hyperlinked website with an overview of information in a friendly, easy-to-scan format is ideal. Then, if they want more information, they can easily find it. Most international electronic news magazines are structured like this, by the way. Boomers want the look and feel of any material to be slick and professional.

Generation Xers (born 1960s to 1980s)

Learning environment

Xers have grown up increasingly frustrated because they feel that traditional schooling is totally out of touch with real life. Naturally, they're not nearly as attracted to classroom-style interaction as the two preceding generations. They know that learning is a lifelong career in itself so they want training that's related to personal skills development and increased personal marketability. They like to absorb this via CDs, videos and computer-based training with access to a human guide and expert when they get stuck. Training needs to be fun and multi-styled. They don't want a certificate. It is real life skills they're after.

Ideal trainer

Your approach should be that of a guide rather than a formal trainer. Age and experience don't matter to them as long as the trainer is clearly proficient in the subject matter. They're not really impressed by long CVs and lists of academic qualifications. The faster the trainer gets going and demonstrates her expertise, the better response she'll get from the Xers. Respect has to be earned; it won't come by default. Xers are highly motivated learners who ask lots of questions and want interaction. Some will do their own research so let them get on with it. Set them on a course and then leave them alone to see where it will take them. Allow them to learn by experimenting. Let them fail and then help them learn from the experience.

Likes

The more role playing you do, the more they'll like it. They want to get involved with what they're learning, to experiment with it and then receive feedback. If theory is required, then edutain (entertain as you impart knowledge). Keep it brief and get back to interactive learning. They're not worried about putting their reputation on the line and will jump in and try something even if it makes them look clumsy in front of others. They also appreciate a facilitator who understands, and respects, their ability to multitask, ie absorb information while doing something else as well.

Dislikes

Boredom – whatever you do, don't let them get bored. Chop and change – surprise them regularly. You will need to change your pace, your process and your style constantly. Know-it-all trainers who won't allow participants to challenge them are not going to succeed with the Xers. And don't indulge in showmanship or hype. It's not their style.

Training materials

They don't read as much as the Silents and Boomers, and even the Millennials read more than they do so keep your notes short. Use lots of visual stimulation such as headlines, subheads, quotes, graphics and lists. Give them options for the format of notes such as print, email, CD or webpage.

Millennials (born 1980s to 2000s)
Learning environment

Millennials are difficult to intimidate and are, on the whole, free of fear. Failure doesn't terrify them. They care about manners and believe in civic action and, for all these reasons, these new workplace arrivals will look for more attention and structure from their bosses than the Xers do. Teachers and trainers need to provide personal challenges and allow them to work in teams. If you have a lot of Millennials in your group, give everyone a task and then, when a quick-off-the-mark few have completed it, encourage them to walk around the room and help others. The structure of the training room should be informal and adaptable to quick seating changes. Forget straight rows and chairs behind desks. Ensure you have good electronic equipment.

Ideal trainer

The best approach is that of an experienced mentor. They respond well to personal authority and respect qualifications and expertise, so spell those out to them. Explain what the practical benefits will be of what they are learning at the start of your session. Use multimedia (as you did for the Xers) and different techniques to get your points across. Ensure that you give constant feedback and encouragement. They prefer a trainer who lets them discover information, rather than one who just hands it to them on a platter.

Likes

Training courses that go beyond teaching simple job functionality. They want to learn about parenting, marriage, personal financial management, health and wellness. And in future companies will increasingly be required to provide such courses. They enjoy training that teaches them skills they can continue to use long after the course is over. They really enjoy mentor programmes.

Dislikes

Very little, actually. Just don't bore them and don't speak down to them. You'll be surprised by how much they know. They appreciate a 'buzz' in the training room and won't keep quiet to let others, including the trainer, speak. Don't let this put you off – just keep on talking. This generation has developed the ability to do what most women do anyway – multitask!

Training materials

Keep them lively and varied. Printed materials should have the same multiple focal points as materials targeted at Xers, with one exception. Millennials are readers, so include printed articles and written information. Provide lots of links to web pages.

Don't panic when you have all the generations in one room ...

For a start, now that you've read this far into the book, you've learnt the sociology of the generations who will be facing you. Make an effort to use their icons, language and values and ensure that your examples include all the generations. There isn't a simple, one-size-fits-all solution so the next best thing is to learn as much as you can about each participating generation. Read chapter 11, Educating the Generations, for more background. Draw up a game plan that will help you to tailor your presentation to their specific preferences and needs.

There are two approaches you can follow:
- Put the generations into multigenerational, layered, small groups. This may produce tension but you can use that creatively.
- Put them into homogeneous groups which will tend to reinforce stereotypical, generational thinking. But it may help you to meet each participant's learning needs.

Whichever method you choose, do so with clear intent and understand the pros and cons of it. If you want to get through to each generation, then include something you know will appeal to each one of them at the start of the course to get them 'on side'. It will be like pressing a button. You will enjoy their positive response!

13

Generations @ Work

Attitude to work:

GIs:	I am grateful to have a job.
Silents:	I work hard because it's my duty to do so.
Boomers:	Work is self-fulfilling; it makes me feel important.
Xers:	I work to fund my lifestyle.
Millennials:	My work will help to change the world.

A century ago the world was slap bang in the middle of the Industrial age, with smokestacks blackening the skies, men (mostly) going off to work at their womb-to-tomb nanny organisations with their sandwiches tucked under their arms. They retired, if they didn't die on the job, from the same company they'd worked for all their lives, at about sixty years of age. Back then, agricultural workers accounted for about half the economically active population whereas now they hardly make up two per cent of it.

Today's Xers (who are mainly in their twenties and thirties) carry their businesses on their laptops, work in jeans at coffee bars and feel little loyalty for companies that tossed their loyal Boomer parents onto the scrap heap during the last economic downturn. They want their pay cheques, company cars, expense accounts and cellphones *now*.

We're going to take you through the massive changes from Organisation Man to Bright Young Things. The former went off to work, dressed in his suit and tie, with the correct, conventional attitude to his lifelong job. The latter, regarded as the slacker, 'whatever', but techno-brilliant Xer, struggles to get to work at the 'correct' time, and when he's finished his project he wants the day off.

Each generation has reacted to the way in which his parents worked and the dominant workplace cultures and ethics that prevailed when he was an impressionable child.

We have, on the whole, grouped GIs and Silents together in this chapter because there are few GIs left in the workplace today as most have retired. Silents, if not already retired, are busy doing so, or are certainly contemplating it.

What the workplace was like when each generation entered it

GIs (born 1900s to 1920s)

This generation began working around the time that the Great Depression started which meant there was very little work at all. Many of them started in the family business or scratched for work where they could. Many a GI today will talk about working on government funded projects created specifically to provide employment, such as building dams, roads or harbour breakwaters. No wonder then that work, when you got it, was regarded as a privilege and a gift, and you stuck with it, not only because you were too nervous to make a change, but also out of deep gratitude to your employer. That loyalty and 'I owe you, Mr Employer' attitude has lasted, more or less, to this day. So no wonder the GIs tell their grandchildren to be loyal and work hard and are outraged if they see them simply walk away from a job.

Silents (born 1920s to 1940s)

It was economic boom time when the Silent generation began working in the 1950s and 60s, but they packaged the same careful attitude to work that their parents had, along with their sandwiches, as they left for work. This was the classic Company Man. He toiled from nine to five in a job that was structured and hierarchical. Work was 'hard'. He arrived home at exactly the same time each day to a polite welcome from his stay-at-home wife and three to four children. His meal was cooked and waiting. Suburbs bloomed and office parks were invented and built close to home to save the company man commuting into town. Certain cities and areas became known for particular types of work – Detroit was home to the car industry, Seattle to the airline industry (now the world's high-tech capital) and New York to the world of finance. Suburbs were built to house workers near these hubs. The massive South African based international insurance company Old Mutual located its headquarters in Pinelands, Cape Town and built a self-contained suburb to go with it. Hershey, in America, built a town for its employees.

Boomers (born 1940s to 1960s)

When the rebellious, questioning and spoilt Boomers arrived at work, this coincided with a steady economic boom that took the world by storm. It was largely fuelled by technology but every industry was expanding and there was a general boom in work. Jobs were, on the whole, exciting and easy to come by, and most governments and corporations gave easy and generous bursaries to anyone who did tertiary studies. When Boomers graduated from school, technikons and universities they had little problem finding employment. Major changes were beginning to take place in the workplace, creating a different environment from that in which their fathers had worked. The three main drivers in the economy were quality, customer service and globalisation. Multi-national companies were becoming more common and rapid growth was considered normal and to be expected.

Generation Xers (born 1960s to 1980s)

They arrived in the workplace just as the economic boom was tailing off and things were beginning to fall apart. Some of them caught part of the Internet wave and many a 20-year-old Xer leapt on to it, made quick millions and, just as quickly, lost them. The wise ones who got out early found themselves millionaires by the age of thirty and retired or trained for a different career. On the whole, however, the Xers feel that the promises made by the visionary Boomers about a brave new working world have fallen apart. Economies and organisations have shrunk, leaving them struggling to find work.

They feel caught in the middle of a transition. Most industries know that change is required at most levels – structural, product and staff changes – and most even know *what* change is required. Yet change is taking too long to be implemented for the naturally impatient Xers.

Millennials (born 1980s to 2000s)

This new generation will enter the workplace just as the world comes out of the present downturn in the global economy, and starts a new wave of development and innovation fuelled by technology, nanotechnology and biotechnology and the emotion economy. The difficulties of the transition that is presently irritating the Xers will largely be a thing of the past. The world of work will look very different from what it is now. The predictions of leading futurists, such as Charles Handy, Alvin Toffler and Tom Peters, will probably have been realised, with careers looking more like a portfolio of jobs and constant change being the order of the day. Flexible working hours and telecommuting will be the norm, not the exception, and we'll be thinking about applying Ricardo Semler's *Seven-Day Weekend* principles.

The emotion economy:

The industrial economy was based on 'make and sell'. Take, for instance, the massive production of Henry Ford's cars and his dictum. 'You can have any colour you like as long as you like black'. (Interestingly, this too has come full circle with black being the hot new colour at the time of writing this book.) But back in Henry Ford's time there was little regard for the customer. The focus was on the production process.

Then, starting in the late 1950s, came the information economy which is based on a 'listen and serve' dictum. Nearly 80 per cent of the world's employees are now in the service industries. Microsoft is the equivalent of the Ford motor company. The focus now is on quality and customer satisfaction: 'the customer is always right'. Market research, segmentation models and distribution channels all contribute to making the customer king. In spite of this, customers are generally faceless because they're lumped together in demographic segments. And the systems in place to meet their needs are, on the whole, inflexible.

But a new approach is now emerging. The emotion economy recognises that companies will have to take service and information a step further if they want to attract clients, and staff, away from their competitors. Go to a banking court and assess the points of difference between banks. Not much, is there? If you're buying cars, cosmetics or hair care products, except for the very sophisticated and expensive, or the really cheap products, there's not much in it today price-wise or product-wise. Take supermarkets – you'll find some are a little more upmarket than others but on the whole you could shop at just about any of them with much the same quality and service. Furthermore, people are increasingly shopping on the Internet: they will call up a trolley of products from one store and compare it with a trolley from another and then make their decision to buy. The same applies to a travel agent or, indeed, any other kind of booking agent. You'll shop around for information on the Internet and then choose your agent, or bypass them all completely and make your own purchase.

Now comes the crunch. Which agent, supermarket, cosmetics and car will you choose? Increasingly, your decision will be based on relationship, connection, trust and emotion, and not on price, quality or speed of service.

You'll buy a car from, and get it serviced at, the garage that makes you feel special and looks after your particular needs, and you'll go to the bookstore with the coffee shop, where smiling staff find that book for you. Indeed, they may provide Internet access so you can search Amazon.com's new 'inside the book' search facility. The travel agent who delivers your tickets knows your hotel preferences and rings you when there's a special on that she knows you'll enjoy will, not surprisingly, be your first port of call. The restaurant maître d'hôtel who welcomes you by name and treats his staff well so that they are pleasant and happy around you, will attract customers. The estate agent who paints your house for you, at her cost because she knows it will fetch a higher price for you both, or fills it with flowers on show day, will grab your attention and custom.

Companies that will attract attention and custom are those that:
- are trustworthy and honest
- make their clients feel special
- provide service tailored to client preference
- understand 'mass customisation' and 'markets of one'
- network with their clients, spreading their good name by word of mouth
- take issues of the environment, corporate social responsibility and sustainability seriously
- treat their staff like human beings and not just biological machines

Other names for the emotion economy include: intimate economy, relationship economy, wisdom economy, transparent economy, and connection economy.

The office environment in which each generation prefers to work

GI and Silent generations

These two generations fought in the World Wars so, not surprisingly, they take a militaristic approach with them into the workplace. They like formal, structured offices, with clear divides between management and staff. In the 'good old days' newspaper editors sat in what we called 'mahogany row' with a line of secretaries dividing them from ordinary journalists. Few editors actually ventured onto the newsroom floor.

In huge corporations the hierarchy didn't even sit on the same floor as the 'workers'. Their wood-panelled, antique-filled offices were usually a couple of levels up and if you happened to climb into the same lift, they would study the ceiling or the floor in order to avoid your gaze. If your eyes met, you greeted them deferentially, in a tone as close to awe as you could manage.

Strangely, some Silent generation, and even Boomer, managers are still creating offices like that today. They just do it more subtly. They have the open-plan approach, so beloved by Boomers, but delineate hierarchy nonetheless, using chairs of different shapes, sizes and textures to indicate your level (or lack) of seniority. The higher you rise on the corporate ladder, the more your carpet colour changes. You're also seated closer to the outside of the open-plan office where the floor-to-ceiling windows overlook the office gardens/ lake/ fountains. The mahogany barrier is now tinted glass but the secretaries are still there guarding the inner sanctum. The boss says his door is 'always open' but only the brave breach the glass moat.

Silent generation bosses, not surprisingly, like silence. Radios and people shouting across the office are not music to their ears. A certain decorum is required. The formal environment demands formal clothes and speech. Fraternising during office hours is not encouraged.

GIs and Silents see work and fun as mutually exclusive. The workplace is therefore austere, functional and 'businesslike'. Offices that look like rabbit warrens, with strictly enforced decor codes, grey, hard-wearing carpets and uniform layout are the norm.

Boomers

As you'd expect, the generation with the rallying cry of 'don't trust anybody over thirty' is a little more relaxed in the office. Boomers introduced chats at the tea trolley or water cooler, radios and piped music. Furniture has become funky, as well as functional. Ergonomics (the science of fitting people to their office environment) was embraced by Boomers who like to think of themselves as 'people people' and that their staff always comes first.

A good Boomer likes the office to reflect him and his product so branding is high on the list. Comfy cafes have taken the place of sterile canteens. The 'look of success' has become more important. Office blocks are massive open-plan affairs with impressive entrances, hanging gardens, fish tanks, precious hothouse pot plants and filtered coffee on tap. Chrome, glass and wood have turned new office buildings into symphonies of light and air through which you can see sky and trees. Fountains flourish, tinkling water is heard everywhere and much is made of ambient noise and white sound. When the offices aren't massive, which they often are because Boomers are fond of dramatic, impressive effects, they are increasingly like big houses. Some sexy companies offer all sorts of subsidised services to their staff, such as dry-cleaning, travel agent facilities, theatre bookings and therapy for those getting divorced or married, and for those with drug and alcohol addictions.

Structure is still strong though and people in the know are aware that there's a pecking order and who's who in the zoo. Nowhere is this more evident than in the complex arrangement of designated parking bays and special access cards. The GIs, Silents and Boomers all have designated parking places and if you want to change them you might as well sell your soul to Satan because it'll be easier to bargain with him.

Xers

As you would expect, the laid-back Xers want a much more informal, flexible approach, with first-come, first-served, parking. They don't understand why Boomers are so concerned about designated parking because, even if it was on a first-come, first-served basis, no Xers are going to get out of bed in time to beat them to it anyway!

Xers like to design their own workplace environment so they can express their individuality. Switched on companies are increasingly allowing them to do just that, in their attempts to attract the brightest and the best. They give staff their own design budget, allowing them to choose their own desk, chairs, couches. A guy working for a creative design company asked for the wing of a Dakota airplane to be dropped through his ceiling for use as a worktop. He got it, and, in his first year achieved way beyond his designated budget, thus paying back the investment.

Xers arrived at work with flexitime and telecommuting. They say it makes sense to stagger working hours so they don't spend precious time sitting in rush hour jams and they prefer to work when their biological clocks ring out their optimum times even if that's way past midnight. If they can work from a computer at home then so much the better.

Graeme, co-author of this book, works from home, as do his colleagues in their TomorrowToday.biz company. But Graeme works in Johannesburg because he likes to make twenty-five calls and do his emailing before breakfast whereas his colleagues, who like to surf (in water) before breakfast, live at the coast. They hold meetings in coffee bars and know which ones in South Africa, London and New York have Wi-Fi (wireless Internet connection) and a power supply for their laptops. They are not surprised when they phone a colleague and hear kids in the background because that's what they expect to hear when they call someone at home. Boomer and co-author Sue, no longer tries to quieten her dogs when the phone rings or turn down the music that plays when she's writing for fear that callers won't take her seriously.

Whatever the office environment might be, Xers require it to have elements of fun and relaxation, and need to have the flexibility to personalise and constantly change it. A Durban-based South African manufacturing company, Barrows, changes its entire office layout every three months. The lost productivity time is more than compensated for by motivated Xers who are inspired and enlivened by the constantly changing environment.

Millennials

When they arrive in the office they will want a family-friendly workplace. They will demand crèches and playgrounds for after school care, and will think nothing of taking their families to work. Gyms and schools in office grounds, and overnight sleeping quarters and hammocks slung up in the office gardens will become normal office environments. Satellite offices and the use of wireless technology will further enhance employees' ability to telecommute and be flexible. The company that is probably leading the way and is the most ready for the Millennials in terms of experimenting with new work environments is Brazil's Semco group of companies, headed by Ricardo Semler. He has documented their approach in his book *The Seven-Day Weekend.*

We would love to hear about other companies adopting a similar approach. Please email us about great workplaces, to: *stories@TomorrowToday.biz.*

Your CV:

The new approach to writing a CV is to write less about what you have done and more about who you are. Include an analysis of the company you're trying to get a job with. Realise that a CV doesn't get you a job – it lands you an interview. In spite of this, people still send in 9-page-long CVs which include a photograph of their high school rugby trophy.

To sum it up, you need to write:
- This is who I am
- This is who I think you (the company) are
- This is what I think the job is about, including the biggest challenges
- This is why I think I am the right person for it

Attracting and recruiting the different generations

There is a war for talent at the moment even if unemployment is rising. In most countries the issue is not a job shortage. There is a skills shortage, an attitude shortage and a shortage of companies offering the type of environment that employees are looking to work in today. Mainly, what we need to understand is that today's prospective employees are nobody's fools. They know what they want in the workplace and how to obtain it. Recruiting, therefore, needs to be part of a holistic approach to personnel development.

GIs

It's most unusual for a GI to be involved in a recruiting drive right now, but we're constantly surprised by reports of 90-year-olds still working, so you never know.

Silents

This generation is definitely going to be both recruited and recruiting! Read chapter 19, Re-tyreing, and you'll see that we believe it's crazy of us to even think of losing the wisdom and experience of this generation. They've experienced every type of economy in the past fifty odd years, from bust to boom and bust again. They've seen and done it all and their experience will be invaluable in these testing economic times. Their greatest attribute is their loyalty and they're good at maintaining the continuity of a company's corporate culture.

Recruit Silents from within your company if you can. If they're reaching retirement age then why not redeploy them? After all, they know your company inside out. They will understandably be nervous about moving posts because, being Silents, they'll have occupied one post for a long time.

Generally speaking, a Silent recruitment interview will be a traditional one. They won't ask lots of questions about the company. They'll expect you to ask them a lot of questions.

Their CVs will be short because they will have worked for one company or in one industry all their lives.

Highlight the fact that there will be training opportunities, because Silents are embarrassed to be seen as incompetent. Reassure them that they won't be shoved into a room full of youngsters when it comes to computer skilling. In short, make it easy for them to come on board and develop their skills.

If you're recruiting Silents from outside, don't make the mistake of thinking that they don't need an orientation course. It's essential for them to feel part of the company, an aspect of working that they love. Give them the company history, its culture, mission and the traditions of the organisation.

Boomers

You will need to sell your vision, mission, strategy, passion and values. Emphasise that not only will your company be in existence for years to come, but that it is also going places. This is vital information for Boomers. Silents assume that the company will last for a lifetime. Boomers do not assume this, and need assurances and evidence of a sustainable plan. You need to assure Boomers that if they work hard they will get ahead, fast.

Boomers will expect a fairly traditional recruitment interview, and will probably be overly formal in their approach to it. Setting out and selling the career path is vital in that recruitment meeting. Silents think it's *infra dig* to ask about career paths, but Boomers say, 'It's critical to know my prospects in this company.' The recruiting process will be less traditional than it is with Silents but the standard interview happens in that you, the interviewer, are still asking most of the questions. You can expect Boomers to want to take home the glossy corporate brochure.

When Boomers start work, ensure that everything's ready and waiting – the phone, the desk and business cards. Silents expect to take a few days to get up to speed. Boomers want to hit the ground running.

They will not be all that interested in orientation courses but, if these are presented in an upbeat and motivational manner, they can enhance the initial commitment of a Boomer to a company and generate energy and even passion.

Xers

Companies have had a huge wake-up call as the Xers arrived in the workplace from the late 1980s onwards. As new members of this generation stream into the workplace they require assurances and evidence upfront that the company they are joining is dealing with the sorts of issues that concern them. You won't have to show off a perfect workplace – it's Boomers who tend to expect and present perfection – but demonstrate your awareness of Xer workplace issues and indicate that you're open to change and development.

When recruiting Xers, you need to note that both the medium and the message have changed. You'll elicit the best response by advertising in multiple media from magazines to newspapers and on the Internet. You may even try, like Ikea, the Swedish furniture maker does, putting handwritten advertisements on the walls of toilets in local clubs.

Xers have changed the rules of the recruiting game. They interview the interviewer. They say, 'That's enough about me. Now I want to hear about you.' Interviewers report being stunned by having the tables turned on them, especially by sceptical Xers who think that the recruitment process, especially if handled by a Boomer, will include corporate branding and spin. And that's anathema to Xers.

They often arrive for the interview in chinos and a jacket. The buttoned up and down suits belong to the Silent and Boomer generations, who wouldn't have dreamed of asking about the salary, leave and working conditions. Those sorts of questions might have implied that their values weren't in the right place or that they weren't prepared to work hard. Xers have changed all that.

Recruiting used to be a fairly lengthy process, certainly at the top rungs of the corporate ladder. It could take a couple of months from the time a company decided it had a vacancy until you heard you'd landed the job. Xers want instant turnaround. Today the process sometimes only takes days. We live in a 24/7 world where technology like cellphones, laptops, and global video recruitment interviews mean that we're able to work non-stop. The beach, log cabin, ski resort, are all online. Talented Xers know the global search for quality never sleeps. If they get a good offer, they're not going to wait for the dozy company to wake up. These days you have to assess a CV quickly, hustle people in, know what you're looking for and what you're going to offer. If you snooze that IQ (and EQ) will disappear out of your office faster than you can log onto your computer. We are, of course, talking about the bright things, the top layer, not the workers, the cogs. They are vital but not the hot property for which a skills-starved world is searching.

Xers prefer an electronic orientation course, or better still, a 'find out as you go along' approach to working out how their new office operates. It's best not to bore them with lengthy histories and background. Trying to 'schmooze' them with motivational talks is not the way to go. Remember, that's Boomer stuff.

Millennials

The older people in this generation are just beginning to come into the marketplace and, because they're so young, their recruitment will be for part-time or student jobs. If you're looking for bright young things, you'll need to link their jobs to tangible rewards; the job alone will not be enough to attract them. You might give them a sign-on bonus, or movie tickets or meal vouchers.

In countries like America, where Millennials are older than they are elsewhere, they need to be aggressively recruited because they're switched on. They don't all hang around shopping malls, drooling over Britney Spears or Enrique Iglesias. In America one third of teenage Millennials are already working twenty hours or more a week. When they arrive for a recruitment interview, they know more about your company than you do about them because they've read it all up on the Internet. That still doesn't stop them asking you questions, so you need to start a recruiting drive or interview by really selling yourself to them.

Some American companies, worried about their future workforce in a first world economy where dwindling populations are the norm, are getting in early, really early. As Lynne C Lancaster and David Stillman write in their book *When Generations Collide*: 'Smart industries are forming connections with schools through internship programmes and mentoring opportunities that can introduce Millennials to their companies in positive ways – long before they're ready to hit the workforce full-time.'

Companies are also not just competing against other companies. They are in future going to need to convince Millennials that they need to work for someone other than themselves. Millennials will start their own businesses, or work from SoHos (small offices, home offices) on a project or part-time basis, in unprecedented numbers.

And the smart Millennials begin building their CVs at school. They go on leadership-building Outward Bound courses, or take extra computer skills courses, anything to put on their CV. Many, like Amy Marshall, daughter of Sue, co-author of this book, take a gap year at the end of school. During this year Amy did a first aid course, an off-shore sailing course, crewed on a 100 foot motor yacht down the Mozambique channel and then worked on a London Thames cruise boat, where her sailing, first aid and waitressing skills easily landed her a job where she worked with staffers much older and more experienced than she was.

Amy and her friends are preparing themselves for a working world that never sleeps. Don't wait to start recruiting them. They're already checking you out.

Orientation courses for Millennials will need to be fun and involve socialisation with their colleagues. The key will be to make them feel comfortable as quickly as possible while letting them sense the company's values and culture by interacting with your existing employees.

Control – the next big issue:

Leaders need to learn a whole new way of managing, or controlling, the staff who work with them. In a world where 'change is the only constant' and people speak endlessly about 'managing chaos', it's not surprising that new ways of running a business to keep it in tune with change are emerging.

Innovation and diversity are essential. If you stifle this by autocratic, outdated leadership your company will not stay afloat. The delicate flower of innovation will only flourish in a business environment where there is democratic or open leadership. In this the CEO needs to learn how to relinquish control, delegate authority, provide information freely and openly and allow room for mistakes. You even need to reward certain mistakes because in doing so you will generate discussion and a sense of freedom, plus the opportunity to live with the consequences of that freedom.

Leaders who don't make this shift will be left behind in the next few decades.

These are the types of leaders that Xers and Millennials want to work with now and in the future they will become such leaders themselves.

How the different generations think about a career

GIs and Silents

They set out to build a career that saw them spending a lifetime with one employer or, at the very least, remaining in one field. Their attitude is that doing a job is something you do all your life. Your job IS your life. They feel a real responsibility towards their employers and their employees. This is loyalty and dedication at the highest level.

Boomers

When this generation set out on a career path they, consciously or not, often selected one that would show their parents and their communities that they amounted to something. They seek challenges. Once they've achieved something they like this to be noticed, either within the company, in terms of grand offices or titles, or in the outside world in business magazines or newspapers, and even on the social pages.

But Boomers are now heading towards that time in life when every generation begins to contemplate the future. This doesn't necessarily mean that they will slow down or stop being workaholics, just that they're starting to question what they've made all the money for. Microsoft's Bill Gates, for instance, is working in the field of AIDS and malaria prevention. His partner, Paul Allen, has given $100 million to fund a project that is mapping the human brain.

If Boomers are setting out on a new career path at this stage of their lives, they will want to know that they are doing something meaningful and not working only for financial reward. Many of them, though, are resigned to seeing out the remaining years to retirement, often feeling trapped in their careers, which they selected decades earlier in another lifetime, in another world.

Xers

This generation is not prepared to stick to one particular company or industry. It saw its parents give their life and soul to companies which then spat them out when the economy nosedived and the company didn't need them any more. So from the time they start working, Xers set out to build a portable career, one they can take anywhere with them. Bruce Tulgan, author of *Managing Generation X*, interviewed thousands of Xers for a research project which showed that nearly 80 per cent of qualified Xers are no longer working in the area in which they qualified. Tulgan, an American, was the first person to really get to grips with Xers as a working generation and ascertain what motivates them.

Graeme, a thirty-something Xer, has heard the same story during his many presentations when he asks audience Xers if they have changed careers. The average 30-year-old nearly always responds in the affirmative.

In a portable career, in a rapidly changing world, Xers should expect to be between jobs at least five times in their lives and to change industries three times. They will need to reskill themselves, almost completely, at least twice during their working lives.

This doesn't mean, contrary to Silent and Boomer generation boss expectations, that Xers are unreliable, disloyal and flaky and will up and leave you at the drop of another offer. Not at all. It is just that they are building their CVs in anticipation of yet another economic downturn, company downsizing or rightsizing or whatever. They're creating options in a world that offers no guarantees. Xers know from their parents' bitter experience that they could be made redundant overnight, and they would prefer to choose to leave before they are told to do so. They also like to leave when a company's on the up and not on the skids.

Employers need to get to grips with this constantly job-hopping generation by providing job portability from within so that staff won't leave them. Identify new areas of expertise in your company where Xers could be retrained and in so doing you will soothe their career jitters. You may retort that if you do this, they will leave you anyway with their newly acquired skills, so yes, it's a dangerous strategy, but one that could pay you better than constantly training new Xers who don't know the corporate culture and haven't even the shred of loyalty that often accompanies familiarity.

A word of advice for Xers: don't shake that company dust off your shoes purely for the sake of doing so. You often need to stay in an industry longer than you feel is necessary and you need to take the time, and have the patience, to be fully competent before you move on. You might otherwise never fully attain your potential.

Millennials

They view work as one big, lifelong CV-building exercise. They were born at a time when they heard their Boomer and Xer parents talking about a cutback in jobs and feeling the pinch of the shrinking economy. They grew up listening to parental conversations about needing to move on and to add to their CVs, so, not surprisingly, that's what Millennials will do – move jobs, not for more money but to add more skills to that CV.

In the 'old days' when youngsters applied for a job in a pub or a restaurant, they didn't have to present a neatly typed CV, but that's what they are increasingly being asked for today, even if they are just doing a gap year before university or college.

Down the track, Millennials will, like the Xers, develop a portfolio of careers. In fact, futurists predict that Millennials will have ten different career changes in a lifetime and will completely change their careers at least once a decade. Some of that changing will not necessarily be from corporation to corporation because both Xers and Millennials believe that career changes are not just *up* the career ladder. They can also be down and even out for a while. In other words, they could leave their influential company post and opt to learn a new skill in another area of the corporation. They will be surprised if this has a negative impact on their salaries as they expect to be paid for their talent and output and not for a position or title. They might opt out of the working world altogether and do some work for the Peace Corps or Voluntary Service Overseas or an HIV/AIDS organisation, which would add to their life skills but not their bank account.

Millennials will have several jobs simultaneously. For instance, a lawyer will work three days at her firm and then two days in her technology company. We know of a vet who's also a chef at weekends because he loves food so much. In countries like New Zealand, job sharing and multiple jobs have become fairly usual. This culture will spread rapidly.

The difference between a Boomer employer and a (future) Millennial one will be that the Boomer, when recruiting, will look for someone who's a world expert with thirty years experience in his field. A Millennial will be more impressed by adaptability and flexibility, all things being equal, than high-flown expertise.

Teamwork

GIs and Silents

These two generations have a model of teamwork that developed during the two World Wars. Their concept of it, which they have carried into the workplace, is that a team has a leader (the general) and workers (foot soldiers). As leaders, they were bossy, spoke down to their workers, didn't give reasons, didn't tolerate dissenting views and carried on regardless of everybody else. Teamwork, therefore, has not been a priority.

As younger Boomer management experts have moved in with their faddish methodologies, from group hugs to river rafting, these older generations have felt left out, ostracised or just downright irritated. Many of them, however, still dominate from behind the scenes, blocking new thinking at the top where they sit safely ensconced in mahogany boardrooms, removed from the people who make their companies tick.

Boomers

They value teams and prefer a lot more equality than the first two generations are prepared to tolerate. They want everybody on the team to be empowered, to have their say, and to experience a common vision and a common way forward.

This is their reaction to their bossy, domineering parents and bosses.

They believe that effective teams are those with common values and are, largely, homogeneous in purpose and approach. That's why in most companies today that are headed by Boomers, there is a vision, a mission and a purpose. There are values and strategic action plans. There is layer upon layer of paperwork ensuring that everybody is on the same page and in the same ballpark; that everybody has the same world view and outlook paradigm. Team building is about having common experiences and a shared outlook. The best way of attaining this state of being is to start a war. As this is usually impossible, Boomers do the next best thing, by simulating war. They expose everybody on the team to extremes like swimming wild rivers and climbing hectic cliffs in an effort to bond them all together. One of the most extreme examples of this was the South African 2003 Springbok rugby team being forced to do extreme activities, naked and at 'gunpoint' in so-called team building exercises.

Xers

This generation is used to adrenalin rushes from their own, voluntary, extreme sports such as canyoning, BMXing and bungee jumping. They're not keen on the Boomer team building at the best of times because their attitude differs starkly. They value the individualistic approach. Xers believe that team members should build on separate strengths. So they don't sit around a table and ask, 'Where do we intersect? What do we have in common?' like the Boomers. They say, 'We are all individuals so what is my point of difference? What is my unique contribution?' This has led to the misconception that Xers are not team players. While their image is indeed one of the lone individual it doesn't mean that they are incapable of working in teams. They're great team players, actually, but in Xer teams and not Boomer-type teams. Xer teams ignore the Boomer approach of ensuring that everyone is 'aligned' to the team's values. They deliberately look for areas of difference between team members. This makes Xer teams a lot more rugged, even intimidating. Team players are encouraged to share differences of opinion but consensus is not the goal. Individuals, or small groups, work on certain tasks, make decisions and are trusted by the rest of the team.

You could argue, therefore, that Xers are more collaborative than earlier generations. They don't get bogged down in political posturing. They simply get on with the work. And they're much more direct in their communication style than earlier generations have been.

Millennials

They will be much more natural team players than Xers. They have grown up in a world dominated by Boomer teachers and role models who value transparency and democracy in team work. Millennials will have grown accustomed to being empowered and included since they were young and they will bring this expectation into teamwork at the office.

They need team objectives, and need their role in a team to be clearly explained. They also like to know the reasons *why* a particular output is required and don't function as well without this background understanding. Teams dominated by Millennials may not be as fast off the mark as other generations and will certainly be much slower than Xers who prefer to dive straight in to a task and work out frames of reference later. But the slower start will bear fruit when energy is converted to action later on. Don't shortcut your Millennials.

The most successful Millennial teams will be those reflecting the diversity of our society because they are uncomfortable in homogeneous, single demographic groups. They require diversity of all types. They will be good at encouraging people of all ages, cultures, genders and levels of experience to have a voice and will be good mediators when clashes of interest or opinions occur. Don't discount their input because of a lack of experience. They will more than make up for it – just watch them go.

The old team approach (GIs, Silents and Boomers):

- Interdependence is key.
- Good work is the result of good working relationships, so we need to focus on team building and have lots of social events and conferences to help us to do that.
- Appropriate behaviour is determined by conforming to group norms.
- Resolve conflict – even if it takes all day ... and all night too.
- Always attempt to empower others.

The new team approach (Xers and Millennials):

- Individual autonomy is key.
- Good working relationships are the result of doing good things together.
- We only need to get together when there is a job to be done; we don't need to have a meeting for the sake of having a meeting.
- Want to manage conflict by agreeing to disagree. There isn't time to reach consensus on every single point in a meeting and we can't sit here all night waiting for everybody on the team, or in the meeting, to make a point, however valid it is, just for the sake of hearing his own voice.
- We will delegate to sub-committees. They go away, make a decision, come back and report it, quickly and concisely. The decision is merely reported back to the whole meeting. It is not debated, ad nauseam, all over again.
- Xers are not out to empower every single person on the team. There isn't time to know everything about

everything. For instance, the financial guru on a company board will co-opt a couple of people to help him make some decisions. Chances are half the meeting hasn't a clue about the financial statements anyway, so why bother them? All we really need to know is 'Are we in good shape, or not?' If we are, let's get on with it. No point in wasting any more valuable time.

Experience:

Experience isn't what it used to be.

By definition, experience is something you get just after you needed it – so experience is only really helpful if what happened yesterday happens again tomorrow. And how often is that!

Of course, wisdom (applied experience) is always relevant, but too many people rely on experience instead of wisdom. In today's rapidly changing environment, few people, old or young, have real experience. It is an unwise company that excludes young employees from decision making or strategy development simply due to a lack of experience. The fact that they have not been stuck in a rut for years, doing the same old things the same old blinkered way, but bringing fresh new insights to an industry may be the most valuable asset they have. Xers and Millennials, if you're good enough, you're old enough.

How generations view rewards
GIs and Silents

For them, the job *is* the perk! Just having a job, being able to say they are employed and working for a particular company, is the 'reward'. So too is the satisfaction of a job well done. And the golden key that unlocks their total career fulfilment and reward is a six letter word: retire. That is one of their greatest rewards – to retire from a life spent working hard and to enjoy their well earned rest. However, many cannot afford to retire. And increasingly, even if they *can* afford to, many find they do not want to. They enjoy working.

Companies who want to reward these two generations, note the following: tell them that they won't be too old to work – they will be 're-tyred'. In other words, you will reskill them to enable them to continue working should they wish to do so. And make it possible for them to work in such a way that you can continue to use their skills in a world where we're running out of workers (Xers and Millennials).

Some wise companies are providing transport for flexi-elders to save them the stress of commuting. Others are allowing them to take extended periods off to visit grandchildren or attend a school sports day or just go on jaunts to the countryside. Others want to return to university, like a retired British judge who recently took up residence at Oxford University. Age is an increasingly flexible statistic and no longer determined by years but by elastic minds.

Sue knows of a 77-year-old accountant who works a three-day week and takes off two days to look after her grandchildren. She also knows a lawyer of ninety who puts in a couple of hours a day at his law firm and when he's finished a project, takes three months' holiday.

Boomers

They have always been competitive because there were so many of them at school, college and university and to stand out they had to make a name for themselves. At work, competing with millions, the satisfaction of a job well done doesn't cut the ice for Boomers in the same way it does for

Silents and GIs. They need to have the 'well done' announced in a front page advertisement or editorial. For this generation of strivers the rewards are all about the corner office, seniority, money, title and a permanent parking spot.

They have become accustomed to disposable income, and are not the world's best savers, so rewards also include: a company car, holidays away from home, plus gizmos and material items.

Time is increasingly an issue for Boomers who, being the Sandwich generation, have to look after both ageing parents and children. Anything that helps them keep their frantic lives together, in terms of services such as on-site car cleaning, car servicing, dry-cleaning, child care, aged care or transporting their ageing parents, or children, to doctors and dentists, are wonderful rewards for them. Retirement planning and help with financial planning are also good rewards.

In addition, as Boomers begin, like it or not, to age, they are increasingly looking for challenging and exciting projects to occupy them that will make a difference to society and enable them to leave a mark behind them when they die.

Xers

Freedom is the only reward worth anything for this generation. 'We will not pay the price for success that our parents did,' say Xers. They won't forget going home alone while their workaholic parents slaved away for companies that often, after years of slog, retrenched them or downsized their jobs.

And the freedom they want is to have balance in their lives. They want to be with their kids, to bathe them at night, watch them at ballet, play the drums, and kick a soccer ball with them at weekends. Few highly paid, demanding, 24/7 jobs are worth the price of not growing up with their families themselves. They are increasingly locating to out-of-town homes, either in villages or the countryside, with their computers, faxes, cellphones and the Internet, where they work long, hard hours but can opt to do so at night when the kids are asleep. The ability to do this is a great reward.

If you want to tie them into a corporate suit, you will need to make their workplaces fun places, where they can dress fairly informally, work hard but have time off when the project's done. They don't want future rewards because they quite rightly point out that not even you know the future and how long your company's going to be around. They want to be able to take their pensions and any accumulated leave or savings with them when they go.

Millennials

Companies that employ teens are using gift certificates to reward them, such as discounts at retail stores, free meals or tickets to movies or concerts. They want to use such rewards NOW and enjoy telling their peers about them which could, of course, prove to be a good recruitment tool for your company.

This approach will hold true as they grow older and enter the corporate world. They want practical rewards that they can use. This often means extending rewards beyond the workplace to impact on their personal lives. They want time savers, like a meal in a box or a coupon to buy a ready-made meal because this is a busy-beaver generation. They, like Xers, enjoy the freedom that laptops, cellphones and the Internet give them.

Another reward for Millennials will be working in areas that are meaningful to them, such as saving dolphins and whales, or conserving rain forests or threatened communities. Millennials will also appreciate grand 'celebrations' because they are sociable and enjoy parties. Conversely, it won't matter to them if a reward is small or relatively inexpensive as long as the process of handing it over is fun-filled and fresh.

It's not a reward if nobody knows about it!

Many of the above mentioned rewards are already being implemented. Some companies headed by Silents are providing dry-cleaning and valet services for their hard-pressed Boomer and Xer workers, but, being Silents, they don't talk about them. Not surprisingly, company employees are often unaware they are available. Potential outside recruits are even less aware of them.

Boomers have for years been providing flexible working conditions, like two to four working day weeks, and changeable holidays. Again, they've not talked about them or put them in their company brochure. Some companies award 'points' for work well and diligently done. Save up enough of these and you could win anything from wine to a deep freeze.

The bottom line here is: if you've got rewards – talk about them!

Feedback and evaluation time

GIs and Silents

No news is good news. If you don't tell them anything then they think they are doing a good job. They don't feel the need for annual reviews. Their attitude is, 'If I am not doing my job, I expect you will fire me. If I hear nothing, I can only assume I am doing just fine.' They can find formal reviews quite intimidating, especially if performed by much younger people. Try, therefore, to keep them short and reasonably formal.

Boomers

They like to have annual feedback, or, if it's a fast moving industry, then quarterly feedback. It needs to be formal with a great deal of paperwork, at a designated time that you have given them ample warning about. There needs to be a policy in place for feedback, how it's conducted, and why. It's essentially almost like a ritualised mating dance and many Boomers don't take it seriously. There are hundreds of books on the market explaining the best and the right way to go about it.

Xers

They want feedback at the end of every project. This can drive their Silent and Boomer bosses mad with frustration because it is exactly the opposite of how they work. Indeed, Xers won't move on until you have evaluated them. When Silents question the need for it, Xers respond by saying that it doesn't matter whether the project is a day, a week or months long, they want feedback so that it becomes a continuous process.

They have the attitude, 'OK, I've done that. Now I can move on? And, by the way, before I do so I wouldn't mind a day off, too.' They appreciate a less structured, informal approach.

Millennials

They will want feedback at the press of a button. They will want to know what you think, right now. In a fast moving world, they will need to have a finger on the pulse, constantly. Take a sales operation. In the past the sales manager would get monthly reports but now receives these on a weekly and, often, a daily basis. But a Millennial will want it *now*. They say, 'Twenty-four hours is like history. I want to know who sold what in the last few minutes.' Or, 'I have just finished a sale. How did I do?'

This isn't surprising. After all, Millennials have had instant feedback from birth. They're used to watching a show on TV, seeing a book or a household item they like, and then hopping onto the Internet, comparing prices by checking out the websites of several suppliers and then ordering. They use their credit cards, then they email confirmation of the purchase and say they want it next morning. As they are waking, the doorbell rings, and there it is. They are used to interactive TV and voting for their favourite competitor by SMS. This is gratification before you even knew you had the need.

The scratch before the itch.

Balance (between 'work' and 'life')
GIs and Silents

These two generations had a similar approach to balance. Work was about production. It was about producing items, goods, food. It was not about fun. You worked hard and there was little balance in your life. Balance kicked in when you retired. Your balance was forty years of hard work and twenty years of no work.

If we want to help the Silent generation (and the few GIs still working) to attain some balance, the best way now is to help them make a proper transition to meaningful retirement. At the moment, a Silent generation person could be a senior manager at work one day, and the next day wake up to the realisation that he need never, ever get out of bed to go to the office again. It's incredibly abrupt. It affects not only the worker but the spouse too, whether or not he or she is working. Suddenly, there's an extra body around the place. We need to help Silents ease into retirement with orientation courses and family counselling.

Another factor to take into account is that retirement is not what it used to be. Sitting around and doing nothing all day is no longer acceptable to most of us. As we've already suggested, bring these Silents back into the office on a part-time basis or reskill them. Send them on computer courses.

This is as good for them as it is for your company. Human beings are not designed to do nothing. We are designed to have challenges in life. And that's why so many retirees who do suddenly stop working often die within a couple of years. If you've got nothing to get up for in the morning, your body probably reasons that it's time for you to leave it and move on. It will shut down.

Boomers

They live to work. They are the 'hooray, it's Monday' brigade. Ask them what time is the best time to leave the office and they will reply, 'ten minutes after the boss'.

For Boomers, work has always been a competitive place. They've always seen work as difficult and never talked to their colleagues about their salaries and packages. They have had the same attitude towards work, by default, as their GI and Silent parents have.

But this generation is now going through a great awakening. They want more balance in their lives and they want it now. There could be a couple of reasons for this:
- Some of them are becoming grandparents and they want to do a better job at that than they feel they did as parents. They want a second chance.
- They see that their Xer children are having a better time at work than they did. Xers are demanding and receiving

paternity leave, taking time off, or refusing to work late because they want to see their child playing the piano at the school concert.

Boomers are beginning to feel that the train of life is moving too fast down the track for them. Time, they realise, is their most precious commodity. The Oscar-winning 1999 film *American Beauty* illustrates the yearning that Boomers now feel for balance in their lives. Many a Boomer can relate to Lester and Carolyn, the couple played by Kevin Spacey and Annette Bening, who begin to question everything from their marriage to their careers. Lester gets fed up with his boring job selling advertising, 'self-destructs' magnificently in order to get fired, and then goes to the local fast food outlet where he asks for a job. The startled teenage interviewer protests, 'We don't have any positions in management right now.' Lester replies, 'Good. I'm looking for the least possible amount of responsibility.' He's jaded, disillusioned and exhausted. He reflects the feelings of millions of Boomers.

The best way a company can retain the services of such employees is to help them attain the balance they want, to give them time off, to counsel them and to retrain them if that's what they want. Let them downscale if that's their choice, and enable them to do so without losing face. The cost of giving them free time is far less in the long run than the cost of replacing them.

Xers

They demand balance. For them it's not a privilege. It's a right. They will resign if they don't have a balance in their lives. We have moved away from an inputs-driven economy to an outputs-driven one. In the former economy you were paid just for being at work, for sitting at a desk. GIs, Silents and Boomers pitched for work and got paid for it, even though some were horrendous slackers and never did an honest day's work in their lives. It is the traditional nine to five approach.

Xers, with the new technology that often enables them to work when and where they want to, question why they need to be in the office at all. They say, 'It doesn't matter what I look like when I work, or how long I spend completing a project, as long as I produce it to your satisfaction. OK?'

They say, 'Don't tell me to be at the office at 8am when I have worked from midnight to 5am because that's when my biological clock tells me to work.'

They are boggled by the Silent and Boomer generations' insistence that they have to be at work on the dot of 8 or 9am and that starting and finishing times are not staggered to suit those who find working the set company hours difficult for myriad reasons.

When they are interviewed, Xers will ask, 'What time off will I get? How many weekends will I have to work?' And if they don't like the answer, they will walk out and find a company that better suits their needs. They're not waiting until retirement to achieve a balance in their lives.

Millennials

There are huge changes afoot for this generation, both in terms of the way they are growing up and the workplace of the future.

Right now, this is one of the busiest and most over-programmed generations ever. Sue's daughter Amy hardly had a free moment in her school day from the time she started at 7.30am until she came home at 5 or 6pm. There were extra maths and science lessons. Drama practice went on night after night. Homework often wasn't completed before 11pm or midnight.

British newspapers report children as young as seven and eight years of age doing homework that takes them two hours or more. Some of it is so complicated and demanding that their parents and grandparents struggle to help them. Often parents are so exhausted by homework demands and the resultant stress on all family members, that they just do the homework themselves. Anything, they mutter, for peace and quiet. Conversely, some schools, like Crawford Preparatory in South Africa, specifically instruct parents not to assist their kids because the world has changed so much that the former have little idea about subject content, especially maths, and end up only confusing their children.

Some parents are so desperate for their children to be accepted in the 'right' school and to be the best that they encourage them in their multi-activity days which are now so busy that even six-year-olds need to keep a diary.

Millennials aren't happy with this state of affairs and are beginning to fight back. When they get to work, they will see it as just one more thing or activity they will need to balance in their lives. They won't put work into a separate category. It will just fit in with everything else they do. This is hardly surprising as they're increasingly growing up with parents working from home, often at night as well as during the day. So companies will have to compete with Millennials for their time. Right now the contract is, 'I own you, buddy. I pay your salary. You work the hours that I tell you to.' Millennials will say, 'You don't own me. You pay my salary. I give you output. I am taking Tuesday off to be with my son.' And they will get the day off. This is because as the nature of work is changing so companies are changing their attitudes towards employees.

Companies increasingly understand that they are not hiring an individual. They are hiring a 'system'. It consists of the employee and his or her family made up of spouse, ageing parents and children. Some companies are already changing their approach to recruitment. They interview the spouse and if he or she is not happy with the way you'll be working, then the deal is off. Company conferences include spouses. They are invited to hear the company's report back on its financial results. They want the family to be part of the organisation in the same way that the company needs to respect that the individual is part of a family system.

So companies increasingly will give you, the worker, the day off on your birthday or wedding anniversary and a half day on your spouse or your children's birthdays.

Companies in this high-tech, unsleeping world where skills and talents are global commodities, need to attract and then ensure they retain the talent they find.

And giving their employees balance in their lives is the big way to go because every generation now wants it, albeit in different guises.

Attitude to work:

GIs and Silents: I worked hard for forty years. Now I'd like to retire.

Xers: I worked hard until lunchtime. Now can I go home?

Office dress codes

Until fairly recently what you wore to work was a given. You put on a uniform in the true sense of the word, or you dressed to fit in with the company's uniform approach. That has changed dramatically in recent years. Here is what each generation now expects of its staff and we offer some tips on this contentious topic.

GIs and Silents

A suit and tie are essential and don't make them too flashy. This generation isn't impressed by multicoloured shirts and wild ties because they grew up in an era of grey-suited office workers and pinstriped bankers. Women, on the whole, tend to wear conservative skirts and blouses and don't display knees or cleavages.

A major difficulty for these generations is their propensity to 'judge a book by its cover'. Many a con artist has duped pensioners simply by looking 'respectable'.

Tip: Try not to view the dress code of other generations as 'dressing down'. It's indicative of the more relaxed approach to work and making it a fun place to be today. GIs and Silents may see this as part of the 'problem' with 'youngsters' today.

Boomers

It was the blue jeans generation that started the trend towards leaving jackets at home. This is particularly the case in the IT world where billionaires wearing sneakers, T-shirts and jeans are almost commonplace. However, as Boomers have aged, they've reverted to conservatism and hauled out more formal suits and ties. The old school tie is often worn by this network-is-my-middle-name generation.

Political leaders in particular all seem to spring from the same mould as they wear their dark suits and white shirts with a monotone red or blue tie.

Women, who entered the workplace in really big numbers in this generation from the 1960s onwards, initially did so in fairly casual clothes. But as they began climbing the corporate ladder and smacking their heads on the glass ceiling, they realised that in order to be taken seriously, they had to dress seriously. By the 1980s the power suit had arrived with huge padded shoulders to emphasise 'bulk' at the boardroom table and offset any silly notions about 'little women'. Blouses with feminine 'ties' were hot and some women went the whole toot in pinstriped slack suits complete with waistcoats.

Men had to keep up so they upgraded to flashier clothes with labels, brand names and designer suits becoming de rigueur.

However, the strain of keeping this up every day of the week proved too much for Boomers. It was they who instituted 'casual day' at the office.

Tip: Boomers, you were wild and free once. Don't forget that as you try to make everybody the snappy dressers you are now.

Xers

This generation took dressing down to its ultimate with their grunge attire, baggy pants and 'just out of bed' hairstyles. They have abandoned suits and ties almost completely, preferring formal open-necked shirts when some sort of formality is required. They can't understand why, if they never leave the office and don't have to meet clients, they can't work in jeans or shorts. If they do have to meet a client, they will wear the suit and tie. They are confused by managers who assume that it's not possible to think, or work, unless they are wearing a tie at all times.

There's been a backlash, recently, against this casual approach. Some companies, such as Deutsche Bank, have reverted to formal dress code policies, requiring full suit and tie. Others require women to wear suits only and even insist on court shoes without peep toes. It's debatable whether the more formal approach will prevail in the long term. We believe the more casual (but clean and smart looking) approach will prevail.

Tip: Xers who find themselves working with Boomers, Silents and GIs would be wise to have a suit and tie handy for critical business meetings. Tame the wilder hairstyles before meetings.

Millennials

Self-expression is a fundamental human right as far as Millennials are concerned and they want this to emerge in their clothing, hairstyles and accessories. They are pushing the boundaries of appearance from body piercings to visible tattoos. They believe, naively or not, that their work should do the talking. Don't assume that long hair for men, or shaved heads for women, or piercings or heavy mascara (for men or women) necessarily constitute signs of rebellion. They often aren't.

It's possible that in future even companies such as banks or airlines, that now require full-on uniforms, may become more flexible and simply require uniformity with some expressions of individuality allowed.

This generation will demand reasons for every dress code you impose on them.

Tip: You don't have to lose your corporate image to fit every Millennial whim. They need to compromise too. Create and explain a corporate image, rather than dress code, and allow them to express their individuality, while enhancing the corporate brand. Be prepared to explain and defend your rules.

Loyalty

GIs and Silents

You, the employer, received loyalty just by providing a job. That was the contract – you get my loyalty if you give me job security. Loyalty was expressed this way, 'I'll go the extra mile for you, the employer.' Or, 'Don't say anything bad about my company.' If you slag off a company that a GI or a Silent work for they will drop the following into the conversation with the intention of shutting you up, 'Well, I work for that company.'

That's loyalty, going down with the company.

Boomers

They will be loyal if you give them challenges that allow them to feel self-fulfilled, and if you give them a clear upwards career path. You can also buy Boomer loyalty by not retrenching them in tough times. Being transparent with them is also highly regarded.

Boomers were shocked when they were retrenched as it didn't tie in with their vision of their brave new world of endless opportunities.

Xers

'If you want loyalty, get a dog.' That's their attitude. They know you can't offer them job security in uncertain times, even if you pretend to do so. If you promise them security, they will say, 'I cannot believe you.' They are not cross or bitter or disappointed. They just know that you cannot live up to what you say.

That sense of impermanence has been reinforced by the collapse in recent years of companies like Parmalat in Italy, Enron and Arthur Andersen in America and Barings Bank in England. No one anticipated that industries and companies would collapse the way they have in recent years.

So if there's one thing that Xers expect, it's that they will have to change jobs. They are, therefore, flabbergasted that you could even suggest that you expect loyalty from them. 'What ARE you thinking?' is their retort.

For them, it's all about a contract. Loyalty and paying dues was like being a slave. For a few years they work slavishly, then they're fast-tracked to management so that in ten years' time they hold down a senior position. But they don't believe this will happen. You and the company may not be around in ten years' time, so they want their reward NOW.

If an employer does however change from the old-fashioned approach to loyalty and enters into a two-way partnership with an Xer in terms of balance, freedom and rewards, this will buy his loyalty. But you need to reinforce that contract on a daily basis. Don't take it for granted.

Someone we know got divorced and ended up without a roof over his head. His employer lent him money, paid his legal bills and gave him clothing. Now that's loyalty and the employee says he will never, ever, leave that company.

Millennials

They will demand a balanced working life. Companies will need to see them as part of a 'system', as part of a family and not as stand-alone individuals. If this is done, they will be loyal. It's a daily contract that works both ways.

Fun

GIs and Silents

'What's that?' they ask. 'Surely not something we have at work!' They had the military model in mind for the workplace. You don't have fun in the military. Well, most people don't.

Boomers

Fun is what you have at a conference away from the workplace, or during a lunch break, or a short tea break. They are highly competitive and view fun as frivolous. It might lose you your position – even your job. No ways!

Xers and Millennials

Fun, enjoying what you do and how you do it are, in their view, critical components of the workplace. If they can't work in pleasant, happy surroundings with cheerful people, they're not going to stick around. One Xer employee was shocked when he was reprimanded by his boss for suggesting that they have some fun. The Silent generation boss snapped, 'Look, we already have one casual day a week. It's called Sunday.'

Generational attitudes to changing jobs:

GIs and Silents: Don't change jobs. It'll stigmatise you.

Boomers: You may have to change jobs but it'll set you back in your career.

Xers: It's a necessary part of career development. I expect to be between jobs about five times in my life.

Millennials: I will constantly be changing my job.

You know you're working in the new millennium when you get this email:

- You try to enter your password on the microwave.
- You haven't played solitaire with real cards in years.
- You email your buddy who works at the desk next to you.
- When you go home after a long day's work you still answer the phone in a businesslike manner.
- You've sat at the same desk for years and worked for three different companies.
- Your CV is on a disc in your pocket.
- You learn that you're redundant on the 9pm news.
- Your biggest loss from a system crash was when your best jokes went down with it.
- Your supervisor doesn't know how to do your job.

- Contractors outnumber permanent staff in your company and are more likely to get the long-service awards.
- Board members' salaries are higher than all the Third World countries' annual budgets combined.
- Interviewees, despite not having the relevant knowledge or experience, end the interview when told of the starting salary.
- You only call in sick when you can't walk, or you're in hospital.
- Your relatives and family describe your job as, 'works with computers'.

The clinchers are:
- As you read this list you kept nodding and smiling.
- You thought about forwarding it to your friends.
- It crossed your mind that your jokes' group might have seen it already but you don't have the time to check, so you forward it anyway.
- You got this email from a friend who never talks to you any more – except to send you jokes from the Internet.

14

Advertising to the Generations

Generational attitude to advertising:

GIs:	Tell me what the product does.
Silents:	Explain why the product is better than anything else.
Boomers:	Must enhance my image.
Xers:	Needs to be surprising and unexpected.
Millennials:	Entertain me.

Attitude to advertisers:

GIs:	Are trusted advisers.
Silents:	They're the experts.
Boomers:	Flatter me … I like it.
Xers:	Don't trust them. Sceptical. Cynical.
Millennials:	I know that they know that I know that they're advertising.

Imagine an advertisement in a yellowing newspaper for a Model T Ford. Underneath the little picture of the distinctive vehicle are lots of words, describing in detail the characteristics of the car. No lurid adjectives. Just the facts. Lots of them. The kind of information that makes you feel it could have been written by an engineer in the Ford factory.

Now, fast forward to a cinema. You've arrived a little late and as you sit down you think, 'Oh-my-gosh, the movie's already started'. Then you relax as you realise you're being entertained not by a movie but an advert.

You have just journeyed, in your mind, from the beginning of the twentieth century, from the GI generation, to the *now* generation, the Millennials.

That's the trip we're taking you on in this chapter. We're journeying from the adverts that your parents/grandparents/ great-grandparents studied, to the adverts that will rivet you, your children and their progeny by their narrative as you sit in a darkened theatre.

Why did the adverts that were effective a hundred years ago, work for that generation? What's happened in between? It's a generational story. The era, the time, the generation into which you were born is one of the major influences on you as an individual. We've established that. So it makes sense that the advertisements that you spent the first ten years of your life reading, listening to, and now watching, have had a huge impact on the kind of message you like receiving from the person or the company that is selling to you today.

'In order to connect most effectively with an individual, the style of advertising to be used should be as close to the style of advertising most popular during the first few years of the person's life,' wrote Graeme, co-author of this book, and Kathryn Robinson of Ogilvy and Mather, in their research paper *Generations and Advertising Literacy.* In 2002 it won one of the South African Market Research Association's top prizes and a merit in the global WPP market research awards.

Point made? Yes? No? Let's take a look at how advertising has worked since 1900. After that we'll look at how people like their advertising messages packaged today and how advertisers, whether they are selling travel, insurance, houses or lipstick should focus their strategies to reach across the generations.

A brief overview of advertising in the twentieth century

GIs (born 1900s to 1920s)

When young GIs were growing up, cars, or automobiles as they were called back then, were beginning to appear on American and British streets, thanks to Henry 'you can have any colour you like as long as it's black' Ford. Fire engines were still pulled by horses, many areas of London were lit by gaslight and people generally regarded the airplane as an eccentric new machine for which there would be little commercial use.

Let's look at advertising against the background of slow, stylised and formal living, with silent cinema in its infancy, newspapers bringing global news a day or two after the event and no radio or TV. The emphasis on advertising at the time was on the manufacturer's painstakingly written description of his product. Early print adverts included small pictures of the product in its packaging with a lot of text about it. If it was a scientist doing the writing, all the better, as GIs wanted to know the molecular make-up of a product and the scientific description even though half the time they couldn't understand it all.

So, a tiny picture of a Model T Ford with detailed descriptions of fuel consumption, horsepower, top speed and gears would impress people wanting to buy a car. In fact, the picture wasn't really that important. It was the detailed printed words that riveted them. It didn't have to be compared to anything. You either wanted to buy it or you didn't. There was no such thing as shopping around.

Silents (born 1920s to 1940s)

Freedom of choice and competition began to creep into advertising in the early years of the Silent generation's childhood. There was a 'reason' given for buyers to purchase one product over another one. This doesn't mean there was anything as promiscuous as competitive advertising which was either legally banned or frowned upon. But the focus moved from the product's attributes to the performance of the product, its desirability and place in the market. Silents remember Pears soap and the picture of the little girl with curly hair called 'Bubbles'. She is climbing back into her bath because she's forgotten her Pears soap. The picture worked because it was so appealing and so innocent and these attributes were projected onto the soap. An advertisement would also have worked if it said 'By appointment to the

Queen', because that was the ultimate stamp of approval in an age where you lived and died for your country, both literally and figuratively.

Boomers (born 1940s to 1960s)

The 'brand' became critically important for the first time in advertising and focus shifted to how the product would enhance the consumer's lifestyle rather than on its utility. This meant that the consumer's profile, the kind of person most likely to buy the product on offer, became important. Image and status became the key motivators for the product. Today, the advertising industry is replete with consultants and agencies that help companies develop complete brand 'personalities'.

So how will a Harley-Davidson improve your image in the eyes of your girlfriend, your mates and your work colleagues? As Boomers currently dominate the advertising industry and are in most cases the primary target market for luxury products, it's no surprise that the lifestyle approach to advertising is hot stuff today. Adverts for cars, watches, perfume, shoes, alcohol and certain clothing brands are not about how healthy or good for you they are, or how well they keep time or do their job, but are targeted at making you feel more sexy, cool, desirable, wealthy. If you buy those products, then you'll be living that wonderful lifestyle.

Boomers are also influenced by influence. If famous people use a brand, Boomers are far more likely to want to use it themselves. They're impressed that Tiger Woods wears Nikes, that film stars use Lux soap and so on.

Xers (born 1960s to 1980s)

For this generation, advertisers have moved on from extolling the lifestyle virtues of a brand to showing the product by way of a narrative story. Adverts have become entertainment in themselves. They are short stories and are often discussed and sent around the Internet. For instance, take the advert about some guys in a truck with surfboards on the roof rack, who are driving from beach to beach looking for good surf. At beach one there are some awesome waves that they get out and admire; then they shake their heads, get back into the truck and drive on to the next beach. Here they see gorgeous girls tanning in bikinis. They shake their heads again and drive on to another beach where the scenery is drop dead stunning but, again, they get back into their vehicle. The message is clear: it's not surf they are after. It's driving in their truck.

The use of music and Hollywood movie-style directing makes this and many other adverts an art form in themselves. Famous global campaigns include Budweiser (*Wazzup*), Reebok (*Terrible Terry Tate*), Mountain Dew (*Do the Dew*) and so on.

In this manner of advertising, the extrinsic side of the brand is assumed – that the truck is rugged, comfy, has an excellent braking system; that the beer tastes great and quenches thirst; that the sportswear is comfortable, durable and scientifically designed for peak performance, and so on. It's not necessary to talk about the brand's attributes. Although they may sometimes be included, they are not the primary objective of this form of advertising. Consumers are expected to buy the product because they are impressed with the advert as an art form rather than with product utility or lifestyle links.

The advertiser and the consumer are, in a sense, both on the same side in this form of advertising. In car advertising you often see the vehicle swooshing through water or climbing up the sides of craggy mountains. It's almost as if the vehicle is on a catwalk.

Some adverts are getting to the stage where they hardly show the product at all. The advertiser knows that if the consumer wants technical specifications, she will find these in great detail by just clicking onto the Web.

Millennials (born 1980s to 2000s)

The Xers started the shift to the advertisement itself becoming entertainment and this is continuing. We've reached the point where everybody knows that's what is happening in advertising, so the pretence that the consumer is being given objective information about a product, which is what the GIs and Silents assumed, is dropped. The advertisers are no longer pretending that the product will enhance your lifestyle, and you know it's just a product and that they are out to entertain you. It's not so much about *what* they are selling now as it is about *who* the advertisers are, and who *you* are, the consumer.

A good example of this is the John West tinned fish advert in which bears are fishing for salmon. A fisherman rushes the bear to wrest the fish from him. It soon becomes clear that the bear is a fake, as it karate kicks the man, and a scuffle ensues, before the man walks off with the fish. The payoff line is 'We endure the worst to bring you the best'. It is hilarious and was posted on the Internet where millions of people sent it to their friends for a good laugh. Companies are increasingly advertising this way. Budweiser beer has close to one hundred of these ads on the Internet. Some of them are long – two to three minutes – and are too expensive to flight on TV. They encourage, and even fund, spoofs of their adverts.

Books such as *The Tipping Point* and *Viral Marketing* understand that word of mouth is a powerful advertising tool. It's not far-fetched to say that one person might influence an entire country with a brilliant, entertaining Internet advert. Graeme's company TomorrowToday.biz sends out a monthly email to over 25 000 people and they pass it on to their friends. So if Graeme punts a certain product, it will have an audience. Many other people are doing the same thing and the clever ones do it selectively and entertainingly.

Celebrity endorsements are out unless they are entertaining. Britney Spears doesn't say, 'I drink Pepsi' or Christina Aguilera, 'I drink Coke.' The advert featuring Christina is about a fan who becomes an extra on one of her video shoots. He faints every time she comes over to him and at the end she drinks a Coke. She doesn't say it's healthy, or sexy or anything . . . she just drinks it.

Tiger Woods wears Nike clothes. He doesn't say anything about them and we all know that they don't make him the world's best golfer but the fact that he's wearing them tells us that Nike is an icon.

This new form of entertaining advertising provides stimulation and fun, sometimes with little or no direct reference to the brand, and when the brand does appear it's usually in a highly symbolic form and its presence is an integral part of the artistic whole.

Millennials love this.

Prediction time ...

Advertisers, marketers, promotion gurus and PRs will need to bear in mind that the Millennials are civic minded and determined to 'save the world', its fauna and flora from extinction and the havoc wreaked upon it by the materialistic Boomers. They regard them as having raped the planet's forests and oceans. They are high minded and crusading on the one hand and easily bored and demanding on the other.

They are the advertising future.

But so are the 'over-60 and overlooked' Silent generation, and, increasingly, the Baby Boomers, who will be the wealthiest and healthiest retirees ever, living it up in their golden years.

We will deal with all the generations and how best to reach each one in a moment, but before we do, we need to understand just how much advertising is changing due to all kinds of pressures being exerted on it.

Today we have moved on from the brand itself as being important. Taking a product and turning it into a 'personality' who shops at certain stores, holidays, travels, eats, drives and wears products in a particular way is no longer the way to go. Today we can't brand a product as if she, or it, were a separate person.

Today advertisers will have to sell not only the product but the company that produces it. Customers want to know what's going on behind the scenes, what's cooking on the production line. That's why Nike and Gap had such a problem over their sweat shops allegations. The backlash meant millions lost in retail and it nearly nailed them. It's why many companies like Total and Shell are going on 'ethics roadshows' and emphasising corporate social responsibilities.

In today's world where there isn't much difference between products or shops, or shopping malls, and with prices tending to even out, customers will choose an airline or supermarket or butcher based on emotional criteria and not necessarily linked to price or quality. They will, however, avoid those that they think are exploiting their workers, whether through overwork or bad working conditions, sexism or racism.

If you have half a dozen airlines to choose from with not much difference in quality or price, you'll go with your gut feel about the airline you feel is 'right' for you.

Having said that, some marketers are advocating a radically different approach to hooking the elusive customer. Stephen Brown's book *Free Gift Inside; forget the customer, develop Marketease* says that in a market where customers are sophisticated, their desires sated many times over, and where all products and services are essentially the same, the time has come to 'tease' the customer.

A brilliant example is the way that JK Rowling's Harry Potter book was marketed in 2003. Stephen Brown says it was marketed on 'absence'. It was made known that copies of it could be sold out overnight, creating anxiety, massive queues and all-night pavement parties the day of its release. We were told that the original manuscript was locked up in a safe after it was 'almost stolen' from the publisher, Bloomsbury. The hype was incredible and resultant sales an all-time record.

Stephen Brown uses the De Beers strategy of manipulating the laws of supply and demand to maintain the desirability of diamonds as an illustration of yet another excellent 'tease' campaign. And let's not forget the upmarket boutique in London's West End where only 'chosen' customers were allowed in and, once in, were often treated with contempt. They loved it.

So Brown suggests that instead of pandering to consumers, it's better to play hard to get, give them a personalised experience and they'll come running for more in an age where every consumer is a marketing expert. They know they're being sold to all the time with promises, come-ons, boasts and give-aways. Marketing has become self-parody, which is why the time has come to market marketing. The marketing must itself be marketed. It needs to become a talking point along with the product it is selling, like the John West fish and

Budweiser's *Wazzup* ad campaign. We certainly have come a long way since that Model T Ford tiny photograph with the intense type beneath it.

As we said at the start of this chapter, in order to connect with an individual, the style of advertising you choose needs to be as close to the kind of ads that were popular when your target market was young, for that is what they relate to.

How to make the most of adverts aimed at GIs (born 1900s to 1920s)

There are a surprising number of switched on 80 and 90-year-olds around and if you want to reach them you need to remember that what they look for are product attributes. They relate to a scientific description of a product. It might not always make that much sense to them but they want to know the chemical make-up of it and see lab-coated scientists discussing it.

Indeed, the GIs look for product attributes even when there aren't any in an ad. Graeme was part of a team with Ogilvy and Mather that presented a series of ads to generations-based focus groups. Of all the adverts shown, at least one advert was produced in such a way that a particular generation was able to relate to it. When each specific generation focus group, eg Silents, Xers, was asked to name its best ad, it was uncanny the way each generation chose exactly the one that Graeme's team predicted it would.

When the GIs saw an advert of a car with a dog's face hanging out of the window, salivating tongue and his fur blowing back hard in the wind, the GIs said the advert was aimed at showing the car's speed. They didn't understand it. In fact it was a Millennial ad, an entertaining advert about a funny looking dog, and this confused the GIs who didn't find it amusing. They wanted the facts.

Key marketing theme: 'Give us the facts.'

The message here, if you want to reach the GIs, is that you need to ensure you include product information and attributes, no matter how outdated an approach that might seem to you. If you're targeting a product at the GIs then don't do something silly with it.

Take the print advert for Poli-grip denture glue. An elderly man and woman are pictured kissing passionately. The line beneath it reads: 'Let your world move, not your dentures'. It is amusing, but only for younger generations who don't need denture glue yet. The copywriter who put the ad together was probably in his late twenties. It's a generational mismatch.

What he needed to know was that denture glue aimed at 80-year-olds should not set out to be entertaining, image or status conscious, or silly. It needs to say, 'Denture glue that will keep your teeth in place for fourteen days. Your teeth will only come out when you take them out', and then give them scientific information about the glue and how it works.

Product information could possibly include details of its usage – as adverts used to do in the 'good old days'.

Tips for advertising to GIs

- Give them the facts.
- Explain product usage.
- Don't try to be silly or funny.
- Don't refer them to web pages.
- Provide postal addresses.
- Longer, information-rich adverts are a good idea, including Home Shopping Network.
- Make use of scientific experts for endorsements.

Silents (born 1920s to 1940s)

They want to know that the product you're trying to sell them is better than, or has the competitive edge on, other products. In countries where competitive advertising is now allowed, this needs to be done subtly in a genteel and gentlemanly manner, not viciously.

Silents like the use of important people, NOT celebrities, for endorsements. The national sports hero (who isn't on drugs or sex abuse charges) is a good one. So is a retired politician of stature like Nelson Mandela or Jimmy Carter or Margaret Thatcher.

But they also relate to testimonials of 'real people' telling them how the product works. Infomercials are largely aimed at them. Probably the longest running ad campaign in South Africa, which ran from the 1970s to the 90s, was for Omo soap powder. It was built around testimonials of housewives who declared that it washed 'whiter than white' and 'it works for me'.

Key marketing theme: 'We're not old.'

Silents who are in their sixties and seventies don't think of themselves as old, whatever Xers might think about them! As *The Economist* wrote, 'Getting to know long-ignored older customers, however, is hard work for marketing youngsters, who are used to lumping all people over the age of sixty into a grey basket of frailty, tweed and stinginess. Advertising's creative types, the people who dream up commercials, are considered ancient by the time they are 35 years old. Finding a way to communicate with an older audience is a challenge for them.'

Car manufacturer Ford came up with a novel way to help its mostly under 40-year-old design engineers to grasp the needs of ageing drivers. They put the engineers into a 'third age suit' which adds about thirty years to the wearer's age by stiffening the knees, elbows, ankles and wrists. It also adds material to the waist – a rotund stomach inhibits people's ability to sit easily – and it has gloves that reduce the sense of touch. Ford's designers also wear scratched goggles so they can experience what it's like to have cataracts. The result? Ford cars are easier to climb in and out of, seat belts are more comfy and glare has been reduced.

Another option could be to employ some of these retirees to act as consultants.

Advertisers targeting Silents need to ensure that everything they write and say is to the point and well written. Silents don't like sloppy grammar and abhor spelling mistakes.

They are philanthropic and have a strong sense of community so if you want to get teenagers to take a specific action, such as opening bank accounts, appeal to their grandparents to do so for them, or even better, with them. You can also ask grandparents to buy products, gizmos like cellphones and laptops, for their grandchildren. This works well if the kids are going to use them for the 'right reasons', such as homework.

Silents value strength and achievement and history is important to them. They are not good ones to whom to launch a new product because they take a 'wait and see' attitude. This isn't surprising when you realise they value longevity, history and success in a product.

Tips for marketing to Silents

- Ensure that your grammar and spelling are perfect and that the voice-over artiste has an 'old-fashioned' and easily understood accent.
- They respect expert opinion and take the view that hard work and not luck is what makes things work.
- Understand that they're enjoying a 'second middle age', but they don't think of themselves as ageing.
- They're spending their kids' inheritance (SKIing) and they're the fastest growing segment of the wealthy market.
- They like buying the market leader.
- They don't want to be rushed.
- Don't be nervous about employing a couple of them. Use them in focus groups to help you really ram home your advertising message.

Boomers (born 1940s to 1960s)

If the Silent generation is 'not old' you can bet your bottom dollar that the brand-crazy, 'wear-the-label-on-the-outside' Boomer generation is even 'less old'. Best of all, delete 'age' from your lexicon and you'll be fine. Any euphemism will do. We know that they know that you know their age, but so what!

The fact is that Boomers spent the first half of their lives idolising youth and they're now set to spend the second half idolising age. We're not saying we'll go back to the days, 150 years ago, when young people tried to emulate age by stooping and wearing padded jackets to make their backs look bent or dyeing their hair silver, but age is set to become a lot sexier than it has been up until now.

Boomers are out there in their Hell's Angels leather bomber jackets and denims, riding their motorbikes and belting out their Elvis and Beatles songs. They're jiving, rocking 'n' rolling to them too because they're the fittest ever generation to reach the age they have. So, whatever your product is – travel, health care, anti-wrinkle creams, hair colour shampoos, cars, climbing equipment, surfing, laptops, motorbikes – Boomers will use them because they're keen, young and fit enough to do so.

They're also wealthier, on average, than any other generation has been before them and they're keeping that wealth for themselves, not handing it on to their kids. One understandable reason for this is that they've no idea how long they're going to live and their money had better last as long as they do. Add to this the natural tendency of Boomers to be self-indulgent and fairly wild in their spending habits, and knowing they now have the time, the health and the wealth to be able to do so, you soon realise that this is a generation that's going to spend even more than they have up until now.

Key marketing theme: 'Make me feel special.'

It's extraordinary, given the demographics, how advertising is still targeting youth as promiscuously as it is. In industrialised countries, for instance, the over-sixties already account for well over 20 per cent of the population – compared with less than 12 per cent in 1950. By 2050 that proportion is expected to rise, on average, to a third, reaching over two-fifths in Japan, according to a feature in *The Economist*. That is mind-boggling – one third of the population over the age of sixty!

No wonder some clever marketers are already jumping on the bandwagon, as indeed they should be because the hands on the levers of power today, in commerce, industry and politics, are overwhelmingly Boomer hands. They're starting to regard 60-years-old as quite young! For instance, hair care products are often about 'go ahead, spoil yourself, look good', which is classic Boomer style. The cosmetics industry is going flat out to market products that the massive Boomer market will snap up, with their urging of women (and, more subtly, men) to wipe away those wrinkles. Remember when Lancôme ditched Isabella Rossellini as its model because, at age forty-two, she was considered 'old'? Compare that with L'Oréal hiring Catherine Deneuve in 2001 when she was fifty-seven, to promote their hair care products. Equally savvy was Estée Lauder asking its star model in the 1970s, Karen Graham, to be its new face for a mature market cream in the 2000s.

Already, this is a massive move, marketing wise, from a decade ago when the sight of silver hair in glamorous shampoo adverts was a shock for many a TV viewer.

The Boomer muscle is also apparent in music sales. At the millennium when everybody was talking 'the top 100 best...' for the past century, Boomer movies and songs dominated all lists. In 2000 the global number one best-selling CD was The Beatles '1' and in the Top Ten were Abba, Queen and the Rolling Stones. No wonder. They are the biggest hits of the Boomer era and Boomers have the bucks to buy five or ten CDs at a time. Who owns Virgin, the world's biggest music store? A Boomer – Richard Branson.

All of this will not be music to the ears of the young, edgy Xers in advertising agencies who can't understand one of their fastest growing target markets – the ageing Boomers. Suddenly your thirty-fifth birthday will not mean your last day in the ad agency after all. And the wise ones just might re-recruit some of the 40-year-olds they've just 'retired'.

Tips for advertising to Boomers

- They are busy and want everything faster, more convenient – and don't mind paying for it.
- Put the label on the outside of the product – make it reek of class and quality. Boomers enjoy displaying their conspic-uous consumption.
- Use 1960s and 70s music – Boomers were the first to put music into adverts and they like 'their' music the best.
- They believe they know better than anybody else, so forget products endorsed by any generation other than Boomers.
- They distrust authority so communicate product benefits straightforwardly and honestly.

- BUT they are attracted by celebrity endorsements and image.
- Use loyalty schemes.

Xers (born 1960s to 1980s)

'Sceptical' is the one word that overwhelmingly defines this generation. And as if that were not enough of a nightmare for marketers, add to it the Xer ability to wriggle out of any 'marketing box' or 'label' that is slapped on them in an effort to define them. They loathe being called the 'lost' or the 'twilight' or the 'indigo' or '13th' generation.

The American generation gap experts, William Strauss and Neil Howe, in their book on Xers, included a chapter on marketing and its title reads 'I am not a target market' with good reason.

Xers are savvy. They know what advertising is about and that it's not objective. If they see a laboratory with a 'doctor' in a white coat, they know that it's a TV studio or was shot in a university research centre. They are used to feeling that advertisers are lying to them, the same way spin doctors lie in the political sphere, so you have to let them know that you know that they know.

You can't buy loyalty from an Xer in most spheres and especially not in products. Advertisers who come up with a brilliant idea for an advert, then try to cash in on their success by expanding it into a variety of their products are not wise. The Xer response is that what grabbed them the first time around was that the advert was surprising and unexpected. In South Africa Omo was able to run its 'whiter than white' ads for about thirty years. Vodacom's got away with something like seven or eight years with its YEBO! GOGO campaign. Xers expect something new. This techno-savvy generation is easily bored, so surprise them.

This is why Xer creative directors are now pushing the boundaries in advertising agencies and are creating the entertaining ads that the Xers want and Millennials think is normal.

Xers, more than any other generation, like to think that a product is targeted specifically at them. They're not attracted to a lipstick advert that's targeting your mother because they don't want to wear the same stuff as her. In fact you want her to be appalled by the lipstick and nail polish you wear. You need to be careful about creating multigenerational ads and if you do, then you would need to run them in media specific to each generation.

Key marketing theme: 'I am an individual.'

It's wise not to create an advert that has a lowest common denominator. It might work for the Silent generation but you will lose Boomers, and Xers won't even come near it. You have to pick your target market. No self-respecting Boomer is going to read the magazine *Puke* and no self-respecting Xer is going to read *Harpers and Queen*.

Branding is huge for Boomers but Xers don't buy into a brand identity. They are too individualistic. Whenever Boomers need to change a brand, such as BP changing from British Petroleum to Beyond Petroleum, or British Airways repainting their planes, it's a huge drama with consultants crawling out of the woodwork and millions spent in the process of months-long agonising.

Conversely, Xers require the marketer to change his brand on an ongoing basis, for example the way Nike has done. It's gone from Nike to Nike with the 'swoosh' and now it's just the 'swoosh'. No doubt it will change again, soon.

Xers would also quite like you not to take yourself too seriously and, with their slightly irreverent view of the world, to maybe poke a little fun at your own brand.

No wonder Xers and Millennials aren't interested in today's average ad. The focus today is neither on the brand nor the consumer but on advertising itself. The ad has to be entertaining and absorbing with subtle messages. They're not confused when they stumble, late, into a darkened movie house with their Boomer parents. They know instantly it's an ad – their kind of ad.

Tips for advertising to Xers
- Give it to them straight – they are smart and savvy.

- They are easily bored so they enjoy clever tricks and the unexpected.
- Entertain them. The advert must be an art form in itself.
- They respond to up to date language that's irreverent, not politically correct and direct.
- Don't be linear – Xers are used to multilayering and enjoy mystery and paradox.
- Xers value friends – don't go for the 'lone ranger' image.
- Conversely, they're highly individualistic in the sense that they value choice, customer options and personalisation. The 'one size fits all' route is totally out.
- Forget product loyalty from Xers – concentrate on selling them a concept instead.
- They have no heroes – only celebrities.
- They are not as brand conscious as Millennials; they buy a brand for its quality, not its image.

Millennials (born 1980s to 2000s)

These kids might want to save the world from the damage inflicted by their materialistic, consumer-mad, energy-guzzling Boomer parents but don't underestimate them as soppy bunny huggers and green beans. They are street-smart, savvy and hip. And they are already impacting massively on consumer spend. It was estimated in 2001 that the average American teenager had nearly $60 of disposable income a week, derived from pocket money, part-time jobs and babysitting. About 20 per cent of them invest in stocks and funds and as many have bank accounts and credit cards. It was estimated in 2001 that 31 million American kids aged between 12 and 19 controlled $155 billion worth of consumer spending, in a survey done by Teenage Research Unlimited, and reported in *The Economist*.

It was estimated that by 2003 this figure would have risen to $248 billion.

This generation, also known as 'Bornfrees' in South Africa, because they were born when apartheid was dying, spend about R4 billion a year and influence their parents' spending to the tune of R20 billion a year, according to research by the University of Cape Town's Strategic Marketing Institute in 2003.

Key marketing theme: 'Entertain me.'

No wonder retailers are obsessed with them. Their spending power extends far beyond what they carry in their wallets. It's not just kiddies' stuff. They influence the cars, household appliances and even the houses that their parents buy. This is because they surf the Internet looking for the kind of car they want their parents to drive, then download the information and present it to their amazed and techno-nervous parents.

In France, Peugeot tapped into this by running a series of ads that showed children encouraging their parents to buy the Peugeot 806. One showed a two-year-old arranging pasta on his plate to read '806'. The payoff line was 'the car that children recommend for their parents'. In South Africa McCarthy Call-a-Car featured an ad where kids called in and ordered the car. Estate agents are increasingly putting houses on the Internet, and guess who's hogging the computer, surfing the Net, and knows mom and dad are looking for a new home? Why Junior of course. And while few parents would allow a 12-year-old to completely dictate the purchase of a house, they ARE giving their kids a much greater say in spending.

These parents are Boomers, so they're workaholics, harassed, spending less time with their kids than they know and feel they should. They make up for it by spending money on, instead of time with, their kids. The Henley Centre Research Organisation in London calls this 'perfect moment time'. If a lot of time is spent driving kids to and from school, then why not let them help choose the car? And we all know the story of the kids whose parents rock up at school in a less than perfect (in the kids' eyes) vehicle and park it, on kiddie instruction, around the corner. Maybe they should just buy a new car!

Marketers have clicked on to this new force and are grabbing these youngsters' attention early on in their lives. Dieter Zetsche, head of Chrysler Global, said in *Fortune* magazine of 24 March 2003 that it is his company's intention to specifically target Millennials with their Jeep and Dodge brands. They can't drive and they don't have money but they do influence their parents and when the time comes for them to buy a car, guess which make will pop into their minds first!

Mazda got caught behind in the new, small, zippy car market, so they gave the outer shell of their proposed car to designers of a video game called *Grand Tourismo*. Two years before Mazda was ready for the road, kids saw it in this game and their watching parents saw it too of course. When it arrived, they were ready for it. Now Mazda has taken this a step further and invited the computer software designer to join their concept team for designing the next range of sports cars. He's suggested that instead of gears, brakes and a steering wheel they have a car using the Sony Playstation video game console.

Millennials will require marketers to be as concerned about the values and culture of the company as they are about the product or service they're selling. This is, technically, what marketing departments should be doing anyway, but in most companies these days, marketers have little say about the internal workings of the company. That will need to change. Every part of your company, from products to adverts, your receptionist, security guards, website, office building design, music on hold, needs to convey the message about who you are. Branding is both external and internal now, and the Millennials are watching you closely. Not just your adverts – they're watching YOU!

Tips for marketing to Millennials

- They are confident, don't treat them like kids. They're so confident they're almost arrogant in their insistence that you don't talk down to them.
- Know how the product you are marketing is produced – avoid skeletons in the cupboard.
- They're plugged in and want messages in sound bites on modem media.
- Make sure your website gives lots of information about who you are, not just what you sell.
- Your staff are a huge marketing tool – make sure they're passionate about your products, and create easy ways for them to generate word of mouth marketing – about the products AND the company vibe itself.
- Time is their most precious commodity, not money. They're prepared to pay for convenience and time-saving devices.

- Endorsements will work with them as they look up to heroes.
- They're extremely brand aware and know if you are 'hot' or not. Word of mouth marketing and capturing the 'influencers' is critical.

Multigenerational advertising

Spare a thought for the products that have to appeal to different generations at the same time, for instance, universities and colleges. It's the students who usually make the decision about which university they want to attend, yet it's the parents who pay for it. It's actually a joint buying decision. But the very things you want to highlight to attract students, 'freedom, campus fun', are the turn-offs for their parents. They're attracted by 'civilised, controlled, academic environment' and that's not grabbing the students right now. You, the university, are appealing to two separate audiences with different expectations and market appeal.

Other products need to be rebranded for a new generation. For instance, Mercedes is considered an old man's car. Yet BMW, its main competitor in Europe and around the world, has successfully established itself with Silents, Boomers and Xers.

There are, unfortunately, no silver bullet solutions for cross generational marketing. The rule of thumb for an established brand is to focus your efforts on the younger of your target markets. But this advice is simplistic if it's not accompanied by a full understanding of the product offering, the consumer market and brand history.

The best option is to create separate brands for each generation.

When Levi's found that young adults didn't want to wear the same jeans as their ageing Silent and Boomer parents, they created a variety of other brands, such as Dockers, for a new generation.

If you can't go this route then the next best option is to run multiple campaigns in different media. This is easier today than it has ever been before due to niche publications, narrowly defined cable and satellite TV channels, radio stations and, of course, the Internet.

Take the example of university advertising. Adverts aimed at parents could be placed in business and women's interest magazines. Those for younger people could be flighted on music radio stations, made available via the Internet or put into extreme sports or Gaming magazines. It will be tough to manage these multi-channel campaigns but the results are worth the effort.

The key is to be sensitive to the different value systems with which you are trying to connect. You've already gained an understanding of this by reading our book. Your skills and experience will do the rest.

For more details and the results of generational research and advertising literacy, see our website at:
http://www.tomorrowtoday.biz/generations

Gender roles:

GIs:
Men and women's roles were strong and distinct for this generation. Men were in charge and they, for the most part, owned women. Women did not even have the right to vote. There was one set of rules for men and another for women. This meant, essentially, that men could do as they wished while women had to conform to strict codes of dress, behaviour and manners. Men earned money. Women, generally, did not. It was this economic bondage that kept women subservient, a situation that still exists in some parts of the world today.

Silents:
World War II emancipated women because they were virtually forced to work to free their men for war. They were also encouraged to make munitions, and hands that had only patted butter and babies' bums turned to

filling bullets with powder. They were, however, not accepted in positions of power – only as workers. After the war, women who had worked night shifts in ammo factories and fought as secret agents behind enemy lines reverted to being acquiescent, and sometimes frustrated, housewives and mothers. Clear gender roles were, once again, established.

Boomers:

These feisty women were not about to be forced back into the 'closet' as many of their mothers had been after the war to free jobs for returning servicemen. Freed by the Pill from unwanted pregnancies, they flooded into the workplace. The feminist movement forced society to seriously reassess its attitude towards women. Gender roles began to blur as men wore long hair and women, like famous model Twiggy, cut theirs as short as men used to. Women wore pants and some men wore kaftans. Rocketing divorce rates saw many women become the family breadwinner.

Xers:

They are blurring the gender differences even more with androgynous hairstyles and clothing. Men, like soccer idol David Beckham, use cosmetics and fragrances and wear their hair long. Women cut theirs as short as men used to and carry briefcases. Often men and women take turns at being the breadwinner, as one or other spouse studies. Men still dominate but there are more single breadwinner homes headed by women in America than there are by men.

Millennials:

The fashion trend, at present, is for women to look more feminine with longer hair and more body curves so gender roles may, in future, become more clearly defined again. But it is still too early to make clear predictions. There's no doubt that increasing female confidence about their abilities will make it less important for women to fight for their rights.

15

Leading the Generations

Generational leaders:

GIs: Nelson Mandela, Jimmy Carter, Sam Walton, Mother Teresa, the Queen Mother, Winston Churchill, John F Kennedy, Billy Graham, Margaret Thatcher, Ronald Reagan, Pope John Paul II, Eva Peron, Malcolm X, Alan Greenspan, Walter Cronkite, Fidel Castro, Louis Armstrong, Walt Disney, Henry Kissinger, Nelson Rockefeller, Ray Kroc, Edmund Hillary, George Bush Snr, Lee Iacocca, Jiang Zemin

Silents: Desmond Tutu, the Dalai Lama, Jack Welch, Muhammad Ali, Kofi Annan, Paul McCartney, Helmut Kohl, Thabo Mbeki, Mikhail Gorbachev, John Major, FW de Klerk, Lech Walesa, Elvis Presley, Jacques Chirac, Neil Armstrong, Queen Elizabeth II, Harold Macmillan, Tiny Rowland

Boomers: Bill Clinton, Tony Blair, George Bush Jr, Gerhard Schroeder, Princess Diana, Andrew Lloyd Webber, Vladimir Putin, Donald Trump, Bob Geldof, Richard Branson, Steve Jobs, JK Rowling, Luiz Inacio 'Lula' da Silva, Bill Gates, Steven Spielberg

Xers: Mark Shuttleworth, Lance Armstrong, Tiger Woods, Jerry Yang, Jeff Bezos, Michael Dell

Millennials: So far… Prince William, Venus and Serena Williams, Haley Joel Osment

Attributes of generational leaders:

GIs: Principled, tough but fair, authoritarian, stoic, civic minded, visionary, gentlemanly.

Silents: Pragmatic, stable, hard working, low key, loyal, balanced, formal, hierarchical.

Boomers: Visionary, idealistic, workaholic, enthusiastic, energetic, bossy, passionate, principled, loud, reward-driven.

Xers: Cautious, creative, pragmatic, realistic, low key, innovative, flexible, independent, adaptable.

Millennials: Will be... civic minded, visionary, confident, optimistic, moralistic, principled, values driven.

Some generations throw up leaders so charismatic and visionary that their names live on long after they've gone. Some lend their names to adjectives such as Churchillian or Stalinesque, and nouns like Thatcherism or Reaganomics. Other generations, however, are characterised by leaders who fade into obscurity, even though they've done their diligent best.

Why is this so?

The short answer is that the historical era into which a leader is born has a determining influence on the leaders who grow up in that time.

The longer answer is that genetic make-up (nature) along with the way we are raised (nurture) are two key factors in creating each one of us the way we are. Your parents will have brought you up in the prevailing parenting style of the times which may have been a permissive, hands-off approach or conversely authoritarian and strict. But they will also have been strongly influenced by the era in which they were living. If they were struggling through a war or an economic depression when you were young, that would have had a tsunami-like effect on their lifestyle, attitudes and finances. Consequently, they are likely to have been cautious with money and careful with relationships. This will, in turn, have affected you and *your* attitude to life.

Some generations are born during exciting, optimistic times which help to shape their outlook. They graduate from their youth as optimists and visionaries, believing there's always a solution to life's problems. Those were the values inculcated in them by their parents and leaders during their youth and teens. As they move into middle-aged adulthood they become leaders themselves and impose their particular brand of leadership style on the environment over which they have control.

And so the cycle of generational leadership is established. In this manner, each second generation has some form of echo of the generation that was in power when they were kids. This means that a pendulum effect flows through history.

In the twentieth century generations have changed from being optimistic to pessimistic, back to optimistic and then pessimistic again. The pendulum also swings from a generation that is proactive in its outlook to one that is reactive. For instance, the Xers (now in their twenties and thirties) are generally regarded as being pessimistic, while the Millennials, who are currently toddlers and teens, are optimistic and determined to save the world from the damage caused by preceding generations.

GIs and Boomers have spent longer in leadership than any other generation. They came to positions of power earlier, are leaving them later, and have a greater effect while in power than do other generations. A good example of this is Margaret Thatcher and Ronald Reagan's special relationship, clearly evident in letters they wrote to each other. They had a belief that God had ordained them. This belief was also shared by John F Kennedy, Martin Luther King Jr, Nelson Mandela and now by George W Bush. Margaret Thatcher made an abortive attempt to hand over power to a Silent generation leader, John Major, but the Boomers said, 'stand aside, we're coming through'. And they did, in the form of Tony Blair and Bill Clinton. Clinton was an unknown when he stood against Bob Dole (GI/Silent generation) who was older, wiser, trying to do the 'Ronald Reagan thing' and nobody gave Clinton a chance. But he was a Boomer and swept the boards.

Boomer and GI leaders have an aura about them that sets them apart from others. When Nelson Mandela whips out his wallet and gives 500 rand to an old age pensioner, he does so with a grace and presence that is legendary. The same can be said of many of the actions of fierce anti-apartheid campaigner, Helen Suzman and Nobel Peace Prize winner, Archbishop Desmond Tutu. South African president Thabo Mbeki and George Bush Junior just don't cut the ice in the same manner.

It's important to note here, once again, that generational history is a generalisation. We're not carving up all the people in the world into five generations and asserting, arbitrarily, that every single person fits into only one generation, *their* generation. There are always exceptions to every rule, we are all unique and influenced by a myriad of different factors. But having said that, it surprises us constantly how many people who grow up in a particular generation do find themselves dressing, eating, working, thinking and leading in a similar fashion.

GIs (born 1900s to 1920s)

This generation was born at a time when the world was being shaped by powerful, global figures. It was a time of phenomenal change and excitement, characterised by new inventions and gutted by two world wars. The GIs were guided and inspired by great men and women of character and determination.

Leaders who influenced them

Jan Smuts, Henry Ford, Mao Tse-tung, Mahatma Gandhi, Cecil John Rhodes, Henry Ford, Vladimir Lenin, Queen Victoria, Charles Lindbergh, the Wright Brothers.

The times they lived in

The early 1900s were characterised by inventions. Thomas Edison had invented the light bulb. Henry Ford set up the world's first car production line making wheels available to the masses, and the Wright Brothers proved the theory of controlled flight in 1903. The Titantic sank in 1912.

World War I (or the Great War) boomed on to centre stage in 1914 and dominated the globe for four years while its repercussions, World War II, haunted the world deep into the 1950s. The Great War was largely a formulaic war, in which troops fought in trenches and advanced metre by metre, step by step. Indeed, it was so formulaic that subsequent generations learnt to their astonishment of British and German soldiers emerging from their trenches on Christmas Day, shaking hands, swapping cigarettes, playing soccer, and then returning to their hellholes to fight and kill each other again the next day. Although the Great War had Gatling guns (the early machine guns) and fledgling air forces, it represented war as it had existed for about 300 years.

The leaders didn't change war tactics. That is partly why society didn't change after the war. Millions of people died, and the lives of equally many families were changed irrevocably but the structure of society as a whole didn't change much after World War I. Geographical boundaries didn't change significantly and political power didn't either. The best example of that lack of change was Germany's retooling itself for a second shot in World War II.

During the first twenty years of the last century, there was no great breaking of the shackles of the Victorian era or even of the Industrial era, even though boundaries were being pushed, a new society was being created and leaders were not scared to tackle the issues of the day.

It was out of this environment that GI generation leaders emerged.

The GI leadership style

They are, on the whole, strong, visionary and principled leaders. The thread that weaves through their style is their quiet, almost conservative, heroism. They didn't set out to shake the world the way you shake a puppy by the scruff of its neck. They just set out, fairly quietly, to change it. They have been doing so for half a century, from the young John F Kennedy to the now elderly Nelson Mandela. Their imprint on the second half of the twentieth century is unmistakable. When Nelson Mandela came home after twenty-seven years in prison on Robben Island, the expectation was that he would storm through South Africa, changing it with each giant step. That belief existed because the leaders at that time were Boomers, like Bill Clinton and Tony Blair, who do tend to slap the world around and get their way. But Mandela didn't. He changed the world his way, the quiet way.

The GIs had a similar and clear view to Bush and Blair that the world needed to be changed. But their approach was steady and calm because it was shaped by the people who were leaders when they were young. And those leaders were, generally, Victorian in their thinking.

The GIs were a visionary generation as they came into power in the 1950s and 60s and they probably assumed their positions of power more slowly than the Boomers have done. In their day you paid your dues first and only expected to rise to leadership positions after a long apprenticeship. Nevertheless, they were often the youngest leaders ever seen. And they were, like John F Kennedy, the first leaders to be born in the twentieth century. They didn't force their way into power, they allowed the power to come to them.

GI leaders had visions and were inspiring. We think of John F Kennedy's push to land a man on the moon; of Martin Luther King's dream for black people to do the then unthinkable – to stand up, be counted and make a place for themselves in history.

GI business leaders included Walt Disney, Henry Ford, Sam Walton, William Hewlett and David Packard, to name a few. They were the leaders as the Industrial era came to a close and the dawning of the Information Age began. Although they were not the powerhouse of the Information Age (the Boomers claim that distinction) they were in charge and were able to see the benefits both in the political and the social spheres.

The GIs were not what we today call powerful leaders in that they had awe-inspiring visions that they imposed on people. That's the Boomer approach. They preferred to lead by inference. They have a vision and realise it, but a lot more slowly and steadily than the Boomers who want their visions installed and operating within weeks of having them. GIs have a much longer term view of how change should occur. It is a conservative leadership style that wants everybody on board with the same vision. They build large groups of disciples or believers around them, who work well with them

201

and take their vision forward. They believe in action, but it is often slow. And it is probably because of this approach that they have had a lasting impact on the world.

Silents (born 1920s to 1940s)

They grew up in an era when the difficult times they lived in, the Depression and World War II, demanded pragmatism and strong, calm leadership. On to the world stage marched Winston Churchill, Franklin D Roosevelt, Joseph Stalin and Jan Smuts. The charismatic leaders who had led the world before them were now regarded with scepticism. It was the Churchills of the world to whom the Silent generation turned for role models. Stern times call for stoic leadership and Winston Churchill probably typifies this best with his speeches made to his fellow Britons, suffering the nightly, deadly onslaught of the German air force. 'We shall fight on the beaches, we shall fight . . . we shall never surrender.' That's what his stout-hearted countrymen wanted to hear and that's what he gave them. The American president during World War II, Franklin D Roosevelt, had the same resilient determination. There was a job to be done. They had to beat the Germans and the Japanese. They did so.

Leaders who influenced them

Winston Churchill, Adolf Hitler, Joseph Stalin, Franklin D Roosevelt, George Patton, Charlie Chaplin, Al Capone.

The times they lived in

The Roaring Twenties were ushered in to the sound of jazz which had become the rage in all social classes, and spread fast due to the popularity of the first wireless stations broadcasting in America and Europe. Flappers feverishly danced the Charleston attired in shifts with low waistlines. Short, frizzed hair, feather boas and cloche hats epitomised 'the look' as men and women searched for oblivion in a not surprising reaction to the horrors of World War I. The 1920s were characterised by Prohibition in America and labour strikes in Europe and England. But just as the older Silents began to arrive on the scene, it all fell apart. The decade collapsed in the 1929 American Wall Street crash with fortunes tumbling all over the world and resultant misery and destitution for the masses throughout the western hemisphere.

The full effects of the Depression hit the world during the 1930s with John Steinbeck's book, *The Grapes of Wrath*, vividly describing those bitter times. The 1930s saw the rise of Facism, Communism, horrendous unemployment, Hitler's rampant ascendancy in Germany and a slow slide into World War II that Europe and Britain were desperate to avoid. Life was changing tumultuously throughout this decade and news that might have been ignored before now blared into most homes thanks to the 'newfangled' wireless. In 1938 Germany mobilised and terrified Jews tried to escape from officially organised pogroms. Britain and France declared war on Germany in September 1939.

America was dragged into the war in 1941 when the Japanese attacked their fleet at Pearl Harbour and by the time peace was struck in 1945 over 30 million people had died. The world was fragmented, nations searched for stability – political, economic and cultural – and countries, cities and towns had to be rebuilt from ashes.

It was time for hard-working, stoic and pragmatic leaders.

The Silent leadership style

Most of this generation lived through terrible times during their childhood. They were hugely influenced by the people in leadership positions at the time, whose approach to life's challenges was 'we will get you through this'. They tended, on the whole, to take a back seat. They weren't the visionary, upfront, charismatic leaders that the GIs would be. They led by delegation, by getting everybody on board through teamwork and shared vision. They were stoic and determined in their approach.

The vision was to get through the Depression and the war, so they gritted their teeth and did so. This affected the young Silents deeply. Their childhoods were spent struggling for survival, learning to save, wondering where their next meal would come from and then having to cope with the threat of death or being subjugated by the enemy. They internalised this external threat, learning to live from day to day and this translated into an approach to life which was more survival than visionary.

They accepted that the world was a tough place and that success would come only by persevering and keeping your head down. 'Get a good job in a big company and stay there,' was the advice their parents gave them. They listened.

It's not surprising therefore, that when this generation came into power later on in life than the GIs had done, in the 1970s and 80s, they didn't arrive as leaders with a rallying call. In fact, when they became leaders the world was once again in crisis. They had to pick up the pieces after Nixon and Watergate. They were handed an America ravaged by the Vietnam War and its economic, emotional and societal consequences. South African leaders had to handle a cruel and vicious apartheid system. Britain was dealing with the post Profumo Scandal which rocked the establishment to its core with its tales of prostitution and spies.

The Silent generation leaders, far from creating new visions, operated instead in a void of vision. It was left to the young Boomer leaders in the 1980s and 90s to stride into this void and project their own visionary approach when leadership was handed over, quite abruptly. Presidents born in the 1920s handed over, often quite suddenly, to presidents who were born in the late 1940s after World War II. But Silent generation leaders who left their mark include Russia's Mikhail Gorbachev who completely changed the 'old' Russia; and South Africa's FW de Klerk who handed over power, willingly and bloodlessly, to Nelson Mandela. Kofi Annan and Thabo Mbeki have both adopted a 'softly, softly' approach to international politics.

Silent generation leaders bring a calming, balancing approach to the environment. They are less vocal than Boomers and lead by example. They believe that leadership should emerge from their character and their being rather than from their words and commands. Squeezed as they are between two

204

powerful generations (the GIs and Boomers) let's hope the Silents are not relegated to the footnotes of history.

Boomers (born 1940s to 1960s)

Boomers were being born when the charismatic and visionary leaders like Churchill, Roosevelt, Mandela and Henry Ford were centre stage on the world platform. When many Boomers were in their teens and early twenties, GI leaders such as John F Kennedy, Martin Luther King and Nelson Mandela began to move on stage. They were the role models for Boomer leaders and the Boomer generation that has dominated the world like no other generation before or since.

Leaders who influenced them

John F Kennedy, Mother Teresa, Neil Armstrong, Pope John Paul II, Billy Graham, Edmund Hillary, Walter Cronkite, Alfred Hitchcock.

The times they lived in

World War II dominated every facet of life, virtually across the world, until 1945, and its aftershocks continued into the 1950s. They were the stirring and devastating times of the evacuation of troops trapped on Dunkirk's beaches; Hitler's concentration camps where six million Jews were extermi-nated; The Battle of Britain; the London Blitz; the bombing of Pearl Harbour that brought the Americans storming into the war as they fought the Japanese and the Germans. The world watched in awe and horror as Hiroshima and Nagasaki were wiped out by atom bombs. 1942 was the darkest year of the war with seemingly imminent defeat, but the next year the Allied Forces began winning major battles and Italy surren-dered. In 1944, the D-Day landings on the beaches of Normandy signalled the rout of Germany and in April 1945 Hitler committed suicide and Mussolini was killed. Germany surrendered and America, in the face of the Japanese intransigence, dropped the first atomic bombs on Hiroshima and Nagasaki. More than 30 million people died. Daily life throughout the world was hard with rationing in some form or other. Across the planet, demobilised soldiers, refugees, concentration camp survivors and displaced people looked for what had once been home.

The world was like a huge jigsaw puzzle and the fledgling United Nations tried to help put it back together again. Grand plans for rebuilding the world and creating great societies were being discussed. Visionary, dynamic leaders soon replaced the more pragmatic wartime heroes.

Stalin was still murdering millions, Gandhi was assassinated, and the new state of Israel was born. As the world moved into the 1950s, so the Cold War began, Korea and then China became involved and new tensions grew.

In Britain, there was a new queen for a brighter age as Queen Elizabeth II was crowned and rationing and austerity gave way to optimism. Britain's Edmund Hillary conquered Mount Everest with Nepal's Tenzing Norgay. Winston Churchill retired in 1955 at the age of eighty-one. In 1955, a black American woman, Rosa Parks, refused to give up her seat on the bus to a white person and sparked the first American race boycotts and riots.

John F Kennedy moved into the White House, taking with him his beautiful wife Jacqueline, who soon lavished her glamour and pizzazz on it. A South African doctor, Christiaan Barnard, performed the world's first heart transplant in 1967 which marked the start of huge strides in the science of prolonging life. Marilyn Monroe posed and Elvis Presley gyrated.

The Boomer leadership style

Boomers grew up in visionary times when John F Kennedy sent a man to the moon and Martin Luther King stirred a mighty nation with his 'I have a dream... ' speech about the sons of former slaves and the sons of the former owners of slaves being able to sit together at the table of brotherhood. Russian cosmonaut Yuri Gagarin became the first man in space, Betty Friedan launched the Women's Movement and the Pill was born.

They were stirring, cutting-edge times so it's hardly surprising that Boomers believe that leaders just need to create a vision and it will happen. They believe that if you just expose a team to one of their visions, this will be enough to inspire people to work hard to attain it.

Boomers enjoy nothing quite as much as having conferences, summits and delegations. All over the world, when there is a political, environmental, trade, or any other kind of challenge (or problem) the Boomer leaders will immediately call for some kind of meeting. Whatever field Boomers are working in, be it charities, faith-based organisations or politics, you will nearly always find them organising some sort of strategic thinking exercise, or what South Africans call a 'bosberaad' or 'bush meeting'. This is usually held over two to three days at an out of town venue. This strategy has been satirised in movies such as *City Slickers*, in which Boomers (the city slickers) visit cowboys on a ranch in an amusing effort to teach them all about leadership skills and what having a vision is all about.

In a typical 'out of town' meeting, the head Boomer, usually the CEO or MD, stands up and shares *the vision*. This is a carefully crafted statement which every leading Boomer has tucked up safely in his/her briefcase. It's explained, carefully, passionately, in an effort to inspire people to buy into the vision.

Having shared it, the head Boomer has to ensure that everybody believes they can achieve it. This process involves activities such as walking over burning coals, abseiling down impossible cliffs or river rafting down crocodile infested waters as they learn that nothing and nobody will stop them or stand in the way of their achieving the vision.

Having shared the vision, the Chief Boomer then shares the 'mission'.

Only Boomers understand the difference between the *vision* and the *mission* and they insist that both are vital to the organisation's success. By this stage, the Xer generation staffers are thinking, 'vision, mission, purpose... just how much more do we need for goodness sake?'

The answer for Boomers is in short: a lot more.

For next comes a list of strategic objectives and strategic action steps. These are written up on a banner and prominently displayed at all company events.

Banner One:
Vision statement
Mission statement
Values statement
Purpose statement

Banner Two:
Strategic Objectives
Strategic Action Steps

Then to ensure yet again that everybody knows exactly where they fit into the scheme of things, each individual is given a list of core competencies, KPAs (key performance areas) and KPIs (key performance indicators).

You are then all divided into small teams where you brainstorm, summarise, categorise, and then write down your findings. These appear on yet more posters which, by now, are hanging from every available bit of wall and even pinned to chairs and couches.

A great number of buzzwords are employed at these meetings. Boomers love them. The only things they love more are acronyms, such as EE, BEE, AA, CSR.* If you don't know what they mean, you are not a Boomer.

Out of town meetings are also useful to Boomers for playing the recognition game. Boomers enjoy recognition, it's part of their mindset (see chapter 6 on Boomers). They like having targets and, having achieved them, they want awards for doing so. Being ranked and classified is important to them – it's a powerful motivator.

Something else Boomers love to use at meetings and conferences is surnames to refer to certain management theories. For instance, they will talk about the 'Handy' model or the 'Drucker' method, referring to management gurus Charles Handy and Peter Drucker. Few people really understand what Boomers mean but that doesn't deter them and they carry on regardless. In fact, often they don't fully

---

* *Employment Equity; Black Economic Empowerment; Affirmative Action; Corporate Social Responsibility.*

understand the terms themselves which is why they're using the label anyway and hoping their bluff won't be called.

A nice example of this happens in the film *Good Will Hunting* where Ben Affleck is being taken apart by a young Harvard intellectual who tries to shut him up by referring to certain theories, dismissing him with 'now, if you'd read the book...' The janitor, played by Matt Damon, then steps forward and nails the student for completely misunderstanding the theory he has just recited and adds to his considerable discomfiture by rattling off a few others to emphasise his point.

The reason Boomer leaders enjoy using labels, surnames and acronyms is the sense of exclusivity this engenders, a kind of Armani intellectualism. Boomers are the most academically qualified generation of leaders ever and they rely on this knowledge heavily. This can sometimes be to their disadvantage. They give too much credence to qualifications when employing staff, or remunerating them. Knowledge is developing and expanding so fast now that the ability to learn on the job and develop continuously is more important than academic qualifications.

Another area that is a challenge for Boomer leaders is their world view. Their approach, and that of the GI and Silent generations, is Newtonian as opposed to Quantum which is a systems way of thinking. In other words, Boomers believe that the world and its organisations work in lots of little, different bits – pieces that each work in a precise and definite way. To understand the whole system all you need to do is have an understanding of each of the parts of the whole system. That is how Isaac Newton attempted to describe and systemise the physical world, which he characterised as a complex machine. The danger of the machine imagery is that it leads to the belief that the key to understanding the whole lies in the study of the different parts.

This is how most MBAs are structured. Students complete courses on administration, human resources, economics, marketing and so on. Students graduate understanding the component parts of a business but not necessarily the whole business. But the Xer and Millennial generations know that it's vital to understand the whole system.

Most Boomers still feel more comfortable fiddling with the components of business and this often results in micro-management. There's a place for this in business, politics and leadership but there's a danger they can end up concentrating on the components instead of the whole system. That can spell trouble if the team, organisation, business or political party, is not managed correctly.

The fall of the Roman Empire, the city of Troy and Napoleon's march on Moscow, all serve as examples of leaders who did not take into account the whole 'system', the big picture, but only parts of it. When Napoleon sent his mighty army into the frozen Russian wastes, he forgot that an army marches on its stomach. And so he lost the war.

From Vietnam to Iraq, and the Falklands to Libya, Boomers have waged wars on the basis of grand visions that may have missed the bigger, and more long term, picture.

The bottom line is that Boomers have tremendous vision but need to temper that with some practical, hands-on application and slightly less idealism.

Generation Xers (born 1960s to 1980s)

This generation was born and grew up during scary times such as the wars in Vietnam, Angola and the Falklands. Watergate blew apart Nixon's administration and, in South Africa, 16 June 1976 marked the student uprising, the beginning of the end of apartheid and years of strife and bloodshed.

Leaders who influenced them

Leaders during their formative years included Richard Nixon, Lyndon B Johnson, John Vorster, Idi Amin, as well as Margaret Thatcher and Ronald Reagan. They were, with the latter two notable exceptions, generally uninspiring role models.

The times they lived in

The Cold War reached its chilling zenith and the Berlin Wall came tumbling down during the Xers' childhood which was, on the whole, a fairly low-key, dismal time during world history. Students in many parts of the world demonstrated and rioted against conscription and war. In America a large group of students were protesting against the Vietnam War when their own National Guardsmen opened fire and killed four of them. The Israeli/Palestinian struggle intensified in the aftermath of the 1967 war and the world watched in horror as Palestinian gunmen killed eleven Israeli athletes at the Munich Olympic Village. Richard Nixon became the first American president to resign from office as a result of the Watergate scandal. His language on taped conversations in the Oval Office taught many youngsters their first swear words. Photojournalism during the Vietnam War produced images that horrified the world and probably none of them so telling as that of naked girl, Phan Thi Kim Phuc, running screaming down a napalm ravaged landscape.

In South Africa, schoolchildren were mown down by police and killed in their hundreds as they erupted against the hated 'Bantu Education' system and apartheid in the mid 1970s. Generally, it was a time of fear, brutal suppression and uncertainty which accounts for much of the Xer values and attitudes.

The space shuttle Challenger exploded on 28 January 1986, killing all seven crew members including Christa McAuliffe, the first woman in NASA's 'Teacher in Space' programme which had been designed to raise public support for space travel. The explosion was seen live in many schools across the world.

The spectre of AIDS began to stalk the world. Millions died in genocidal Rwanda but because it was Africa, the world was slow to respond. Thousands died of starvation in Ethiopia.

But the equivalent of a new 'industrial age' was happening to offset the gloom. Bill Gates and Paul Allen founded Microsoft. Steve Jobs and Steve Wozniak founded Apple. They changed the world by putting computers on the desks and in the homes of everybody who could afford them. Life on earth was changed for ever as computers began speeding up every facet of our lives.

Margaret Thatcher's election in the late 1970s put the first ever female British prime minister into Number 10 Downing Street. It changed the face of both British politics and Britain.

The Xer leadership style

It's probably too early yet to produce a comprehensive description of the manner in which Xers will lead, although by the age of thirty many Boomers were already making their mark felt. Xers seem to be taking longer to assume leadership positions.

We need to see this against the background of this generation's childhood. They dragged themselves out of bed as teenagers, afraid to face the day. They are, in a time of AIDS and rampant cancer, obsessed with their health. For them the world is a scary place. Their political role models have, on the whole, not been exemplary pillars of wisdom and vision.

In business, the dominant, bossy and optimistic Boomers can't understand the seemingly disloyal, pessimistic Xers. We are currently experiencing the biggest generation gap in history, between Boomers and Xers.

Boomers are dismayed when Xers won't stay for after-work parties and slip out of the bonding weekends and out-of-town strategy meetings so beloved by the conference-organising, endlessly meeting Boomers. Xers cannot understand the Boomer fixation on long term planning when the world is changing so fast and flexibility seems to be the key survival skill. Xers are regarded by their bosses as rude slackers, who hang out in coffee shops, tapping away at their laptops, while simultaneously sneering at corporate culture to their friends on their cellphones. Xers believe in enjoying life NOW. Their predecessors believe you work hard so you can enjoy life in retirement.

Mix the different generations together in leadership positions and you don't have a heady recipe for a successful business/political/organisational pie. Boomers thrive on teamwork; Xers appear to thrive on individuality.

The key difference between Xer and Boomer leaders when they are bringing a group together is the Xer approach of finding the unique aspect in every individual. Boomers concentrate on finding the common thread that binds them all. Xers are innovators and want to discover the new, the cutting edge, the difference that will enable them to excel.

Boomers, on the other hand, want to share values as they believe this will make their teams into cohesive units. Xers scoff at this approach, insisting that if they focus on what they all share they won't be able to grow. Xer leaders are, therefore, more inclined to see their roles as facilitating instead of directing, story-telling instead of controlling, and stirring instead of calming.

Boomer leaders look for alignment so that everybody will work in the same way. This is well illustrated by Sam Walton who founded the supermarket Walmart, the biggest employer in the world. He knows how to get the best out of his Boomer-dominated workforce and he personally leads every annual convention with the Walmart war cry. Everybody has to join in. In fact, they have to join in each morning when the stores open up throughout the world! Disney, Hewlett Packard and IBM have had similar approaches to corporate culture and team building. The term the 'big blue' comes from a memo sent out by IBM in the 1950s in which staff were told to all wear blue. The idea was to align people around a common set of values and principles as well as a common dress code in the hope that they would bond and the business would boom. They did, and it did.

This approach has best been documented in Collins and Porras' bestseller, *Built to Last*, in which they profile eighteen Industrial era companies, each one older than fifty years. Many of the principles outlined in their book, such as 'cult-like cultures' and 'alignment', have been blindly implemented in companies that are trying to retool for the information and connection economies. Xer and Millennial leaders realise that although these approaches have been the key to the most successful companies of the twentieth century, they are not the key for the successful companies of the twenty-first century.

Now in the time of quantum theory, the only constant is change. 'If you're not confused, you don't know what's going on,' according to Jack Welch, General Electric's former CEO. Boomers struggle when they are called upon to rapidly put new working groups together. This is because they first want to bring everybody in the group up to speed with their core values, principles and objectives. Xers, conversely, find it easy to build ad hoc teams overnight because they are looking for points of difference between participants – and the more the better. They're able to build and dismantle teams swiftly, whereas Boomers, having spent considerable time and energy in building up a team, are loath to rip them apart. They want them to last for ever.

Authors and consultants are trying to come to grips with the changes and are writing insightful, esoteric books, like Meg Wheatley's *Leadership and the New Science*. She says, 'There are increasing reports of organisations that have given up any reliance on permanent structures. They have eliminated rigidity – both physical and psychological – in order to support more fluid processes whereby temporary teams are created to deal with specific and ever-changing needs.'

We live in a hot paced world where innovation is desperately needed to stay ahead in the game. Wise companies will put Xers into the hot seats where they'll be allowed to 'do the impossible'. They need to be allocated new job titles like Head Innovator, The Cannibaliser and Director of Story-Telling. As Peter Dames, Toyota's e-commerce chief said, 'It's better to shoot yourself in the foot than to have a competitor shoot you in the head.'

No wonder, as we all work in this fast-moving world, which Xers will increasingly dominate, that they've been labelled the 'generation in a hurry'. They want twenty years of experience in two years flat. This attitude is amusingly illustrated by a cartoon in the book, *Geeks and Geezers,* which portrays two balding men facing each other across a desk. They are doing an annual review and the boss asks, 'So Jim, where do you see yourself in ten minutes?'

Another cartoon in the same book has an Xer boss leaning across his desk, saying to the Silent generation worker, 'I'll have someone from my generation get in touch with someone from your generation.'

However, as we have repeated throughout this book, the generational theory is a general one and there are many people who are old at twenty while others are trendy at sixty. Graeme was contracted as a consultant for a firm of accountants where it was decided that some younger blood was needed in the partnership. Graeme was duly invited to meet the new young partners in their late twenties. He was astounded to shake the hands of the oldest twenty-somethings he had ever met. They were older than the company's Boomers and were in fact, clones of its leaders, the Silent generation, wearing grey suits with neat shoes and matching hairstyles. It was a time warp gone wrong.

Xers are asking some searching questions of the business world in particular as they look for new role models. Mavericks, such as Ricardo Semler, author of *The Seven-Day Weekend,* are providing some hope with challenging questions, such as:

- If I work on a Saturday, can I watch a movie on Tuesday?
- If I take work home, can I bring my family to work?
- Can I retire a little now?

Interestingly, Xers who are the echo generation of the Silents, will, like them, come to leadership positions late, if at all. They do not, on the whole, expect to lead. If they do, it will be in less blazingly public ways than the Tony Blairs and Bill Clintons of our world who were youth leaders in their parties. Today few people know such leaders amongst the British Labour party and the American Democrats. The same goes for the African National Congress (ANC). Where are their Peter Mokabas? They are, it seems, 'missing in action'.

Our message to the Xers is: understand that the process of becoming a leader is going to take a little longer than you thought it would but don't give up on doing what you know is the right thing to do.

Millennials (born 1980s to 2000s)

They are making their appearance on the world stage at a time of economic upturn, of hope for a better, kinder world which they will save from the ravages visited upon it by previous generations. Yet down the track lies the possibility of a devastating slide into chaos and anarchy. In many ways, it could be an echo of the GI's childhood a century ago.

Leaders who influence them

Bill Clinton, Tony Blair, Vladimir Putin, Nelson Mandela, Junichiro Koizumi of Japan, George W Bush, Richard Branson and Bill Gates are some of the leaders who have been and will be the role models for this emerging generation.

The times they live in

This generation is, at once, both the most protected and yet the most vulnerable we have seen in decades. Child pornography, drug dealers in the school playground, date rape drugs, child trafficking rings, child labour, the rape of infants and toddlers, coexist with some of the most pampered, cosseted, loved and spoilt children in history. They are the most pressurised, and yet the most encouraged and supported kids the world has known.

The images of this generation, captured by 24-hour television news coverage as well as the tabloid press that leaves no celebrity unscathed in its unrelenting glare, include: Princess Diana's funeral, the Spice Girls, Posh and Becks; the Gulf War which was the first war to be viewed by the planet from the safety and comfort of their sack potato couches, thanks to CNN; Harry Potter, both in print and on movie; the one hundredth birthday and then death of the world's most beloved grandmother, Queen Elizabeth the Queen Mother; Nelson's Mandela's massively televised long walk to freedom and the making of an icon as we watched his every step; the idolisation of the heart-throb British Princes, William and Harry, and the never-ever-to-be-forgotten day that the Twin Towers were demolished by terrorists in New York, rendering the world in one horrendous blitz a once more unsafe place to live in. Mother Teresa, a saint in life, is now being made one in death.

The Millennial leadership style

We are going to try and predict this because of their youth. They will be an echo of the GI generation with its civic minded, community oriented, visionary leaders. Already the pundits are predicting that this generation will, given the choice, opt to wear uniforms to school and will be happy to be conscripted. Volunteerism is currently at an all time high in many countries and growing as young Millennials use their school holidays to do community work and not just for lazy pleasure.

They want to save the world. Youngsters all over the world, from New Zealand to Russia and America, flock to join organisations such as Greenpeace to save whales, wetlands and wildlife. They fight trade wars at economic summits, highlighting the injustice they perceive the rich First World is inflicting on poverty ravaged Third World economies.

They will, we predict, become leaders early on in life with a boldness and confidence that was displayed by their GI generation great-grandparents.

The Xers realise, not without a sense of pique, that the Millennials will be handed the planet on a platter, and will emerge as powerful young leaders just as the Xers sort out, or at least manage to contain, problems such as AIDS and terrorism. The Xers will manage the idealised, but imperfect world that the Boomers hand on to them and the Millennials will inherit a bright, new world when they are in their mid-thirties. Biotechnology will be a massive force, giving us rice in the Sahara and mealies in the Kalahari. New, and hopefully more stable, global economic systems will emerge.

Millennials will be asked: is the world going to emerge free of hunger or suffering from global starvation?

They will probably shoulder this problem with the determination that is one of their abiding characteristics. They will also have to deal with AIDS. Is it likely to be conquered within the next decade? Or will we be subject to something far worse than AIDS as scientists now hint darkly at the emergence, due to our abuse of antibiotics, of a new super bug?

Increasingly, philosophers, historians and writers talk about the biggest threat to world peace being that of a clash of religious fundamentalists, whether they be Christians, Jews or Muslims. Millennials will probably be the generation that needs to confront and solve the issues that such fundamentalists foment in their narrow-minded, bigoted approach to each other and the world at large.

Millennials will probably also have to learn how to deal with the 'moral grey', because although most people believe that morality is either black or white, it is in fact many shades of grey. Millennials will probably need to be proactively peaceful as they cope with moral ambiguity. Nothing in their world will be as clear-cut as it was for their echo generation, the GIs for whom there was only one way – the right way. Life was easier then. There were only two sexes back then. And one kind of family which consisted of dad, mum and children. Roles were clear-cut. It was tough for those who didn't fit the strict mould – they were cast on to the ash heap of life. Millennials will be kinder and more encompassing, more compassionate, in their world view.

We need to help Millennials along their tricky way as they grow up in a wonderful and yet dreadful time. We need to help them grow up untainted by fundamentalism.

They need to experience:
- Diversity. In the past, most Westerners couldn't interact with Muslims because they never saw them in Bognor Regis or Washington. Instead, they marched off, sword in hand, to the Crusades in the Holy Land to kill an 'infidel'. Now Muslims *are* living next door in Birmingham, Johannesburg and San Francisco. In most cosmopolitan suburbs there are mosques, synagogues and churches, virtually side by side.
- Technology. Millennials will use it far better than the Xers who have been swamped by consumer technology, media and junk (spam) without being able to analyse it. We are suffering from information overload and the Millennials will need to 'sort it' in a manner we have not been able to do. We need to help Millennials to analyse and criticise without becoming cynical in the process.
- Balance. Between work and personal life. Millennial leaders will need to learn that the Silent generation men lived and often ended their days working for 'the organisation'. Boomers were, and still are, hopelessly out of kilter workaholics who don't know when to go home to their families and will learn their lesson too late. Xers are trying hard to get the balance right. Millennials will, hopefully, succeed.

Tips for leading the generations

GIs/Silents
- Make changes slowly, don't surprise them, make announcements well in advance.

- Alert them to your experience and your credentials. These include academic studies, achievements and previous leadership positions.
- Look the part – always aim to be a degree more formally dressed than your team.
- GIs and Silents prefer formality; use surnames and titles. Ask for permission to address them by their first names.
- They prefer clear lines of command. Stay away from matrix structures and cross functional teams. Ensure they each report to only one boss.

Boomers

- Make rewards and recognition public.
- Boomers will rely on you to generate energy and dynamism. If it means having an energy drink before every management meeting, then do it!
- They want to be involved in all decisions. They are passionate about transparency and democracy in decision making processes. Include them at all stages.

Xers

- You will need to earn their respect, yet they will take a while to demonstrate that respect for you. Act with integrity and they'll come on board soon enough.
- Give surprise rewards for unusual achievements.
- Fun is serious business! A little humour, something silly, practical jokes, even a little bit of irreverence will help to create a stimulating, and productive, workplace.
- Try a reverse mentoring programme in which younger staffers are assigned to older executives, to help them get up to speed with technology, consumer culture and information analysis.
- Don't look over their shoulders all the time – it irritates them.

Millennials

- Lead. This generation has grown up structured and supervised by parents who believe in boundaries and are active role models. They respond to leadership with integrity.

- Provide mentors. Millennials enjoy interacting with older generations, and learning in a hands-on manner.
- They like to be challenged. Assign them to projects where they can truly learn.
- They like trying new things. Boredom is your, and their, greatest enemy.
- Let them work with their friends as they are sociable and sharing.

Respect:

The way in which different generations approach respect is one of the major causes of generation gap conflict in the workplace today.

The **GIs and Silents** believe in respect for authority and position. They are likely, when meeting someone for the first time, to accord him respect, almost by default. As time passes that respect might well diminish or disappear. But they will not call attention to this publicly. Their respect is demonstrated in physical ways, including addressing people by their titles and surnames, standing when people enter a room, or moving aside to allow for entrance.

Boomers, the questioning, rebellious generation, need respect to be earned. They will not give it easily or quickly. Once gained, respect is willingly bestowed.

Xers and Millennials need to respect the individual intrinsically, not the title, position or rank. They take their time to develop respect as they get to know the person, his ethics and integrity. They expect people to work for that respect.

16

Politics and the Generations

Politicians need to be:

GIs:	Truthful, disciplined, dedicated, authoritative, visionary, heroic.
Silents:	Self-sacrificing, obedient, self-controlled, responsible, trustworthy.
Boomers:	Energetic, visible, achievers, masters of the sound bite, image conscious.
Xers:	Truthful, believable, inclusive, technologically wired, pragmatic, relaxed.
Millennials:	Holistic, caring, visionary, interactive, inclusive.

Who makes history – is it politicians and leaders or is it the people who put them into power? It could be argued that George W Bush is the president of America because a few thousand Silent generation voters in the state of Florida got off their butts and voted for him in a cliffhanger of an election. A few thousand votes amongst an American population of 300 million were cast by a generation in their sixties and seventies, who believe that voting is 'the right thing to do'. Their votes changed the course of history. If Al Gore had been elected, maybe America might not have gone to war in Afghanistan and Iraq with momentous consequences for the entire world.

If the British hadn't got rid of weak-chinned Neville Chamberlain and put pugnacious, never-say-die Winston Churchill in his place, Britain might have been yet another Nazi vassal state.

'History creates generations, and generations create history,' write generational gurus Strauss and Howe. This is powerfully illustrated by the generational gap between George Bush senior and George W Bush junior. Bush senior is from the GI generation and his son is a Boomer. The stark difference between them is powerfully described by Washington columnist Jurek Martin, who wrote in the *Financial Mail*: 'The father fought honourably in war and knew its costs. He was an internationalist in his bones, a vice-president, head of the CIA, ambassador to China and the UN, and knew that the Cold War meant America needed friends and allies. He called Texas home but was a Yankee patrician at heart, diffident about public expressions of religious faith and steeped in the arts of diplomacy.

'The son, who avoided military service during the Vietnam War, is a proud Texan, disdainful of the sophisticated eastern establishment (Washington, New York) that was the paternal milieu. He never hides his religious convictions and believes in biblical concepts of good and evil, love and hate. Freed of the constraints and obligations of the Cold War, he sees a world where might is right and where America is, by a country mile, the mightiest of all – yet simultaneously the most threatened and misunderstood. His duty, as he conceives it, is above all to protect its security in a dangerous new world, by whatever means necessary.'

So there you have it, father and son, two totally different personalities, shaped by the generational times into which they were born and grew up.

If the Democrats had pitched their campaign at a different constituency, might Al Gore have tipped the scales in his favour? Did the Governor of California, Arnold Schwarzenegger, win the 2003 election because twenty-and-thirty-something Xers, tired of political hype and spin, decided that an actor was as good a person to occupy the seat of power in their state as any career politician, using their, 'so what...!' rallying cry to swing their vote.

Today politicians all over the world are worried about voter apathy which is at a historical high. Voters are unimpressed by the image conscious and young (by generational standards) presidents and prime ministers strutting the world stage today. George W Bush, Tony Blair, Gerhard Schroeder, Luiz Inacio 'Lula' da Silva, Junichiro Koizumi and Vladimir Putin, to name a few, are all Boomer generation heads of state. Their political campaign managers and their press officers are often slick spin doctors and the Xers who have been brought up on a junk food diet of sound bites and spin have had their fill. Shrewd politicians will need to take note of this state of affairs. The next spate of general elections, in 2004 to 2005, will be fought mainly on issues concerned with national security and terrorism. The elections that will take place at the end of this decade, however, will be strongly coloured by generational issues such as retirement age, pensions, work benefits, education vouchers and health care.

Politicians will need to take note of generational issues if they want to be successful in the near future.

The political leaders each generation gets (and deserves?)

GIs (born 1900s to 1920s)

GI politicians were, on the whole, a visionary generation of winners and achievers. History remembers them with fondness because throughout their lives they've been heralded as a generation that achieves great things. Many of the twentieth century's most powerful politicians come from this generation, including John F Kennedy, Margaret Thatcher and Nelson Mandela.

In his inaugural address Kennedy described his generation as 'born in this century'. He was, indeed, the first American president born in the twentieth century and GI presidents dominated the White House for much of it – for an unprecedented thirty-two years.

GI political leaders were the antithesis of the 'spin' leaders we see today because they knew how vital it is to connect with people.

It was in pursuit of the aim that John F Kennedy, who was the first American president to travel in an open car, died tragically as a direct result of his openness. He knew that in a time of growing electronic media, he had to be accessible to the public and so he insisted on the open top car, against the advice of many of his aides.

A characteristic of many GI political leaders is their bold and honourable approach to their jobs. When they were caught out they took the rap. Kennedy made a huge mess of the Bay of Pigs but was strong enough to say so. Richard Nixon resigned in the wake of the Watergate scandal. He lied. He accepted, eventually, that he had lied and he went. He has faded into obscurity. That honourable course was not followed by Boomer president Bill Clinton when he lied. He pretended that he did not lie and he did not resign. And he and his family have not faded into the political background. But GI leaders did the honourable thing. They fell on their swords.

Those who did not have to fall, still stand strong and true, into the autumn of their lives, exuding confidence and energy. They remain busy in retirement, many of them not retiring, in the true sense of the word, at all. Nelson Mandela is a brilliant example of this with a daily schedule that would flatten many a Boomer with its multifaceted demands. He opens a new school that he's been instrumental in getting built, virtually every week. Former American president Jimmy Carter's face is often to be seen in the troubled spots of the earth, lending his clout to causes such as AIDS prevention and Habitat for Humanity, a volunteer organisation of which he is patron.

Silents (born 1920s to 1940s)

The Silent generation has virtually been a sandwich generation when it comes to political leadership, filling in between the long-serving GI presidents and the early-into-power Baby Boomers.

Mikhail Gorbachev, John Major and FW de Klerk were all Silent generation heads of state. History will remember Gorbachev in particular for his brave loosening of the iron rule of the Russian heads of state with his Perestroika, and De Klerk for his vision and pragmatism in handing over the reins of power to Nelson Mandela. But, they did not stay in positions of power for long. They did what they had to do and they moved on.

In America, the Silents have produced three decades of top presidential aides, from Kennedy's era to Bush, but no presidents so far. In jumping from Bush Sr to Clinton and then to Bush Jr, the Presidency has jumped from GI to Boomer with no Silent president in between. Additionally, according to American exit polls, as a generation they have voted for the losing candidate in every close modern election.

But, the key is that they do vote, and the politicians who ignore this generation do so at their peril.

Boomers (born 1940s to 1960s)

Boomers came to power earlier than it was their generational 'right' to do. We expect most politicians to be in their sixties and seventies when they take high office. When the Boomer presidents like America's Bill Clinton, Russia's Vladimir Putin, Britain's Tony Blair and Germany's Gerhard Schroeder arrived in office, they were in their forties and fifties. It's also interesting to note how many Boomers have taken over from GI heads of state in virtually every country.

Tony Blair took over from Margaret Thatcher with John Major sandwiched in between them. Vladimir Putin took over from the ill and ageing Boris Yeltsin.

Japan's Junichiro Koizumi was in his sixties when he took office but he deliberately acts like a Boomer. The new Chinese leader, Hu Jintao, does the same because, like Koizumi, he realises that politics today is about being a Boomer.

George Bush senior was followed by Bill Clinton, the second youngest president to be elected at forty-eight, that America has ever had. Even after two terms in office he remains the country's youngest ever ex-president.

Once Boomers develop a taste for the world stage they love the spotlight so much they tend to flit around the globe sorting out international problems rather than concentrating on the ones back home. This is certainly true of Tony Blair who was severely criticised, not only by the Opposition Conservatives but by his own Labour Party, for taking his eye off domestic problems such as the appalling rail system and disintegrating National Health Service in England.

Thabo Mbeki, the South African President, comes under the same critical fire for not dealing with the horrendous AIDS epidemic at home (nearly a quarter of his countrymen are infected, and dying, from the disease). He is so intent on promoting Nepad (New Partnership for African Development) and saving the African continent from being labelled the dying continent, that political commentators are suggesting he takes a holiday in a foreign country – his own.

Boomers are visionaries and speakers and they like their voices to be heard as they flit from conference to conference. But, as feisty South African MP Patricia de Lille says, 'We are suffering from "conference-itis." The poor don't need a conference to be told they are poor – they know it!'

The GI generation had global visions but they didn't strut the world stage talking about their role in creating them. They tended to do so in private. When they set out to reconstruct Germany and Europe after World War II, it was called the Marshall Plan – not the Roosevelt or the Churchill plan.

Boomers are concerned about their image and how they are portrayed in the media. They employ an army, or should we say a 'gaggle', of media consultants, speech writers, analysts and spin doctors. They ensure everything they say and do is portrayed to maximum effect for that 24/7 TV news camera. They've hardly finished speaking and they've already turned to the opinion polls to see how they have been received.

More importantly, before they utter a word, it is analysed and pored over by speech merchants. If George W Bush, America's president, is talking about the family he (his speech writers) will agonise about how they can best avoid antagonising single parents, mothers, fathers, divorced people... the list is endless. While this is, in a way, praiseworthy, it says something about our age and stage that few heads of state today speak off the cuff, or from the heart. Everything is staged and spun and polished.

Which head of state said the following, 'Politics is like waking up in the morning. You never know whose head you will find on the pillow'? Or, 'When I am abroad, I always make it a rule never to criticise or attack the government of my own country. I make up for lost time when I get home.'

That was Winston Churchill, who also said, when asked what qualities a politician required, 'The ability to foretell what is going to happen tomorrow, next week, next month, and next year. And to have the ability afterwards to explain why it didn't happen.'

His passionate and heartfelt comments struck home in a way that many a politician's do not today. If you pick up a book of quotations by Roosevelt, Churchill or Jan Smuts, chances are you're doing so in order to write or repeat them to emphasise a point.

But George W Bush is more likely to have one parodying his quotes such as, 'My enemies have misunderestimated me.'

When he flew out to announce the end of hostilities in Iraq in mid-2003 (note he used the carefully chosen word, 'hostilities' and not 'war') Bush did so on an aircraft carrier off the American coast. He wanted to appear to be far out to sea, not off a civilian coastline, in order to justify arriving by jet instead of a standard helicopter. In order to have only ocean in the background, the carrier had to be manoeuvred 90 degrees at a tremendous fuel cost. To add to the atmosphere, Bush wore a metallic grey jump suit and carried a helmet under his arm.

Back in the aircraft hangar, and before he stepped up to the podium, it was noted that all the men standing behind him were wearing ties. Bush's media managers gave instructions that they should be removed to create a more informal appearance. To the average person it seems quite extraordinary, if not bizarre, to go to such lengths in order to create the 'right' impression for the American public.

When Al Gore, the former vice-president under Clinton, was fighting to be the Democratic Party's candidate, he gave his wife Tipper a kiss that would not have gone amiss in Hollywood for its intensity and duration. This was to emphasise that he was a committed family man and far removed from the Monica Lewinksy sexual shenanigans of his boss.

American presidents are not allowed to use email because it is considered too instant and too informal a mode of communication – and might well land the presidential user in trouble in an era where every single word is seized upon by the media. A single gesture in the camera's glare is worth more than a million words. Take Margaret Thatcher's dropping of her handkerchief over the tail of a British Airways model of its then new, and now discontinued, ethnic branding. She acted out her feelings. Brave (GI) woman. Would a Boomer head of state dare to be so spontaneous today?

As Boomers grow older, in spite of themselves, the spectres of global economic collapse, international terrorism and ecological burnout, all threaten our sense of safety and well-being. These issues dominate the current political framework. Boomer leaders are making their influence felt on issues ranging from sex, profanity and violence in the entertainment industry, to smoking, pornography, sex slaves and drugs. As they go on their value-focused way, the Xers increasingly regard them as moralistic, hypocritical and domineering.

Xers (born 1960s to 1980s)

Even the oldest of the Xers aren't elderly enough to be top level politicians yet, so give us a few years before we rattle off the names of their leaders. In the meanwhile, let's discuss them as constituents; a role they are reluctant to play.

They are, on the whole, not interested in politics which they see as a manipulative process. Xers recognise and dismiss the slick, clever presentations that pass for political debate. They know a spin doctor when they see one and have the most sophisticated spin detectors of all. They see right through the sham. Remember, this is the home alone generation that was not pampered or coddled, but grew up caring for themselves and learning to think on their feet.

Some people argue that the young(er) generations have not, as a rule, been interested in politics. Flip through the many books, however, that were printed to mark the new millennium and that focus their camera lenses over the past century. They show that marches and protests (think Vietnam, the atomic bomb, the Cold War…) have been hugely youth-based.

Edward Docx, a Generation Xer writing in the British based *International Express*, puts it succinctly, 'Now, even eight-year-olds stand around thinking (of a Cabinet Minister's visit to a local school), "he's only here for a photo opportunity." Indeed, advertisers will tell you that the youth market contains the most cynical consumers in the country. They decode all the strategies and they can detect exactly what it is they are being asked to think, and how, and why. The default setting on the hard disc of this generation is not belief, it is disbelief.'

In the 1999 South African general election, youthful turnout at registration points was so low that the National Youth Commission approached twenty-five sports, music and business personalities to endorse its voter registration campaign. But only three of those approached agreed to have their famous faces attached to the campaign at no charge. This was regarded as a serious setback to a spunky campaign to get first time voters and people under thirty to vote. The apathy of the mainly young black voters infuriates their parents who have fought for, been imprisoned, tortured and died in their efforts to win the right to vote.

A survey, *Youth Trend 1*, conducted by the University of Cape Town's Unilever Institute among young people aged eighteen to twenty-four at the beginning of the new millennium, showed that youngsters were indifferent to politics. They were embarrassed by government and regarded money, not politicians, as the most important source of power and self-assurance. The same trends are evident in Britain, Europe and America.

The pragmatic Xers would rather volunteer than vote. They have an aversion to institutions and giving up control of anything that belongs to them.

Bill Clinton successfully wooed this generation by being the first president to initiate a live televised presidential debate on MTV. He appealed to the young as the sax-playing guy next door and his appeal was embellished by his savvy, young election team.

As we write this book, before the 2004 American, Spanish and South African elections, and the expected 2005 British elections, it's predicted that Xers will, once again, not turn out to vote in healthy numbers. Yet a party that wants to see itself in power by 2010 will need to connect with Xers.

Here are some pointers:

- Use more technology. Howard Dean from New Hampshire in America raised more money than any other politician has done in the run-up to the primaries for the 2004 US presidential election by using the Internet and getting Xers to help him in his campaigning. He uses credit cards and communicates through the Internet and SMS – the Xers' main forms of communication. He wasn't as successful in his efforts as he had hoped to be but he has shown the way to the future.
- Drop the spin doctors. Politicians are going to have to get back to ad-libbing and being more real. They need to speak from the heart without the fear that they will be misunderstood. And if they are, then they need to be honest and straightforward about clearing up the misunderstanding. They need to develop their principles without concern for pressure groups and analysts.
- Benjamin Zander, world famous orchestra conductor and motivational guru, first advocates that everybody follows Rule Number Six: 'Don't take yourself too seriously'. When asked what the first five rules are he says, 'There are none, only rule number six.' Politicians who want to attract Xers might like to follow this rule and ethos.
- Be surprising, be controversial. Put it out there. Xers will admire you for that.
- If you are wrong, say so. Californian governor Arnold Schwarzenegger refused to take part in televised debates. He said they were too predictable. When he was accused of touching and feeling women in the past and making inappropriate suggestions, he said he was sorry. He pointed out, 'At the time I was trying to be Mr Universe and an entertainer, not the governor of California. I have learnt my lesson.'

Finally, Xers, like the Silent generation, are not going to pant to be politicians, leaders and heads of state. The few who do are likely to be revolutionary and to change the way politics are run today. But, on the whole they will prepare the platform for the Millennials who will follow them.

Millennials (born 1980s to 2000s)

This generation will, like the GIs and the Boomers, make an early appearance in the political arena. We believe and hope that they will restore integrity and trust to political office. This is what their generation's voters will demand of politicians. The wise will listen – and win.

Political pointers for the generations

GIs and Silents

Realise that younger generations don't take economic prosperity or family stability for granted. They need governments to assist them in achieving more balance in their lives. This includes protection of the family as a unit, paternity leave and flexitime. Providing incentives for small business is essential. Don't forget the older voters. They, like you, are living longer than they thought they would.

Boomers

You came of age as a generation chanting, 'make love, not war'. Realise that what you meant by 'love' (a self-appropriated, God-given right to make decisions for others) contains the seeds of wars you may foment without foreseeing the long term consequences.

It's time to see Boomer politicians abandoning spin and getting real with their constituencies. It's a well worn joke that nobody trusts politicians but it's never too late to start trying to change that perception. A week has always been a long time in politics but it's longer than ever now with the rapid pace of the twenty-first century and the unblinking stare of the media spotlight. Show your potential Xer voters that they can trust you and they will do so, just drop the schmoozing, it bores them.

Xers

Stop thinking that you can avoid civic life (voting) and history for the rest of your lives. You can't and you won't.

Xers may have their greatest impact by guiding Boomer and Millennial visionaries. It was the young Xer, George Stephanopolous, who masterminded Bill Clinton's first presidential campaign and got the sax-playing, Arkansas governor to 'rock the vote' on MTV.

As Xers move into leadership positions, it's the wise ones who will remember that today's old people are the most active and powerful they have ever been at their age. They can't be ignored.

Millennials

Learn to work in teams, do good deeds for your community, and apply peer pressure for the right reasons. In this digitally connected age, individuals can make a difference and age is no longer the barrier it used to be. Use your power. Today's children should be seen and heard.

Understand that people who are older than you will, in time, come to expect greatness from you – for the simple reason that you are the generation that you are!

17

Generations at church

Attitude to God:

GIs:	God is distant and aloof.
Silents:	God is distant but approachable.
Boomers:	God is familiar – we can feel His power working through us.
Xers:	God is a friend, guide, companion and healer.
Millennials:	God is the nation builder, provider and protector.

You may be inclined to skip this chapter, especially if you don't attend church regularly. However, the church has probably played a role in your life at some stage, whether you welcomed it or not, so this chapter just might ring bells for you and help you to understand where you are now in terms of religion and spirituality in your life. Additionally, some of the advice offered to those involved with the church may apply to other areas of life and other religions too.

The Christian church has, until relatively recently, ruled practically every facet of life in the western world. In medieval Europe and Britain, as well as all the Spanish, Portuguese and British colonies, it owned massive tracts of land, which governed virtually every waking moment of peasants' lives. The lives of the peerage and the wealthy were also inextricably intertwined with power and politics. The defining moments of a person's life were church dominated. You were born into a church, baptised, married and buried in it.

The focus in this chapter is on the Christian church from a generational perspective and is aimed at the popular church-going movement. This has dominated Graeme's life and is where his expertise lies. But the generational insights gained from looking at the Christian religion could be equally applicable to other major religions, especially Judaism and Islam.

By the early 1900s, when the GIs were born, the church's hold, although still strong, was lessening. The Great War, World War I, devastated Europe, Britain and, to a lesser extent, the latter's mighty Empire and its colonies. Few escaped its harsh fallout. In times of great hardship and sorrow, many people turn to God. But others in times of death, misery, chaos and uncertainty, question like never before. The two world wars, the Cold War with its threat of annihilation by the atomic bomb, combined with science, innovative thinking, philosophy, and overwhelming technological advances, has resulted in an unprecedented wave of questioning of life, its meaning and the role of God and church in it. It is this era into which the GIs were born and the following four generations have continued with this questioning trend, each one overlaying it with their own characterisation, attitudes and style.

There are few areas in our lives where the generation gap is greater than it is in the church, where grey hairs and beards are a switch off for jeans-clad youngsters with urgent queries about sex, morals and violence.

Throughout the world the church is in crisis as an increasingly greying clergy is not attracting youthful priests. Youngsters don't relate to people a generation or two older than them as role models. And so a vicious circle is set up of falling figures, both in church attendance and people prepared to don clerical robes. The same is true of rabbis and imams, with very few mainstream and traditional religions reporting massive growth over the past few decades.

Is it possible to breach this generation gap and, if so, how?

Read on for an understanding of the generations in the church. With understanding comes insight and vision, and problem solving follows hot on its heels.

GIs (born 1900s to 1920s)

This is the generation for whom the word teen was invented. Prior to this, adolescence as we know it today, with all its attendant hype, had not been categorised or labelled as clearly as it was from 1900 onwards. The youthful GIs were not only the first teenagers, they were also the first Boy Scouts and Girl Guides.

So interestingly, and not surprisingly, the GI generation became the first one for whom youth ministries were started at local church level. Sunday schools became more prevalent, and not just with an educative function, which is how they started in England, but with a socialising function. Sunday schools became a mini-church for the young. It was, in fact, the same as the church their parents were sitting in but was overlaid with a young people's approach. It was at the time a completely new approach to 'doing church'.

The GIs grew up, as do all generations (so far) with the concept of God as Father. At the time, fathers were aloof and reserved and so that is how God was seen. As GIs expected their dads to protect them, so they looked on God to do the same thing, someone they could call upon in times of trial and need. Going to church was a contract with God in terms of GIs doing their bit. Church and worship were seen as traditional and formal experiences. You wore your Sunday best, suits for boys, frocks for girls, often with hats.

It was during this period of the GI's youth that the Azusa Street Church revival began, in 1906, and the Pentecostal movement started. It was manifested by the outpouring of the Holy Spirit with many signs and wonders. The Azusa Street Pentecostal Revival really took hold in the 1920s, an era of seemingly endless potential and innovation, when America was rich, the economy was booming, and the wealthy partied.

GIs have dominated the church growth consultant industry for most of the past century, and have sparked many revolutions in Christian ministry. This generation produced many powerful evangelists, such as Billy Graham who ministered to several American presidents over the years and packed his audiences into massive stadiums. In the 1950s, he was the first full-time employee of Youth for Christ, sparking off the parachurch (ministries not linked to a specific church or denomination) youth ministry movement. GIs also had a huge influence on the church growth movement, spearheaded by C Peter Wagner, amongst others. Another evangelist, Robert Schuller, first gained attention in 1955 when he used a movie drive-in to house his rapidly expanding congregation. He later founded the imposing and awe-inspiring Crystal Cathedral in Garden Grove, California, a massive building of steel and glass with over 10 000 windows.

Each generation's early experiences of church and religious life will form the foundation for them of what is right, good and normal in terms of religious expression and institutions. For GIs, religion is largely about experiencing God and having a relationship with Him. They were raised during an inner-directed era, when faith is largely expressed in experiences. 'In such periods, those traditions with the greatest emphasis on the personal life and religious experience of the "believer" will thrive. It is also in these periods that new groups spin off from existing institutional structures,' explain Mike Regele and Mark Schultz in *Death of the Church*. However, the GIs' emphasis on faithfulness and dependability has led them to see these experiences as being governed by strict discipline.

What they want in church

The GI generation prefers a formal church environment with no unexpected departures from the norm and where everything is done in an orderly manner. Even those involved in the Pentecostal Revival movement believed that a certain amount of order was required. They like worship that stirs people to action in their fight against the onslaught of evil. They believe that 'God helps those who help themselves', and they can appear very forceful and demanding at first. They prefer no-nonsense preaching that lays down a clear morality and allows no compromise or shades of grey.

It's a great shame that older generations have been allowed to withdraw from active service because they feel too old to make a contribution. The GI generation is rich in wisdom and while they have the strength to do so, they should be connected to younger generations by mentoring them. It's worth sharing with them, and learning from their solid, lifelong commitment to their faith.

Silents (born 1920s to 1940s)

This generation grew up in a profoundly difficult time in the aftermath of World War I, the Stock Market crash, the Depression, famine and then World War II. It was a time when, to quote the Bible, 'darkness lay over the land'. Its dark overtones are captured in the threatened middle earth in JR Tolkien's *Lord of the Rings*, which he wrote during these times. Although he insisted that it was not a parable for World War II, generational history tells us that you cannot divorce the experiences and influences of the times in which you live.

The 1930s and 40s were terrible times and people drew together to find solace, understanding and some sort of peace in shared worship. Churches were packed, both during World War II and for many years afterwards as the rationing and suffering slowly diminished and the world licked its wounds.

Not surprisingly, the approach of the Silent generation was a conservative one. We're not amazed that they called the church 'the sanctuary' for, indeed, a sanctuary and a laager is what it was during those dismal times. And today this is what they want the church to be – a place of calm and stability in a chaotic, shifting world. Their memories of church are of the days when men wore suits and ties, women dressed their best with hats, long skirts and high collars, and children wore scrubbed faces and shiny shoes. The general demeanour was one of awe and quiet reverence. In fact, as church buildings were built in the 1950s and 60s, many of them had a single verse of scripture emblazoned on the front wall: 'Be still and know that I am God'. This is the Silent generation's instruction for church.

Church services followed a set routine. They lasted an hour. You sang hymns accompanied by an organ. In between, there were Bible readings, psalm singing, collection, and a sermon/preaching, which lasted a set time. Half the congregation could be asleep and nobody would notice. Little reference was made during the service to the outside world. At the end of the service you lined up quietly outside to greet the minister and his wife. The men-only pastors had to be married, in their late thirties to fifties, with a wife and children. They fulfilled clearly detailed instructions from the church in terms of sobriety and conservatism.

Boomers have frightening memories of being forced to sit through repetitive, stifling services and if the Silent generation had had its way, that's how church would have remained. Unfortunately for them, many churches are a very different place today with shouting youngsters running around in back to front baseball caps, noisy music and not an organ in sight. The Silents feel that church is no longer church, they feel abandoned. The world where religion had always been a solid foundation is, some feel, now lost to them.

Their experience of the church and faith was shaped by the institutions their next-elder young adult GIs created for them (eg Inter Varsity Christian Fellowship 1923, Young Life 1941, Youth for Christ 1943, and Campus Crusade 1951). For the Silents, faith is expressed best in doing. The ministry focus is on building the institution and creating programmes and structures. As Silents grew into young adulthood in the 1950s and 60s, there was a decline in experiential expressions of faith, and the rise of the mainline denominations. It was the height of evangelicalism, and had such leading figures as Francis Schaeffer, Billy Graham, John Stott and the influence of writers such as CS Lewis and AW Tozer.

As GI and Silent veterans of World War II returned, having been exposed to foreign cultures and faraway lands, and as modern transportation options made global travel more feasible, the Silents spearheaded a renewed interest in foreign missions. They were seen as a means of expanding the Christian church at the 'edge of the Empire'. They often had political and cultural agendas as well as spiritual ones. To this day, foreign missionary endeavours are still heavily funded by the Silents and GIs. Younger generations are not getting involved in the same way, a fact that should give mission agencies sleepless nights.

The Silents' programme-based approach dominated until the 1970s when the Boomers were old enough to demand change and began to wrest control from them. A new type of church was emerging.

What they want in church

The Silent generation's frugal approach to living is most evident at church. They are loath to get into debt, especially if that debt relates to facilities. They do not like ostentatious buildings, preferring a more spartan feel. For example, they may have air conditioning in their offices, cars and even homes, but won't spend the money to cool down their churches. If the church treasurer is a Silent then only a miracle will be able to extract significant funds for expansion and growth.

The Silents have a strong allegiance to their denomination and theological position, and do not change churches as easily as some of the younger generations. They resist change. They like the order, structure, even the decorations in the church they've been attending for decades. When making changes in these churches, care must be taken to affirm past ministries, presenting the changes as an extension of the past rather than as something wholly new.

Silents enjoy in-depth study of the Bible, and respond best to analytical sermons that focus on theology and eschatology (the study of the last times, the end of the world) and solid Bible teaching. They will require the preacher to focus on accountability and a commitment to changeless truth.

Tim La Haye's latest book, *Mind Siege*, or Josh McDowell's series on *Evidence That Demands a Verdict*, are examples of the type of approach that appeals to the Silent generation. They are intolerant of those who are different from themselves, and believe that knowledge of the Bible is the key to living a good Christian life. Gary McIntosh, author of *One Church Four Generations* writes, 'Most believe that if anyone knew enough of the Bible, they would do the right thing. Bible study focused almost exclusively on the content of the Bible.'

Worship must be structured, orderly and restrained. In many churches there are strict rules and procedures laid down for worship leaders, to ensure that they do not stray from this approach. Silents have a very authoritarian approach to leadership (see chapter 15 on Leadership), and use bureaucratic structures to enforce their own style on the rest of the church, relying on positional authority and claims of biblical truths, rather than on relationships and winning people over to their way of thinking.

Boomers (born 1940s to 1960s)

When the Boomers were little kids they attended churches, built by their visionary GI grandparents, which dominated the landscape. GI personalities also dominated public space, with stadium events and high profile campaigns, rallies and crusades. Billy Graham was one of the first to perfect this technique, starting out in Youth for Christ. He moved on from that to form the Billy Graham Evangelistic Association, now headed by his son Franklin Graham. There can be few Boomers who had access to television or saw newsreels at their local movie house, who will ever forget the sight of stadiums packed to the rafters with people belting out hymns and listening to Graham's pounding words.

Their early experiences of faith and religious life were focused on the Silent generation's emphasis on structure and institution, when church was a central focal point in the community.

Boomers have grown up with high expectations of the church, especially of how it should be done. But, as some of their dreams and ideals for the future have been shattered in troubled times, and the church has been unable to respond adequately, they have become disillusioned with it. As they rebelled against the stifling environment of their upbringing, so too they rebelled against church and God.

Some Boomer characteristics include a moralistic view of the world and an overinflated self-opinion. They believe that they have all the answers to problems, and probably don't need the church. Those who remained 'true to the faith' saw their generation begin to slip away and, under the guidance of the structured and programme-driven Silents, devised methods to draw the Boomers back. Many of these have proved effective. Boomers seem to be returning to the church in large numbers – especially those who have children who they wish to bring up with spiritual and moral values.

From the early 1950s onwards, movements such as Youth with a Mission and Scripture Union were born with their emphasis on the conversion, discipleship and development of young people. It was this approach that saw Boomers sweep into church with the same approach they employed in the workplace, namely that the church had to grow in order to be worth anything. The Boomers did to the church what they did to business – they strategised, re-engineered, rightsized and outsourced. The church mirrored business models.

They needed, they said, to be centres of excellence. So the slightly shabby, 'comfy sofa' approach to church was out. The fairly shambolic environment with its polysterene cups and cheap coffee made way for better (Boomer) branding. The huge concrete block churches that typified the Silent generation gave way to multifunctional, 'community centre' churches with many auditoriums and flip up or removable seats.

Boomer pastors modelled themselves on professional CEOs. The churches were based on a powerful and dynamic Boomer leader, similar to those you will find in chapter 13 on @ Work and chapter 15 on Leadership. They were dominated by powerful, charismatic personalities who brought everyone in the church together.

Churches advertised. They attracted people with the use of pictures of smiling pastors and their smiling wives and happy children. And, as Boomers are wont to do, the dynamic pastors were into burnishing their image, selling themselves in order to sell their churches. As so often happens with high profile people, some fell into the trap of believing in their own power and might, and high profile cases of adultery, divorce, embezzlement and misuse of church funds began to hit the headlines. The church, still battling to recover from this blow, has recently been struck again with the child abuse scandal rocking the Catholic church in America. This mirrors the fate of many high-flying Boomer businessmen, who face the collapse of their companies and investigations by national fraud and corporate governance prosecutors.

Boomers' determination to have high standards of excellence meant they began to stage-manage their Sunday services, meeting during the week to practise, and putting together service management teams. Some even paid their singers and musicians, thus attracting talented musicians. Preaching was focused on the power approach with dominant TV evangelists pounding on the pulpit, shouting at the heavens and firing people up. Indeed, many a motivational speaker today was once a pastor in a Bible belt church. They emphasised the health and wealth doctrine, which is: God doesn't want you to be sick and poor. Christian television channels expounded the best methods of attaining health and wealth and in the process, many a church Boomer created wealth for himself.

But there are many good news stories as well. In particular, Boomers were largely successful in applying new models of ministry to their growing churches in the 1980s and 90s. New approaches to church also developed as Boomers founded and grew the mega churches of today. From Bill Hybel's *Seeker Sensitive* approach, to Rick Warren's *Purpose Driven* strategy, every large church was churning out books, manuals and video series on how to grow the church properly. Today, Boomers enjoy vibrant communities filled with like-minded people, all enjoying their brand of 'rock 'n' roll' worship, inspiring 'how to' type sermons and motivating small groups.

The two biggest dangers facing a church dominated by Boomers are that the church will become a haven for Boomers, not creating a place where other generations can also find a niche, and that the church will succumb to the lure of materialism. Like the rest of their lives, Boomers may package church in a convenience store way, so that they can pick and choose their involvement, and not allow it to impinge on their personal lives. All too often Boomers make it too simple to become a Christian, and too easy to simply warm a seat on a Sunday. There is very little challenge, and the discipline and hard work ethic of the GI and Silent generations is largely absent. Volunteerism is slowly choked, and the church itself begins to die.

What they want in the church

American generations guru Neil Howe points out that 'A generation that came of age in an era of "Is God Dead?" is immersing itself in spiritual movements of all kinds, from evangelical fundamentalism to New Age humanism, from transcendentalism to ESP. By a substantial margin, Boomers are America's most God-absorbed living generation.' But the church must beware – the new Boomer-fuelled quest for the spiritual is not a quest for traditional Christianity.

The Boomers want a visionary, fast-moving environment at church, as they search for fulfilment and achievement. They will be most attracted to a church that thinks and acts boldly, and where these grand visions are clearly communicated. They value involvement and teamwork, and want to feel part of a team or community that can shape vision and be involved in implementing it. They prefer leaders who provide vision, but then allow others to act as coaches and mentors.

Boomers require church staff to be professional, effective and efficient. This also applies to facilities. They are attracted to churches with well-maintained buildings, ample parking, good child care facilities, comfortable chairs, clean toilets and a good sound system.

Boomers are action-oriented people and want the sermons they hear to be filled with 'how to' applications, rather than dull explanations and analysis. Powerful preachers, who use the techniques associated with motivational speakers, will have the most impact. The use of seeker sensitive services (church meetings aimed specifically at non-church going people) is now quite common, and a great strategy for attracting world weary Boomers back to church.

Music has always played a huge part in the lives of Baby Boomers. Rock 'n' roll has been part of their history since birth, and they bring this to the church. The music and worship must be lively, upbeat and uplifting. Unfortunately, what most Boomers consider to be great, up-to-date worship is already about two decades out of date. They don't believe that any good music has been written since Elvis died (in fact, some don't believe that Elvis is really dead!). In order to reach out to the next generations, their music will need to make way for more up-to-date styles, like hip hop, techno, house and kwaito.

Xers (born 1960s to 1980s)

Xers have grown up in churches dominated by the battle between Boomers and Silents as each generation tried to impose its own style and feel of church on the other. At present it is the Boomer structures and systems that are dominant, and the large independent churches are still under Boomer leadership.

In the same way as Joshua failed to mentor the next generation (see page 251), so today Boomers are not mentoring the Xers. They're also not standing aside and allowing the Xers to develop their leadership skills and make changes. The same thing is happening in the Boomer-dominated business world. The lack of new leadership, worldwide, is being felt keenly by the church. In Britain, church attendances have been falling steadily for years with estimates that only five to ten per cent of the population attends church regularly. The Church of England has launched a massive advertising campaign to raise the profile of the priesthood as a good career for young people.

In America where there are over 60 million Catholics, with new converts yearly, they are suffering from a shortage of priests. Almost half of all diocesan priests are aged between fifty and sixty-nine, according to the Centre for Applied Research in the Apostolate at Georgetown University. The number of parishes without priests has risen fivefold since 1965. So the Americans are advertising too as they worry about reports that while 24 per cent of the clergy in the Presbyterian church were aged twenty-five and younger in 1975, today only seven per cent are that age. In the Episcopal Church the percentage in that age group has declined from 19 per cent in 1974 to a paltry 3.9 per cent today. In recent South African research, done for the largest denomination, the Dutch Reformed Church, the same frightening trend was observed.

This trend is also true in other faiths. Of the twenty-three students who entered the rabbinical school of the Jewish Theological Seminary in 2002, eight were already over the age of thirty. Rabbi Gerald L Zelizer, rabbi of Neve Shalom, a conservative congregation in the American New Jersey area, said that many are worried that older clergy won't be able to attract younger people, who are least likely to consider religion as important in their lives.

A survey by Gallup in 2002, found that only 50 per cent of those aged eighteen to twenty-nine considered organised religion very important, compared with 60 per cent aged thirty to forty-nine, 61 per cent of 50 to 64-year-olds and 75 per cent of those who are at least sixty-five years old. Charismatic and pentecostal churches are also beginning to join the decline that mainline churches are still experiencing. Churches with a radically new approach will be attractive to Xers who will lead Millennials into them.

Xers may not be religious but they are a very *spiritual* generation, having spent their early years in the shadow of the Boomers' spiritual awakening in the 1960s and 70s. They are seeking a spiritual home where they can truly belong – but this is outside of traditional religious structures, traditions and forms. Their early church experiences have been dominated by the clash between Boomers and Silents. This ongoing battle between different styles of worship, preaching, church structures and governance methods has resulted in many Xers adopting a cynical view of the church's relevance.

Most Xers, by nature a non-confrontational generation, have felt that taking on the Boomers was NOT the best route to go. Those who do challenge Boomers have concentrated their battles in the arenas of music and worship style. They have, however, encountered stiff Boomer resistance.

Infighting has produced a church divided. Xers will spend most of their lives either putting the churches back together again or leaving and starting their own inclusive churches. Maybe they will just leave altogether. It's too early to say and a lot depends on the church's approach over the next decade.

The Xers' childhood experiences of broken relationships (divorce) has resulted in small group experiences being attractive to them, especially when there is an emphasis on family and relationships. For them, faith is best expressed in a small community where the reality of the daily outworking of faith can be expressed so they can see faith translating into action.

But many Xers have also shot themselves in the foot by creating alternative and parallel youth structures. Many of the large churches have separate buildings where youthful congregationists worship while their elders do it their way, nearby. The youth services are often very different in style from the adult congregation, with a more upbeat sermon and more modern music. Smaller churches without such facilities often split services with older members attending mornings and younger in the evenings – a situation which doesn't suit those families who wish to worship together.

This separate arrangement may have solved the crisis for now, but it's not a long-term solution as many churches lose their young people in this manner. They reach university age and find there's no adequate bridging between them and the adult church. And not surprisingly, they opt out. Again, this is mirrored in the workplace where there's no bridge between Xers and business in terms of acclimatising one generation to the needs and aspirations of the other. So Xers hop from company to company, eventually opting out to become entrepreneurs.

In the same way, they hop from church to church, but ultimately turn their back on it.

Their style of churchgoing is very different from the Boomers' 'bigger is better' approach, with mega churches or large stadiums. Xers prefer a more individualistic approach to religion and spirituality with the emphasis on making individual connections with God and a feeling of being cocooned in their own music and own space. The Boomers' kneeling, standing, singing and chanting all together at the same time is not for them. The expression of their religion is a far more personalised experience and those churches who offer this will attract the younger generations.

Flexibility and unpredictability are the bywords for Xers, so churches that have a stable base but include ongoing surprises and changes will succeed in connecting to Xers. Xers would probably have been impressed by the new approach to being fishers of men by one Baptist pastor who raised global interest with his innovative plan to get white people into his predominantly black Louisiana church in America. He offered to pay whites $10 each an hour on Sundays and $20 an hour on Thursdays. The money, Bishop Fred Caldwell told his congregation, would come out of his own pocket. The spin-off was that the church did indeed receive phone calls from whites, and here's the nice part, several of them offered to forgo the money.

What they want in church

Generation Xers are largely disillusioned by a fractured and divided church. They don't understand why broken and bruised people don't go to church for healing, choosing instead to don their Sunday outfits and pretend that everything is OK. Xers want to create a place of spiritual healing, where all those 'who are weary and heavy laden' can come and get rest. Xers see God as the healer of an injured world, the father of the fatherless and the comforter. Close-knit relationships are critical. For this reason, most churches aiming to attract Xers have found the cell church concept helpful. These are churches that meet in formal small groups only, and not in large gatherings or services. The entire church doesn't need to convert to the cell church model, but it's essential that small groups meet regularly within the church.

Worship for Xers requires a sense of the spiritual and the eternal, of mystery and symbolism. They want to feel spirituality and prefer worship to sermons.

Preachers need to use more multimedia and styles that allow for more interaction. This may include stories, debates, dramas, readings and discussions. Sermons that are focused on systematic, analytical explanations will be considered too intellectual and not emotional enough. Any gratuitous 'bashing' of other religions or denominations is a definite no-no. Xers prefer preaching that provides comfort, compassion and acceptance. This does not imply compromising a theology but rather packaging it differently. It could be argued that this is more authentically biblical, as Mark's gospel tells us that Jesus only ever used stories when he spoke to the crowds. He did not 'preach' as we know it today. And he certainly wasn't boring.

Xers enjoy relaxed, informal settings where children also feel comfortable. They don't dress up for church and avoid titles, preferring first names.

They are often reluctant to become involved in ministry and in order to attract them a clear vision must be communicated with a short term (six to twelve months) commitment required.

Millennials (born 1980s to 2000s)

Most Millennials are still children so it's too early to describe in any detail what the church represents for them and their present and future roles in it. Sunday schools are, on the whole, somewhat outdated in their approach to these kids, often still working with felt boards and 1960s-type cut out and paste books and colouring-in books. They've not moved into the twenty-first century and will lose their constituency unless they do so fast. This is, after all, the generation programming your video machines and teaching you how to SMS. Likewise, many of the lifestyle issues such as drink, drugs and sex are confronting them at a far earlier stage in life than was the case with the Sunday school teachers to whom they listen. And there are many other areas of moral ambiguity which churches tend to ignore completely. No wonder Millennials regard them as out of touch fogeys who are too embarrassed, or ignorant about 'real life' to touch base with them on the problems they experience. This is a prime example of the generation gap.

For these Millennials, the emphasis should be more directed towards 'doing faith', which means seeing their beliefs in action that changes the physical world, and links them to a God who works in the world. As Millennials grow up they'll be concerned about the earthly expressions of God's kingdom as opposed to the GIs' concern about heaven and hell. Millennials will be involved in hands-on ministries, working with the church in areas such as hospice, orphanages and with people living with HIV/AIDS. They will also work with communities to help them develop small businesses and will take the leading role in society in terms of developing micro-enterprise hubs in their churches, thus responding to the unemployment crisis in the world.

Their holistic attitude to life will probably see them link their church, business and family lives together.

What they want in church

Where Boomers once stood up and chanted, 'Jesus is the answer', Millennials are now responding, 'What was the question?' Millennials do not want a place where easy answers are trotted out before the questions have even been understood. Their style of learning (see chapter 12 on training and chapter 11 on education) is inductive, meaning that they prefer to discover information for themselves, rather than have someone tell it to them. It's not for nothing that they have been nicknamed the 'Why Generation' – they want to ask tough questions without being regarded as heretics.

Millennials also want to move away from seeker sensitive approaches that strip the church service of its uniqueness and mystery, making it little more than any other large crowd gathering. They want to connect with God, with 'the other', the 'higher power', the creator and sustainer of the universe, and they want this to be done in a spiritual way. Churches that have strong but relevant liturgies will have an advantage with Millennials, as long as they understand and react to some of the broader cultural changes mentioned.

Millennials use technology all the time to communicate, and are disappointed when their church doesn't even have a web page, let alone a pastor who is comfortable chatting by email or SMS. If you want to connect with this generation then you need to acquire technological expertise. They also want the pace of the service and Bible study to be speeded up, dramatically. The prolific use of multiple media in communicating will not be enough on its own to satisfy this media-raised generation.

Having grown up in a diverse, integrated world, these young people will be disappointed and uncomfortable with the homogeneity of most churches. They will expect to see people of different cultures, different ages, men and women, rich and poor, ministering alongside one another. You cannot create this level of diversity overnight in a church, but you should have a strategy for developing it if you want to attract Millennials.

Multigenerational Churches

Lynn Robinson, a doctoral candidate in the sociology of religion at Princeton University in America, and a practising Episcopalian (Anglican), says that each age group in a church is seeking 'A generational message that corresponds to its needs... For the young it is sex; for those in their thirties and forties it's marriage and family; and for the elderly it is ageing.' He fears that 'an older clergy will be unable to deliver the message for younger people, who will then not be energised to serve.' And, he adds, 'the church risks becoming essentially an institution for the elderly to bond.'

The good news is that so many clergy in churches ARE concerned about diminishing interest in them by the general population. Disconcertingly, there are equally many who are not in the least concerned. They prefer to stick to their old, set ways of worship, labouring over the same boring sermons that challenge neither them nor their congregations, week in and week out.

For too long churches have been able to enjoy the ease of a 'one size fits all' approach to ministry. This is no longer possible, if you want to be relevant to every generation. Michael Armour and Don Browning, in *Systems-Sensitive Leadership*, suggest that today's church leaders need to focus on four key areas in their churches, if they want to develop strong multigenerational environments:

- Develop a congregation-wide atmosphere of forbearance, and a love for unity.
- Maintain feedback loops in decision making, ensuring that the leadership continually hears from the congregation about the acceptance of each change implemented.
- Make constant changes, and ensure that the entire system is managed, without talking about 'systems management'. In other words, in some cases it's better to just do it, rather than talk about it.
- Constantly emphasise and communicate the vision.

Loring Leifer and Michael McLarney in their book *Younger Voices, Stronger Choices* highlight three main conditions that must be in place to ensure successful multigenerational programmes:

- Adults must be willing to share their power and responsibility.
- Young people must be willing to take on responsibility.
- Both young and old need the skills to work together.

250

It's become clear that multigenerational ministry is not simply a case of adults 'allowing' young people to attend events they plan. They need to actively involve young people and to respect them. It needs to be ministry *with* and *by* young people, not *to* or *for* young people.

Additional resources

A book that offers many practical tips, and a broad systems-based approach to implementing multigenerational ministries is *Systems-Sensitive Leadership* by Michael Armour and Don Browning. It is not an easy book to read, but is worth the effort.

Graeme's Master's thesis, largely on the issue of multi-generational ministry, is also available online at http://www.tomorrowtoday.biz/generations/minresource002.htm

---

Moses, Joshua and mentoring:

There's a biblical analogy that may help in under-standing the current generational shift. It also serves as a stark warning to the church at the moment. When Moses led the children of Israel out of Egypt, he had a torrid time of it, managing over a million unruly people in the desert. His father-in-law Jethro advised him to stop trying to be all things to all men and, instead, to organise younger men to lead smaller sections of the nation. This made a huge difference, and Moses spent more of his time mentoring and leading than doing day-to-day management tasks. If Moses is a Silent generation 'type', conservative, cautious and self-doubting, Joshua is most certainly a brash, bold, visionary Boomer 'type'. Joshua was identified as Moses' successor, and in typical Boomer style, he immediately saw not the difficulties but the potential of moving into new lands.

He scouted the Promised Land which was filled with frightening giants. But, it also flowed with milk and honey. Joshua urged Moses to cross the River Jordan and occupy the land but Moses, swayed by the people, refused. Eventually, it was Joshua who led the Israelites across the river, took the land, and created a new era and society. But Joshua then made the mistake of not identifying new potential talent in order to develop a new generation of leaders. In spite of having spent forty years being mentored by Moses, he did not, in his turn, mentor anyone, with disastrous results for Israel.

Churches built by different generations:

GIs: Ornate, impressive, grand, with spires that rise majestically skywards.

Silents: Functional with aesthetics downplayed. Cold and draughty because church isn't supposed to be comfy. Built from great blocks of concrete.

Boomers: Professional approach; look like a campus with office park gardens and education centres.

Xers: Meet in barns and warehouses, same sort of places you meet for raves. They're practical, flexible, adaptable buildings.

Millennials: Will want aesthetically pleasing buildings, elegant, and technologically wired.

God is...

GIs: My protector against supernatural forces.

Silents: The God of truth where I find right and wrong, good and evil.

Boomers: Rampant, powering through the universe, a God of vengeance and justice.

Xers: Healing, protecting, nurturing, guiding, the 'mother' God.

Millennials: Our Father, the nation builder, provider and protector.

Style of worship:

GIs: Formulaic. Attracted to religious events that are rich with pomp and ornate ceremony.

Silents: Quiet, reverential. 'Be still and know that I am God' approach.

Boomers: It's a Big Message so spread it in a Big Way. Slick, professional.

Xers: Intimate, non-judgemental, personally connect with my God.

Millennials: Integrate all the spiritual threads of my life. Wants to explore other religious traditions.

Church music:

GIs: Hymns and organ.

Silents: Same as GI but add a brass section.

Boomers: Rock 'n' roll religion with James Brown 1960s type music. Militant, forceful, sing about greatness of God. Electric instruments, keyboards and drums.

Xers: Sing TO God and not about him, less reverential, more familiar with emphasis on the personal. Simple, unplugged acoustic sound.

Millennials: Quite eclectic and merging a lot of the different sounds. Computers and synthesisers.

In church:

GIs: Sit in the family pew, know the minister well, servants sit at the back.

Silents: Wear formal attire, always sit in the same seat and speak to the same people. Seldom meet anybody new.

Boomers: Gregarious, like to sit in big groups of friends they know well. Speak up given half a chance to do so.

Xers: Individualistic. Prefer small group ministries with people they can be real and authentic with. They like the 'home church' movement.

Millennials: Will move back into a large group ethos and will create music and hymns that deal with achievements and victories.

Weddings:

GIs: Formal, followed convention, a pre-determined service whatever the religion.

Silents: Often married in uniform due to World War II.

Boomers: Bucked tradition, married in meadows and made up their own vows.

Xers: Took the Boomer trend and made the less formal and more individual ceremonies mainstream.

Millennials: Are continuing with the trend towards more individuality but may return to the formal, conventional style of ultra white in Western weddings.

18

Healthy Generations

Attitude to health:

GIs:	Called doctor only if strictly necessary.
Silents:	Grinned and bore it (pain).
Boomers:	Doctor must cure me – now!
Xers:	I'll fix it, myself (alternative therapies).
Millennials:	Will be obsessed with keeping healthy.

Health issue that defines their generation:

GIs:	Flu.
Silents:	Bacterial infections.
Boomers:	Cancer and heart attacks.
Xers:	HIV/AIDS.
Millennials:	Obesity.

Health is a powerful generational issue. A large part of understanding what drives your parents, teenage children or grandparents concerns their health and their attitudes to wellness and ageing.

The stage-hogging generation, the Boomers, now in their forties and fifties, refuse point blank to accept ill health. A doctor, a drug, something must fix it. Even more important to them is ageing. They're 'not going there'. Wrinkles, sags, dentures, arthritis, you name it and it's not on their menu. They are determined to live longer and do so more beautifully and physically fit than anybody has ever done before.

For the elderly GIs and Silents keeping healthy and painfree is their single biggest expense and it almost dominates their lives. As youngsters they had no idea that modern medicine, nutrition and hygiene would extend their lives, keeping them earthbound well beyond what they consider to be their sell-by date. Many of their retirement plans do not cover their longevity.

International icon Nelson Mandela celebrated his eighty-fifth birthday in 2003 in the global spotlight, doing his famous soft shoe shuffle with former American president Bill Clinton, Virgin's Richard Branson and stars like Barbra Streisand. He's in pain but he's not going to let it slow him down. Veteran South African struggle hero who fought the anti-apartheid fight from outside prison bars, Helen Suzman is close in age to her friend Nelson. She too is amazed at how long she's been alive, exclaiming to friends, 'It's time I was off, you know,' in her precise manner. Comedian Bob Hope celebrated his one hundredth birthday before he moved on to greener pastures. Film icon Katherine Hepburn was such a powerful personality that when she died in her nineties, she was remembered and mourned by millions the world over.

Today we accept longevity as our due. So it's a shock to learn that when the Mandelas and Hepburns were born, life expectancy in the United States was only forty-seven. Only 26 per cent of men born in England in 1900 could expect to reach retirement age, and even if they did, most of them died shortly afterwards.

Nearly 90 per cent of men born in the UK can expect to make it to retirement and enjoy many healthy years of it too. In the past century, hundreds of thousands of people all over the world have lived twice as long as they were supposed to do. Every year the number of people celebrating their one hundredth birthday doubles. Half of all the people who have ever turned eighty are alive today, reported *The Economist* in its Millennium edition.

Xers, now in their twenties and thirties, accept with a certain weariness (and wariness) that they are going to HAVE to live a long time and will keep paying taxes and propping up sagging medical aids to pay for the health care needs of the Boomer and Silent generations. So they're pumping iron and watching their cholesterol counts in a manner their parents and grandparents would never have dreamt of doing when they were hardly out of their teens.

The Millennial generation who are now children and teen-agers are determined, in an age obsessed with image and glamour, to be equally slim and beautiful. Think of the impact that metrosexual David Beckham and his Spice(y) wife Victoria have on millions the world over. Metrosexuals, incidentally, are men who love grooming products and fragrances but are not necessarily homosexuals.

Millennials are pumping even more iron than the Xers and sweating the treadmill circuit.

In addition, they cannot afford to be ill. Increasingly, Xers and Millennials will work for themselves today, not in big womb to tomb nanny corporations. A day spent not working is a day without pay. That is why for them the definition of 'being sick' will increasingly be 'sick'... as in 'you can't walk', or 'you are in hospital'. Nothing less will do.

The luxury of the Silent generation's mollycoddling a cold at home with feet in a basin of steaming water is not for them. Most Silents were able to take a day off work as sick leave without losing financially. The Silent generation can't under-stand why their (sick) grandchildren never give their bodies a chance to heal with bed rest. Xers and Millennials are amazed that anybody ever takes to their beds when ill.

A story about American banker JP Morgan illustrates how the world of healthcare has changed in tandem with the changing lives of generations. Wealth definitely didn't guarantee health in days gone by.

A century ago, JP Morgan was one of the world's richest men. He financed the rail and steel industries that were the basis of America's industrial might and his name still adorns financial institutions today. Yet, as the London *Sunday Times* reported in December 2002, Morgan who, if measured in today's money, would have been a billionaire many times over, lacked many of the things we take for granted today.

The newly married Morgan was honeymooning in Europe with his wife, who was only in her twenties, when she died of TB. Later on, he was travelling from America to Britain by ocean liner when his father suddenly became ill and died soon afterwards. But there were no satellite communications and no way of getting a message to him.

So JP Morgan was handed three telegrams when he arrived at Liverpool, England.

Dad taken ill.

Dad dangerously ill.

Dad dead.

Morgan died young in 1913 and his death was preceded by years of poor health.

So while money does not buy happiness, it has certainly brought huge improvements in health and longevity. Even the poor can today live healthier lives than JP Morgan and his wife did.

GIs (born 1900s to 1920s)

The Industrial era was in full swing with large factories, big business and manufacturing dominating the world when GIs were born. Nobody was expected to live much beyond their fiftieth birthday, although people lived a bit longer in the developed world. Women often died during childbirth and one fifth of all children died before the age of five. A visit to most turn of the century cemeteries reveals little graves that bear mute testimony to the struggle for childhood survival.

Diseases such as smallpox, polio, measles and mumps carried off millions. The great flu epidemic of 1918 killed millions all over the world. Leading causes of death in the United States were pneumonia and flu, tuberculosis, diarrhoea, heart disease and strokes. Healthcare expectations were fairly dim.

Antibiotics and insulin hadn't been discovered. Coca-Cola contained cocaine instead of caffeine; and, even more startling, marijuana, heroin and morphine were all available over the counter at chemists/pharmacies. One pharmacist told his clients back then, 'Heroin clears the complexion, gives buoyancy to the mind, regulates the stomach and the bowels, and is, in fact, a perfect guardian of health.'

More than 95 per cent of all births in the United States took place at home. The number of American homes that boasted a bath was a paltry 14 per cent. Most women washed their hair only once a month, using borax and egg yolks for shampoo, a habit that would horrify our daily-shampoo generation.

The focus on healthy lifestyles that we take for granted now didn't exist in the GIs' youth. They probably had home cooking nearly all their lives. Processed, fast food and junk food hadn't been invented yet. They grew up in an era when food didn't have to be sexy. It was just food, and today's average family would probably regard it as bland, if not downright boring. There was one big advantage, however. It was balanced with the right proportion of proteins, vegetables and carbohydrates. Food was fatty, diets had a high meat content and vegetables were boiled almost to death. Salads were scarce. People ate this way for centuries and, probably because fewer chemicals were used on farms, natural food was healthier back then than it is today.

In addition, GIs probably did well on what we today regard as relatively unhealthy diets, because much of their daily work was physical. They didn't need the gym and exercise routines that we follow today. They got most of it from just living their lives.

They had none of the issues we have with smoking and drinking. Indeed, one advertisement for Player's Navy Cut cigarettes depicts a golden-haired toddler sitting in the nursery holding up three cigarettes in his pudgy fingers while others spill from the packet lying near his teddy bear. The copy reads, 'The name Player on a packet of cigarettes guarantees the quality and purity of the contents'. This was no doubt a play on the quality and purity of the innocent child holding what we regard as cancer sticks today.

Yet another advertisement, this time for Craven A, depicts a close-up of a beautiful and elegant woman with the words, 'Craven A are always cool, fresh and kind to my throat.' Compare that with the cutting-edge, anti-smoking advertisement that made an appearance at the turn of the new millennium. A young woman sits at a table with a variety of instruments ranging from an axe, hacksaw and spikes to lethal knives. Beneath her are the words 'Smoking Kills'. We've come a long way since the turn of the twentieth century in our attitudes towards smoking and a host of other health issues.

Some GIs who are well into their nineties are astounded at what they regard as obsessive or neurotic behaviour about food and health. 'We ate fatty meat, drank and smoked and we're fine,' they exclaim. 'You just need to keep a balanced approach to everything,' they insist, and there's a world of wisdom in their words.

The elderly today are fitter than people their age have ever been. The sad aspect of physically surviving as long as they have is the mental deterioration resulting from diseases such as Alzheimer's and senile dementia.

Health tips

- Keep an active mind – play bridge, chess, cards.
- Play memory games.
- Don't just sit passively in front of the TV.
- Read as much and as often as you can.
- Walk, however slowly you do so. It stimulates circulation and drains lymph glands.
- Do some form of creative activity such as painting, carpentry, arranging flowers or pottery.
- Write to friends and family. Feeling loved is vital for health and happiness.

Silents (born 1920s to 1940s)

They grew up in the Depression and World War II when food and healthcare were scarce. All over the world jobless men worked for food instead of wages in an effort to keep their families from starving. John Steinbeck's book *The Grapes of Wrath* depicts in chilling detail the battle families had to find work and food in the United States.

The seven years of World War II brought rationing. Many a Boomer child with a British background has heard her Silent parents talking about a childhood where they rushed home from school, hungry and desperate for buttered toast, and rashly ate their meagre weekly ration of butter in one high tea. No wonder they wanted to give their Boomer children everything they never had on the one hand and, on the other, were horrified when those same children tossed date-expired food into the bin. Some Silent generation women in their seventies, living in fairly affluent homes, still cannot help themselves as they retrieve old food from the bin, so deeply ingrained is their urge to save.

It wasn't only the countries fighting the war who suffered but also colonies trying to meet the food demands of battle-blitzed England. South Africa, Australia and New Zealand made a lot of money from the British contracts they signed to supply lamb, beef and wheat but still there wasn't enough to meet the demands of that ravaged island. Stripping the Commonwealth meant these countries, too, were short of basic foods.

From the 1930s to the mid 1950s, when the Silent generation were children, even those who grew up in reasonably wealthy and middle-class homes didn't receive the nutrition children need to grow up strong and healthy.

And as the Silent generation began bringing up their Boomer children in the 1950s and 60s a number of new health problems arose with the arrival of fast food and junk food.

In the 1970s as information and advice about how to live healthy lifestyles proliferated, they began turning to vitamins, health food and medicines that were an alternative to drugs. Indeed, many a Silent generation person is popping up to twenty supplements, vitamins and allied health pills a day to keep healthy and fit.

Health tips

- Keep active. Run. Go to gym. Walk. But keep moving.
- Pilates or yoga will help to keep your mind and body supple.
- Avoid being 'silent'. Loneliness isn't good for healthy minds – join community organisations. Sing in a choir. Babysit. Be someone's grandparent.
- Steam vegetables. Eat fruit instead of sweets and biscuits.
- Make amends with your children for past hurts. Nursing anger is not healthy. (Read chapter 10 on Parenting).

Boomers (born 1940s to 1960s)

Many a Boomer looks back on their childhood and is frankly astounded, in terms of today's high levels of hygiene and warning labels on every tin, bottle and household appliance, that they survived such a lethal period.

Nifty little fences to keep children from tumbling down stairs were unheard of. So were protective covers for electricity plugs. Parents kept their children warm with asbestos heaters that were not unknown to emit clouds of asbestos dust when first switched on.

They ate worms and wild berries, licked their mud pie cakes, scraped food up that fell on to the kitchen floor and lived to tell the tale. Back then that was considered normal and mothers didn't grab the nearest auto-pump disinfectant bottle and wipe both faces and floors. Life for parents and children alike was a lot more relaxed.

Some Boomers can remember their Silent generation mothers taking them off to a neighbour to play when the children in that house had been diagnosed with mumps, chickenpox or some other disease your mother wanted to 'get over and done with'.

It's the Boomer generation that has taken healthcare to the next level. They professionalised healthcare. They privatised healthcare in terms of GPs, medical suppliers and in creating and expanding medical aid schemes. Becoming a doctor in the Boomer era was almost as good as printing your own money, it was so profitable. The medical industry is a multibillion dollar global business today.

Boomers have fuelled the industry with their desire for eternal youth, health and wellness. Cosmetic surgery is one of the fastest growing segments of the medical world today. Mr Silvio Berlusconi, the prime minister of Italy, appeared in public towards the end of January 2004 for the first time in more than a month after a facelift. Boomer Michael Jackson has totally reinvented himself with plastic surgery and few will forget his near 'melt-down' in a Coca-Cola advertisement when his plastic face got too close to the lights. Singer and film star Cher Bono is reported to have succumbed to the surgeon's knife to such an extent that she even had a rib removed to make herself look slimmer. Venezuela, which has recently produced more beauty queens than any other country in the world, expects its beauties to submit to the knife as a matter of course. Those knives are held by Boomer doctors, and their patients are largely Boomers.

But it's not just the stars and celebrities who opt for cosmetic surgery. Eavesdrop on any well-heeled Boomer ladies' lunch in New York, Los Angeles, London, Johannesburg or Sydney and they will be discussing the latest nip and tuck. Indeed, it's reached such heights that any Boomer over fifty-five years of age who admits she HASN'T had plastic surgery, is regarded as a bit odd.

Boomer men, particularly those in the visible professions such as the film industry, television and advertising, are also queuing for surgery. Indeed, heart-throb Robert Redford, now in his sixties, felt compelled to mention that he *didn't* plan to have his wrinkles erased. The implication, of course, was that many around him were!

Men in their fifties and sixties have either shaved off all their thinning hair, going for the Telly Savalas, 'sexy bald' look, or have had hair implants. But before Boomer men turn eighty, wig jokes could be a generational eccentricity. Research into treatments with hormones holds the promise of a cure for hair loss within a generation. And another development will be the manipulation of melanin production in the hair root to eradicate greying.

For Boomer women (and men) the cosmetic knife may not be necessary for ever. A new generation of drugs is apparently going to reverse some of the damage the sun has done. The United States Food and Drug Administration is considering allowing the use of a drug, Dimericine, which contains an enzyme that helps repair DNA. Boomers might not only succeed in holding back the ravages of time but could even end up looking younger than they really are.

In his book *Age Power*, Ken Dychtwald writes that other drugs have been deployed in the battle against ageing. These include Lipitor to lower cholesterol (a rapidly booming Boomer problem), Aricept to boost memory, Celebrex to eliminate the pain of arthritis without creating gastrointestinal problems,

Ambien for restful sleep, Evista to control bone loss and prevent osteoporosis, Detrol to halt urinary incontinence, Rogaine and Propecia to foster hair growth, Meridia to promote weight loss, Renova to banish wrinkles, and hundreds more.

In the same book, Dychtwald details five emerging, new life-science technologies that could become the bio-tools with which human enchancement and life extension are brought about. They are: super-nutrition, hormone replacement, gene therapy and the manipulation of cellular ageing, bionics (cyborg humans), and lastly, organ cloning that will produce spare body parts.

He predicts that in future, it will be common for us to visit anti-ageing doctors to have our hormone levels checked, and get prescriptions for 'custom-tailored cocktails' that will help us stay fit and youthful. And he mentions that today there are more than 100 000 anti-ageing research projects being conducted in numerous disciplines all over the world. More progress has been made in the battle against ageing in the past decade than in the whole history of the world.

Mental deterioration is as frightening as physical age for Boomers. Three decades after they launched the physical fitness craze – remember how Jane Fonda's aerobics swept the world – the spectre of forgetfulness has led to another type of training. This time it is mental aerobics. What's the point of a lean, mean, beautiful body if your brain's flabby? Never slow to sense a commercial opportunity, the greying of 79 million American Boomers has led to a proliferation of books, software, videos and brain-training programmes to keep those brain cells jumping.

On average, individuals begin forgetting at thirty-five, according to Fred Chernow, author of *The Sharper Mind*. You start by misplacing your car keys and glasses and then it progresses to 'where did I park the car?' Ironically, one of the reasons for forgetfulness today is the information overload that requires us to remember more than we ever have before. When Chernow (70) started working, he was expected to know his name, address and phone number. Today we have to remember our credit card pin numbers, medical aid numbers, cellphone and fax numbers, our armed response numbers and so on.

Boomers are attending memory classes, where they're taught that mental exercise, ranging from crossword puzzles, playing chess, bridge, using both hands instead of just your dominant one and learning another language, all help to stave off mental decline. It's the 'use it or lose it' approach.

The United Nations has predicted that mental illness will overtake most other medical conditions in the western world with one in four suffering from them by the year 2015. It is affecting Boomer men more than women because men are less willing to talk about depression and their misery expresses itself in ways that exacerbate their problems, such as drinking and drugging.

One of the greatest fears that Boomers face is the prospect of looking after their ageing, Silent generation parents who missed out on all the food supplements such as Barley Green, Ginseng, soy milk, vitamins, omega 3 and 6 fats, antioxidants and so on. Consequently, the Silents are suffering the brunt of heart attacks, osteoarthritis, strokes, senile dementia, Alzheimers and degenerative eye conditions, to name a few, which are landing them in old-age homes. Boomers, who'd looked forward to inheriting the family home, are having to sell it to pay for their parents' medical care.

At the other end of the age spectrum, Boomer women who were desperate to establish themselves in careers, paid little heed to the ticking of the biological clock until, as they reached their mid-thirties the alarm bells began ringing. Typically, they refused to accept that motherhood had passed them by and fertility mania hit. Louise Brown, the world's first test tube baby, born on 25 July 1978, is now an Xer but the world held its breath as her birth was announced all those years ago.

Today IVF (in vitro fertilisation), hormone treatments, AID (artificial insemination by donor) and AIH (artificial insemination by husband) are rife. Cindy Crawford, Demi Moore, Sophia Loren and Madonna have had babies in their late thirties and forties. Cherie Blair, wife of Britain's prime minister Tony Blair, had her fourth baby at the age of forty-five in a healthy and natural birth. During the last decade, the number of births to women over thirty-five has jumped nearly 50 per cent with profound implications for the configuration of the family.

The health food conscious Boomers are taking a keen, and some say interfering, approach to GM (genetically modified) food. Woolworths in South Africa pulled GM food from their shelves as their major, Boomer, buyers protested against it. Their stand against genetic modification has more to do with fear and the possibility of something going wrong, rather than any scientific proof. However, Boomer heads of state Tony Blair and George W Bush have strongly advocated the use of GM food. This is likely to be a brief, but intense, Boomer-dominated issue that may win, or lose, at least one major election in the near future.

Fear didn't stop Boomers making nuclear bombs and conducting a nuclear arms race but it's stopping the world now in the development of new biotechnology and health-related advances. There could be an intergenerational war between Boomers and Xers. The latter are determined to be pragmatic in their approach to ending famine by creating wheat that grows in deserts, and ending malnutrition by putting vitamins into basic foods like rice and bread.

As Boomers head into true middle age, they've begun to turn their backs on the massive drug companies they helped to create – opting increasingly for homeopathy either as an alternative or as part of conventional medicine. They're also concentrating their formidable energy on a whole range of exercises that will help them slow down the ravages of time. Pilates, Shiatsu, Kung Fu and yoga classes are de rigueur. Reflexology, acupuncture, chiropractic, iridology and aromatherapy are but some of the treatments they are passionate about.

Health tips

- Start saving for your future medical costs. Your children will be unable to pay them.
- Exercise. Walking and jogging are free. If you do nothing else, exercise. It's one of the healthiest activities you'll ever undertake.
- Have regular check-ups for blood pressure, cholesterol and sugar levels. You're entering heart attack and stroke territory.

- The big 'C' (cancer) lurks. Prostate tests, pap smears and mammograms are important. Many cancers can be cured today if you act early enough.
- Stress kills. Pause in your workaholic, driven lives to assess what's really important. Smell the roses. Hug your children and your ageing parents. You will be healthier for it.

Xers (born 1960s to 1980s)

Xers, born to careerist Boomer mothers and workaholic fathers, are the generation that have largely been left to get themselves out of bed in the morning, grab a hasty breakfast on the trot, with the TV blaring, and head for school. Babies and toddlers were dropped at crèches and pre-schools by their parents en route to the office. They're the latchkey kids who had to let themselves into their homes, reached for micro-waveable food and plonked themselves in front of the TV for the rest of the day.

It was Boomers who invented junk food, the takeaway pizza, hamburger, hot dog – all nice to eat but not particularly healthy. They ate junk food 'on the side'. BUT it became the staple food for Xers brought up by Boomers who didn't have time to cook. Cleaning up the 'dining room' meant getting the fast food bags out of the back seat of your car. It's not unknown for some Xers to refuse to eat any food that is NOT processed. They regard it as 'unhealthy'.

Today, the consequences of that way of eating are kicking in. As the older Xers start to move into their late twenties and early thirties, some of them are having families and starting to go for medicals for insurance and their companies, and realising that their TV-couch-potato and Internet-surfing lifestyles have created a largely sedentary generation at risk of high cholesterol and blood pressure. In America, young army recruits are discovering during stringent medical tests that they have high cholesterol levels and clogged arteries. Some of them in their twenties are on the verge of having heart attacks.

Consequently, they're reaching for the vitamins, the minerals, the food supplements, the diet boosters and supplements in the same way the Boomers are. They check the ingredients on a can of chicken noodle soup to see if it contains echinacea and they know the fat content of everything they eat. They're realising they can't abuse their bodies for ever and it's dawning on them that their health and their bodies are the most important natural assets they have – and that they need to care for them. The plus here is that they're doing it at a far younger age than the Boomers did.

They're filling gyms, pumping iron, spinning and stretching as often as they can. Xers, the dot-com generation, are the first generation to seriously contemplate changing our minds with technology. In her book *Tomorrow's People: How 21st century technology is changing the way we Think and Feel,* Britain's best known female scientist, Lady Susan Greenfield, has described the fate of human individuality and relationships in a future where direct modifications can be made to the brain.

A range of technologies such as the Internet, nanotechnology, virtual reality, genetic modification, mood-altering drugs and silicon prostheses for the brain would break down the differences between people, says Greenfield, director of the Royal Institution in London, in the *London Telegraph* in June 2003.

Reproductive technologies, begun by the Boomers, will steam ahead in the Xer generation, undermining the traditional idea of sexes. Renting out your womb to help childless, and often older, parents is on the verge of becoming acceptable. News was released in 2003 that a technique enabling womb transplants is likely to be ready for use, by both sexes, by 2006. At the same time we were told that it is now possible to create life from terminated embryos, so that a child may technically have an aborted foetus as a mother. It could be possible, in theory, to create eggs from men or to reprogram eggs with the genes of a post-menopausal woman.

Stem cell technologies to repair and replace organs will in future further erode the difference between children, the middle-aged and the elderly by keeping people younger for longer. Some mothers will look as young as their daughters.

Xer men are increasingly reaching for face scrubs and moisturisers in one of the world's fastest growing sectors in the consumer products market. Homosexuals used to dominate the male grooming market. Now they're making way for the new market category called metrosexuals. These are men who aren't gay but enjoy using the ever increasing number of male colognes and toilette water, face masks, body scrubs and hair care products. Their fathers and grandfathers used Lifebuoy soap. *The Economist* quoted Marian Salzman of Euro RSCG Worldwide, a leading advertising agency, saying tests showed that about 32 per cent of young men in the United States have metrosexual tendencies. They regularly buy skincare cream and fragrances, and are, increasingly, spending money on waxing unwanted body hair. Soccer star David Beckham is the perfect Xer example of this manly attention to looks with his waxed, bronzed, lithe good looks and his constant changes in hairstyle.

Manufacturers are also targeting younger men for products like shower gels and hair colouring. Many an Xer's 'Christmas stocking' contains at least one such product from The Body Shop. Their Silent generation grandparents shake their heads in wonderment and sniff, 'Where will it all end – what are we coming to?'

Health tips

- Change your sex habits. HIV/AIDS and STDs (sexually transmitted diseases) have made sex a life-threatening activity.
- Become more informed about the food you eat. Buy a steamer as well as a microwave. Get rid of the frying pan.
- Eat three meals per day. Never skip breakfast.
- If you're not eating a balanced diet, supplement with vitamins and minerals.
- Exercise regularly. Extreme sports, every so often, do not compensate for aerobic activity (getting your heart pumping) three times a week for twenty minutes.

Millennials (born 1980s to 2000s)

This generation is naturally still reliant on its mainly Boomer, but some Xer, parents for healthcare. They're probably the most health angst-ridden generation ever raised, subject to constant exhortations by anxious mothers not to 'run your fingers over that germ-ridden handrail and don't eat food off the floor'. Visiting toddler friends are checked for signs of runny noses and hacking coughs that could spell colds and flu. Fear of contamination results in them being ripped out of the sandbox, if they're lucky enough to be allowed to have one in this intense hygiene-aware age.

ADD (attention deficit disorder) is rampant and at the first signs of it children are often slapped on to Ritalin. From an early age they are aware that it's not OK to be fat. Their Xer/Boomer mothers are skipping lunch in favour of diet milkshakes. One four-year-old, told by her best friend that she looked 'fat' in her tracksuit, refused all exhortations by her Xer dad to wear it on a cold winter's day. 'I want to look like my Barbie,' she insisted.

Twelve-year-olds are only eating salads at lunch time. Teen-agers' tuck boxes reflect the obsession of 'thin' as anorexic circles of friends eye each other warily at school break time. Women's magazines, often edited by Boomers but increas-ingly by Xers, are filled with skeletal models draped with designer label clothes that the coat hanger shouldered Millennials rush to the ever-increasing shopping malls to buy once school is out.

The end of school/matric dance is increasingly turning into a fashion show. Seventeen and eighteen-year-olds, who need every ounce of energy in a challenging last year at school, begin dieting for it the moment they return from their Christmas holidays. Bulimia and anorexia reign.

Conversely, obesity, particularly in the United States and increasingly in Britain and South Africa, is on the increase. Poor eating habits, lack of exercise, and nutrition-lacking junk food as well as just too much food are amongst the reasons for this.

Never have we been so obsessed with being thin, and never have we been so overweight. Food has lost its function. Dr Susan Jebb, head of nutrition research at the British Medical Research Council says that obesity is going to do more than anything else to transform the way we look, live and die. Even if the startling pace of its spread over the past twenty years slows down, the majority of humans will be obese in a hundred years. 'The outlook is bleak,' she says.

Andrew Prentice, a professor of international nutrition at the London School of Hygiene and Tropical Medicine, went even further, describing the resultant changes in body shape as one of the most dramatic shifts in evolutionary history. He predicted that in the future obese children would die before their parents.

Concern about children's diet is flooding schools with experiments being carried out worldwide to determine the effect of diet on school performance. One such experiment carried out in an American school in Wisconsin in 1997, saw vending machines removed, fast food burgers, and fries and chips disappear. They gave way to fresh salads, meats prepared with old-fashioned recipes and whole grain bread. Fresh fruit was added to the menu and so was good drinking water. A couple of years on, the results show kids who behave, the hallways aren't frantic, the school principal seldom has to sort out discipline problems in his office, and the children's school marks are consistently higher than they were before the diet changed.

Similar reports are coming in from Britain where some researchers even claim that poor diet may help turn fidgety children into criminal teenagers.

Many a Millennial kid was raised on a slew of antibiotics, resulting in impoverished immune systems, that in time resulted in more frequent infections. Desperate parents turned to alternative cures such as homeopathy, and doctors, particularly in Britain, have increasingly incorporated these disciplines into their practice. Within the Millennials lifetime, it is conceivable that modern science and medicine will both solve some existing crises, such as AIDS, TB and malaria, and also create some new ones, with antibiotic resistant superbugs and the threat of biological weapons of mass destruction.

In an increasingly safety-conscious age, Millennials have never known bottle caps that aren't childproof, screw off and plastic. They take bottled water to school instead of drinking it from the school fountain as their parents did and wipe public toilet seats before using them.

They've only ever cooked popcorn in a microwave.

Life in a mother's womb has become almost as endangered as it was for their counterparts a hundred years ago when so many babies were stillborn or died in childbirth. Today, abortion in China and India is threatening to reduce the number of girls as the Chinese, legally forced to have one child, opt for boys, and in India girls have no economic value.

Millennials appear destined to have the best and the worst of it in the years to come.

Health tips

- Millennials are likely to see a vastly changed health system during their lifetimes with the emphasis being on doctors keeping you healthy, rather than treating you when you are sick.
- Medical schemes may insist on members fulfilling certain basic criteria, such as exercise and weight control, before they will enrol you.

Life expectancies at birth in 2002:

	Total average	Male	Female
America	77.04	74.50	80.20
U K	77.79	75.29	80.84
Australia	80.00	77.15	83.00
South Africa	45.43	45.19	45.68
Japan	80.91	77.73	84.25

Source: United Nations World Factbook

Where the generations were born:

GIs: Born at home with a midwife in attendance, with minimal qualifications, or a neighbour. No men on the scene.

Silents: Also born at home but with a qualified midwife or even a doctor. Some mothers began delivering in hospitals.

Boomers: In hospital. The incidence of Caesarean sections and epidurals increased rapidly.

Xers: In hospital. Doctors set the birth date so that holidays were not interrupted. Water births and 'natural' births (without drugs) arrived.

Millennials: The trend to return to home births will strengthen, aided by superior obstetrics and technology. Water and natural births will continue.

Where fathers are when their children are born:

GIs: Standing outside in the cold, or at a neighbour's house.

Silents: Waiting in the pub for the phone call, with friends and a pile of cigars.

Boomers: Pacing the hospital corridor outside the delivery room.

Xers: Inside the delivery room, complete with video camera.

Millennials: Setting up the live webcam to broadcast the birth via the Internet to family around the world.

Attitude to doctors:

GIs: Didn't call out the doctor, didn't want to 'bother' him. Life was hard, things hurt and there was no reason to make life easy for the sufferer.

Silents: Never challenged the doctor, his was the 'last word'. Kids died. You died ... at home. Doctors paid house calls.

Boomers: Challenged doctors, insisted on being viewed as clients as well as patients. Regarded illness as a horrid intrusion in their lives. 'We have a RIGHT to be well.'

Xers: Doctor doesn't know everything. Insist on alternative complementary treatment and not just drugs. Trawl the Internet for information and cures. Call the doctor by his first name. Challenge medical 'mystique'.

Millennials: The risks of smoking, drugs and sex (AIDS) are drummed into them at school so they make deliberate choices, knowing what they're doing. Will expect doctors to make house calls.

Drugs of choice:

GIs: Alcohol (forget Prohibition). Often died of liver cirrhosis.

Silents: Tobacco/nicotine. Film stars like Humphrey Bogart added to the allure.

Boomers: Marijuana, LSD, speed. Invented drug use as an art form. Marijuana was mild in the Swinging 60s compared with some of the toxin-laced stuff today. LSD and Speed took you out of reality, 'on a trip, man'.

Xers: Ecstasy, heroin and cocaine speed up your metabolism so you can work and play 24-hour days. They dehydrate and can kill you. Make life excruciatingly real (opposite of LSD). Also 'escapist' drugs, including alcohol.

Millennials: Energy drinks. Creatine which suppresses the body's ability to create lactose acid so you can gym longer. May decriminalise certain drugs.

Mealtimes:

GIs: When they were children big families sat around dinner tables and were waited on by servants. They had three meals a day.

Silents: Fewer servants around the table when they were kids. Conversation was subdued. Shared breakfast and supper as a family. Dad was at the office for lunch.

Boomers: Still sat down for dinner with their parents but there was noisy chatter and they expounded their views on the issues of the day.

Xers: Ate dinner on a TV tray. Dads, and sometimes moms, were still at work. Mealtime wasn't sacrosanct. Xers often skipped breakfast.

Millennials: Meals are constantly interrupted by cell-phones and telephones. Pre-packed healthy foods abound.

Eating habits when their generation is in control:

GIs: The hired cook in nearly one fifth of American homes and in well over half of white South African homes, cooked a three course meal consisting of meat or fish with vegetables.

Silents: Mother produced healthy, hearty breakfasts, and roasts for supper with two vegetables.

Boomers: Invented fast foods to help them in their frenetic, workaholic lives. Women were out there in the workforce in earnest.

Xers: Inconsistent eating habits, no set times or procedures.

Millennials: Will return to the more family structured regime of turning mealtimes into social events.

Dentistry:

GIs and Silents: Suffered excruciating toothache alleviated eventually by tooth extraction. Now wear dentures.

Boomers: Extractions decreased as fillings saved teeth.

Xers: Fluoride had arrived and fillings decreased.

Millennials: Some have never had a filling in their lives. Railroad tracks (bands) have resulted in perfect teeth.

Medical aids:

GIs: The system (State) must look after me.

Silents: The State or my medical aid will pay.

Boomers: Medical aid must pay ... or else!

Xers: Will look after ourselves but share some of the risk with insurance.

Millennials: Will focus on 'health' care as opposed to 'sick' care.

Medical aid

In many countries, including America, Britain, New Zealand and Australia, the state provides health care. Those who can afford it, and don't want to wait in queues, pay for their own medical aid.

In South Africa the elderly expect medical aids to care for them. They believe that someone else should look after them. If you do your sums correctly, this concept does not work. Money, medical aid subscriptions, collected from the GI and Silent generations by medical aid schemes, has not been enough to cater for their needs. Actuaries believe that sums collected in the past, based on life expectancies then, are outdated as people live into their seventies, eighties and nineties. Medical aids and insurance companies that are funding the costs of older generations, who are becoming increasingly frail and sickly, are going to run out of money by the time Boomers become elderly.

This is really bad news for Boomers who are used to calling the shots. They're not keen to hear that medical aids aren't wielded by genies who can rub a magic lamp and produce enough money to fund expensive heart bypass operations. In future, medical aids will probably not cover the rarer and most costly diseases. A century ago you would have died of them.

In future, as South Africa's futuristic Discovery Health has proved with its Vitality reward programme for staying healthy, medical aids will focus on keeping their clients fit.

Maybe a straw in the wind is the approach one province in China has where doctors are rewarded for keeping their clients well. They earn only when their patient is well. If we followed their example, the scenario would be that you post your doctor a cheque when you are well. Every time you are sick you stop paying and thus your doctor has a vested interest in keeping you healthy.

Sex:

GIs:
Sex happened in marriage only, and it was for procreation, not recreation. Well, that was the conventional approach because, as we all know, prostitution flourished in Victorian times. But on the 'right' side of the sheets, you didn't discuss sex, not even in marriage. Unmarried mothers were sent to the country to have their babies which were then adopted and never mentioned again.

Silents:
Attitudes towards sex began to change as women's emancipation and the Suffragettes' fight for the women's vote became a force to be reckoned with. Women no longer silently acquiesced to their husband's affairs and visits to prostitutes.

Boomers:
The arrival of the Pill in the 1960s created one of the biggest revolutions in history as Boomer women openly enjoyed sex, freed from the fear of pregnancy. In the Swinging 60s sex became recreational with Woodstock and other music festivals becoming venues for nudity and public sex. Sex became a 'release' to the extent that American president John F Kennedy confided in the then British prime minister Harold Macmillan that if he didn't have it for three days he could develop a headache. Pregnancy outside wedlock lost its stigma although pressure was still exerted on couples to marry.

Xers:
They are wary of sex with the advent of HIV/AIDS and STDs (sexually transmitted diseases) and know each time

they have it with a stranger that sex can kill. A few
nihilistic Xers have used sex as a message of mass
destruction, with the attitude that they're going to die
anyway and so use it as a form of Russian roulette.
Conversely, there are worldwide campaigns urging
youngsters to be celibate before marriage. Sex is openly
discussed at some dinner parties without eliciting
blushes.

Millennials:
They will probably make the strong link again, as did the
GIs, between marriage or a committed relationship
before sex.

Discussing sex with your children:

GIs:	Didn't!
Silents:	Some mention of birds and bees the night before a wedding.
Boomers:	No choice but to be open in view of their own behaviour. Lots of sex films to send their kids to for education.
Xers:	Frank and free discussions. Use correct anatomical descriptions, eg vagina, penis.
Millennials:	Will probably be less pushy with the facts and totally comfortable discussing them.

19

'Re-tyreing' the Generations

Attitude to retirement:

GIs:	Spent a lifetime planning for it.
Silents:	Deserve it and are looking forward to it.
Boomers:	Don't want to retire, love working.
Xers:	Won't be able to because won't be able to afford to.
Millennials:	Retirement won't exist – it will be a thing of the past.

The Baby Boom generation has rewritten the rules of life as they have reached every stage of it and they're still doing so as they move into their fifties. The generation that once warned 'don't trust anyone over thirty', is fast turning fifty. Indeed, every seven seconds in America, a Boomer turns fifty which means that in a few years' time, a Boomer will **retire** every seven seconds. 'Hope I die before I get old,' sang rock group The Who in their classic 1960s anthem, 'My Generation'. Most of them are, however, ensuring they don't die by swallowing as many vitamins and health foods as they can stomach.

They have, unilaterally, decided that ageing and retiring are out. When they were young, gyrating to Elvis and swooning over the Beatles, age was a no-no. Now, not only are they changing their attitude with slogans like, 'ageing is not for sissies', but they're also moving the goalposts. Now the odd little wrinkle denotes character, not age, and grey hairs, hidden by streaks and highlights, allow Boomers to look more 'interesting'.

These fairly superficial matters, although important to Boomers, pale beside the issue that many predict will be one of the most serious of this coming century. It is the clash, or the contrast, between young and old, between youth and age. In a nutshell – there are too many ageing Boomers and too few young Millennials in rich First World countries.

As the large wave of Baby Boomers starts to retire from the workforce, wanting and needing their pensions, there will not be enough Xers and Millennials left in the workforce to pay for them. Furthermore, by the time the younger generations reach their retirement age, the Boomers will have emptied the pension coffers of their contents. The pension larder will be bare.

The Economist reported in its millennial issue that even in the developing countries, at least those where AIDS has not reached plague proportions, a time looms, perhaps nearer 2050, when that same problem will arise. A large group of elderly needing pensions and healthcare will need to be supported by a small group of younger workers paying the taxes and earning the profits. And unless those countries are by then much richer, the pain imposed by this imbalance will be much nastier than for the wealthy west.

If all those demographic predictions come about, then battles between the young and the old could, in both the poor world and the rich, come to dominate politics in the same way as battles between unions and companies, workers and bosses, rich and poor, did in the past.

Internationally respected futurist Peter Drucker, as sharp-witted at ninety-four years of age as some are at thirty, wrote in his book *Managing in the Next Society* that falling birth rates all over the world would be the 'basic disturbance' of the twenty-first century. He said that America is the only advanced country where there are enough babies, 2.2 per woman of reproductive age, to replace the population. But that was only because of its high immigration.

He believes that nothing like the shrinking of the younger population has happened since the dying centuries of the Roman Empire. He writes, 'In every single developed country, but also in China and Brazil, the birthrate is now well below the replacement rate of 2.2 per woman of reproductive age.

'Politically, this means that immigration will become an important – and highly divisive – issue in all rich countries. It will cut across all traditional political alignments.

'The homogeneous mass market that emerged in all rich countries after World War II has been youth-determined from the start. It will now become middle-age-determined or perhaps more likely, it will split into two: a middle-age-determined mass market and a much smaller youth-determined one. And because the supply of young people will shrink, creating new employment patterns to attract and hold the growing number of older people, especially older educated people, will become increasingly important.'

No wonder we're beginning to see features in financial and business magazines and newspapers with headlines like 'Life begins at 50'. That's to help change the mindset of those who hoped their working days might soon be over. Far from it, they will be working for at least another twenty years.

Europe's working age population is set to fall by 40 million, or 18 per cent, by 2050 according to *The Economist*. At present, the European Union's population is some 90 million greater than America's but by 2050 the latter could have between 40 and 60 million more people than today's EU member states.

No wonder pensions have become a regular election issue and that by 2030 fixed retirement ages for people in reasonable physical and mental health may, according to Peter Drucker, have been abolished, 'to prevent the pensions burden on the working population from becoming unbearable. But politicians everywhere continue to pretend that they can save the current pensions system.'

Some Boomer-dominated governments who are looking ahead to the looming pensions crisis, are trying to start taking action now. Their wake-up call has also been the crashing world markets where bearish equities have wiped billions off pension funds. Headlines in magazines like *Fortune* have blared, 'Some $300 billion of pension assets have been wiped away since the bull market ended.' And 'We're faced with the worst financial situation since the Depression.' In an article in December 2002, headed, 'Beware the Pension Monster', *Fortune* magazine reported that big corporate pension schemes in America owed some $1.2 trillion to their current and future retirees, and for the first time in years companies don't have enough money stashed away to pay for those benefits. The size of the shortfall was more than half of what they were expected to earn that year. The day of reckoning had arrived for corporate America and 'the pension monster is going to suck the blood out of those corporations'.

In the short term, an economic upturn might replenish those pension bins, but in the long term, unless there's another quick baby boom, the future looks bleak for pensioners. Already we are seeing demonstrators marching in European countries like Austria and Italy to show their displeasure at their governments' attempts to change pension systems that will enable them to pay less, later. They want to scrap sixty-five as the retirement age and extend it into the seventies.

This might not necessarily be a huge problem for Boomers turning fifty, who feel, look, and act far younger than their parents ever did and who are workaholics anyway. However, it'll certainly be a shock for those who have indulged in that favourite Boomer exercise, living the materialistic life and creating nightmare mountains of debt. And for those who have saved little, or nothing, financial newspaper and magazine headlines that read 'Bye-Bye Pension' will translate for them into 'bye-bye' to peace of mind and enjoyable sunshine years.

The British, for instance, do not save. The Association of British Insurers warned, in a feature in *The Economist* in September 2003, that there was a 27 billion pound gap between what people in Britain were saving and what was needed for them to enjoy a comfortable retirement. About one-third of Britons were not saving anything at all, while a fair number of the rest saved for holidays or cars but not for their long-term welfare.

That situation spells disaster for those not taking account of the new youth-age demographics.

For the Silent generation, the disaster is already upon them. Those who worked hard for a lifetime of forty years and more, did so with the dream of a golden retirement they imagined would last at least twenty years. Now that dream is beginning to fade for many of them and it causes anger and resentment.

This is all pretty sobering stuff but there are some things we can do that will let some sun shine on an otherwise fairly stormy scenario. Our goal in this chapter, therefore, is to try to provide understanding and advice to generations in their different life stages.

GIs (born 1900s to 1920s)

When GIs were born they thought they would be lucky to reach the biblical three score years and ten. Global life expectancy was about fifty. If they did make it to seventy they considered it almost a sign of God's blessing. And, as only a few people were expected to reach this venerable age, it's not surprising that most didn't make plans, from a financial perspective, which would support them through a longer old age than their elders had experienced. They expected to work from sixteen to sixty and if they were lucky, they would live a bit longer, and be able to enjoy a bit of 'balance' and relaxation.

Retirement was traditionally considered to be a time of seclusion. You removed yourself from the mainstream of life, found a little cottage or house near the seaside and sat on your porch. You rusted at the coast, much like old cars do that are left out in the rain without care.

And, like cars, if the parts aren't kept oiled and in working order, they seize up. If your brain's not stimulated, it stops working. So it's not really surprising that people who retire to 'do nothing' just fall apart and often die within a few years of retirement.

When we hear about people, like an American judge aged one hundred who still sits on the Bench, or veteran anti-apartheid campaigner, Helen Suzman who's still speaking her forthright mind aged eighty-six, on issues ranging from drugs to justice, we are amazed. Living legend, and old age 'superstar' Nelson Mandela, who is eighty-five, follows a punishing schedule that leaves people half his age flagging in his wake. Sue knows of a South African businessman aged ninety who drives to his shop every day to supervise his staff. Their common thread is that by using it (their minds) they don't lose it (their memory).

GIs were the first generation in America and Britain to have state-funded pension schemes and they are the first generation to have spent all their lives planning for retirement. Before the GI generation, you just died on the job. Paid retirement, as a concept, did not exist anywhere in the world until it was introduced in Germany in 1889. Then, the German Kaiser Otto von Bismarck initiated the pay-as-you-go system which has worked well, as long as the active workforce vastly outnumbers the retirees. This it did because retirement was set at seventy and the average life expectancy was only forty-eight years of age. Retirement, therefore, was only for the fortunate few who lived longer than 'normal'. Pensions were only introduced in England in 1908, to law-abiding British subjects from the age of seventy. America had to wait for the 1930s for pensions to come in and that was in response to the Depression. So, pensions, set against a historical backdrop, are a relatively new phenomenon.

If we used past projections for deciding on retirement age it would mean, with our fast changing life expectancy graphs, that pensions might only kick in at about age ninety-two for future generations. If you cannot begin to imagine retiring at that advanced age, it'll give you an indication of how financially flat-footed many a GI has been left because they are still alive long after they expected to be. They're running out of money because of their longevity and because life's got more expensive than they ever imagined it possibly could back in the years when they began working.

In Germany, for instance, the average life expectancy of a male, now sixty-five years old, is expected to rise to about eighty by the year 2020. In Britain it's already seventy-six and in France seventy-seven. These are averages! We have, in just over a century, nearly doubled our lifespan. The number of people celebrating their one hundredth birthday now doubles with every passing year.

Silents (born 1920s to 1940s)

This generation has been reaching retirement age for the past few years. They, and the GIs, have lived through what is probably the greatest period of societal and human change in the history of the world. They have emerged, physically, mentally and emotionally, largely intact.

They have lived careful lives, working hard and spending frugally. Saving has been a way of life. They, like the GIs, have spent a lifetime waiting for their retirement, their 'balance' in life to come, delaying self-gratification and putting duty before pleasure. Some men and women who are over sixty-five are frail and have low incomes, but because so many of them have led such an abstemious existence, they are the wealthiest ageing generation yet. They have ironed used Christmas and birthday wrapping paper and put it away for the following year. Little bits of soap cakes are melted into one big bar and food scraps are saved to make risotto. They make cream cheese from sour milk and a dropped egg is scraped off the floor and into the pan. Others may laugh but then others didn't survive the Depression and rationing during and after World War II.

Given this background of self-denial, it's no surprise that there are howls of protest from this generation when proposals are mooted to move the mandatory retirement age to seventy – as it was recently in Britain. The government there has promised to remove age discrimination by 2005.

In America, the Bureau of Labour Statistics has forecast a 33 per cent increase in the number of people aged between sixty-five and seventy-four in the workforce during the period up to 2010.

These fast-changing demographics mean that people who don't have a flexible attitude towards retirement are going to struggle. And that goes for both sides of the working 'fence'. Management will need to get its head around having older people in its workforce as we discussed in Chapter 13 on @ Work.

We know of a 72-year-old woman who recently started a senior citizens placement agency. She updates their computer skills and then sends them out into the workforce on a contract basis to companies who are sensible enough to want wisdom, experience and consistency on their staff. Indeed, we know of many women in their seventies who are still working, many of them in support positions at schools, in pharmacies and small businesses.

And there are 70-year-old professionals, doctors, dentists and lawyers who cannot afford to retire, who are working, many of them happily. We can predict that they will lead long and fulfilling lives, retaining most of their faculties because they are using their brains and are motivated and busy.

An 80-year-old friend of Sue's emails and SMSs her large extended family on a daily basis. She's joined the University of the Third Age and is constantly excited by learning and expanding her considerable knowledge. Graeme's nearly 90-year-old grandmother emails her grandchildren around the globe from her home in England. His other grandmother, in her seventies, had not set foot outside South Africa until recently. She has made up for lost time and has now visited nearly every continent in the world.

Indeed, Silents have both the financial means and the physical energy to do the kind of travelling that keeps massive floating hotels like the Queen Elizabeth and Queen Mary afloat. It's those of the Silent generation who are lively and positive who will live long and healthy lives. Instead of dreaming about the good old times and wishing that life was slower, they are doing their best to get up to speed with new technology because it's keeping them in touch and young.

It's attitude that counts the most – the attitude that keeps actress Joan Collins lively, beautiful and writing columns for the British intellectual magazine *The Spectator*.

Boomers (born 1940s to 1960s)

Boomers spent the first half of their lives ensuring that the world glorified youth. Now they will spend the second half of their lives ensuring that it glorifies old age. They are, quite simply, refusing to go 'gentle into that good night'. They are already, in poet Dylan Thomas' immortal words, raging 'against the dying of the light'.

And as some older (and younger) people sniff, they are doing a lot of things that would not have been considered age-appropriate a couple of decades ago. They won't stop rocking for a start. They started in their cots, rocking to Bill Haley and The Comets, carried on with Elvis Presley, sang themselves hoarse to, 'will you still need me, will you still feed me, when I'm 64?' with The Beatles, and gyrate their jeans-clad hips when 60-year-old Mick Jagger and the Rolling Stones, the most successful touring group in history scream, 'I can't get no satisfaction.' They're successful because the Boomers roll up in their many thousands, all over the world, to the Rolling Stones' concerts to recreate their youth. They are, after all, going to be eighteen for ever, 'in the summer of '69'.

In the advertising industry, where if you turn thirty-five they call you 'grandad' and out of touch with youth, they are having to redefine their mass market. Indeed, any company that doesn't have a campaign for the older generations is going to miss the next big boom market.

French actress Catherine Deneuve became the 'face' of French cosmetic house L'Oréal, at the age of sixty-seven. Four decades ago, women of that age were knitting jerseys for their grandchildren and darning socks. *Moulin Rouge* star Nicole Kidman has become the face of Chanel No 5 at the age of thirty-six. So, suddenly, a totally unwrinkled, baby face is no longer a prerequisite before you can 'face' an advertising campaign.

When Boomers decided something was 'the rage', like hula hoops, the whole world bought them. Likewise with miniskirts, Rubik's cube, flower power bell bottoms, Levi and Gap jeans.

Now that Boomers have decided not to age, the growth industries are cosmetic houses, gyms, hair care products ranging from rinses to dyes, and the health food industry. Vitamins, hormones, minerals and any other health and age-defying products are flying off drug store shelves. The Boomers are being Botoxed and facelifted in a manner that would have left Cleopatra swooning in her milk-filled bath. Men are not being left behind in the anti-age race either. They are dyeing their hair, having facelifts, slapping on nourishing face creams and ensuring the suntan lotion industry's turnover keeps on turning over. As we mentioned in chapter 18 on Health the prime minister of Italy, Silvio Berlusconi, spent a month out of sight having his facelift before emerging in January 2004 to show the world his new look.

The news that Boomers will have to go on working for far longer than they anticipated doesn't really bug them all that much. They are, after all, workaholics. The GI scenario of rusting away quietly at the coast in humble cottages was never their scene, anyhow. Too quiet. Too rusty. They like to sparkle and shine, and if it's in some spotlight somewhere, so much the better. After all, what's the point of having a bum-lift, fat suctioned out, and breast enhancement if there's nobody around to see the result.

No wonder South Africa's skin safaris are all the rage. The country's cosmetic surgeons, who are amongst the world's best, will lift, tuck, scrape and remould you, send what's left of you on a safari to mingle with the elephants and lions in total luxury. You return home younger than you've looked for years with most none the wiser for the reason.

Boomers are forgetting age appropriate behaviour, creating precedents and rewriting the ageing rule book. Take Bill Clinton, who was America's youngest ever ex-president. He's not following the example of other American ex-presidents who faded from the spotlight when their terms were over (with the possible exception of Jimmy Carter). Like so many Boomers, he's just redefining the role of an ex-president because the 'old' one doesn't suit him.

And, in typical Boomer style, this generation is redefining how age is described too. The average American today is living twenty-nine years longer than he did a century ago, but those years are being tacked on to 'middle age' not 'old age'.

Lydia Bronte, American author of *The Longevity Factor*, conducted a study of the careers of people aged over fifty. Almost half of the study participants had a major career peak after they hit their half century. Julia Child wrote *Mastering the Art of French Cooking* when she was almost fifty and her career took off. Nearly one third of Bronte's study participants had major career peaks after the age of sixty-five.

An interesting feature, written for the over-fifties who want to go on working, by Kate Windleton, president of the American 5 O'Clock Club, provides some interesting insights into how to sell 'age' to the workforce. She writes, 'Exploit your age and experience by saying you hope the company wants a mature person, someone who's been around the block.' Many companies, she says, are overrun by kids 'and want a few grey heads around to call on the big corporate clients. They also help the company avoid making the big mistakes.'

She adds, 'Appear energetic, talk about going skiing or hang-gliding.'

And, of course, that's increasingly what ageing people *are* doing. Richard Branson, one of the world's most famous entrepreneurs, is into age-defying exploits all the time. He runs his multibillion business from an island in the Caribbean where he manages his global companies from a beach hammock complete with laptop and cellphone. He best sums up the Boomer flash with his age-defying smile, long hair, 24/7 brain power, vision and charisma.

Boomers are into 're-tyrement' and not retirement. They are tuning their internal engines, rewiring their brains, oiling their biological body clocks and putting on new running shoes as they re-tyre for the future.

They're learning new working skills and planning how to make retirement work for them. In an age where youth is still revered in corporations, they are choosing different ways to work. A childhood friend of Sue's left the company where he was managing director when he was in his late forties, with three of his colleagues, to open a consultancy. Today they are so busy they need to contract in other consultants for experience and skills similar to their own. They work the hours and the way they want to.

Far from being 'washed up' on some retirement beach, they are surfing huge waves of success.

Xers (born 1960s to 1980s)

The Xers will live much, much longer than any generation before them due to biotechnology, nanotechnology and the extraordinary strides being made, almost on a daily basis, in medicine and medical technology. Who would have thought when South Africa's Professor Christiaan Barnard made history by having the raw courage to do the world's first heart transplant, that just over thirty years on, surgeons would begin transplanting an entire face.

Anybody who is under thirty years of age can now easily expect to celebrate their one hundredth birthday. Xers therefore don't plan to retire. The word simply doesn't exist in their vocabulary. They are doing what they love – creating a balance between work and leisure – so why would they want to stop working simply because they have turned sixty-five or some other arbitrary age?

Xers have a big problem in countries where retirement is largely government funded like America, Britain and Australia. Those countries have big social security systems, and the pension money in the state coffers is drying up. Many countries do not have pay-as-you-earn systems. Consequently, there is not enough money in the system to pay the pensions of the increasing numbers of retirees. They have always operated on the principle that there are more workers coming into the system than there are people retiring from it. But instead of saving today's workers' money to pay the pensions of Xers in the future, they are using the money to pay for people who are leaving the system **today.**

A much better way to fund retirement would be for each individual to pay for his own retirement by saving throughout his lifetime. That money you save would be the money you get when you finally shake the working dust off your feet. By diligent saving in such a manner, the pension system should not go bust unless there has been fraud or bad investment.

Some predict that social security in Britain and America will collapse in the future. So Boomers are fine for now. But, down the line Xers won't be and that is why so many people believe there will be generational clashes between the Boomers and Xers.

These two generations already rub each other up the wrong way because they think and operate from such different perspectives. Toss into the generational cooking pot the fact that Xers might have to fund Boomers' retirement and then end up with nothing left in the pot for themselves, and you have a big potential flashpoint.

As we've already said, Boomer politicians are trying to pretend that everything will work out fine in the future even though they know it's a nightmare situation. But it seems that some are adopting the approach of the French Sun King, Louis XIV, who said, 'après moi, la deluge' (after me, the deluge).

Some futurists are more optimistic and believe that age/youth lines are blurring and that, in the future, they are likely to become even more blurred as generations extend their shared love of The Beatles, Rolling Stones and jeans into other common areas.

The Economist commented in an editorial: 'If it is allowed to by governments, that trend ought in time to ease those conventional worries about too many pensioners and too few vigorous youthful workers, for the line between work and retirement ought also to fade as more people choose to carry on working, either full or part-time, well into their seventies or eighties. If that comes about, it will greatly ease the potentially divisive problem of an unequal tax burden as well as providing a welcome freedom of choice to the soon-to-be numerous old.'

Hopefully, this will transpire. However, one way that things might help with the pensions crisis and ageing, is the workplace attitude of Xers who, as you will see in chapter 13 on @ Work, are continually retooling themselves for ongoing different careers.

It's not unusual now for thirty-something American Xers to have had as many as eight different careers. Every time they make a change, they are learning new skills, a youthful form of re-tyrement which will continue well into their old age.

Millennials (born 1980s to 2000s)

Retirement will be out of date by the time the Millennials reach their sixties. It will be an unused word. If it hasn't been consigned to the Oxford English Dictionary rubbish dump, then it will only become relevant when this generation reach their eighties or nineties.

Saving for their own retirement will be vital. Millennials should choose savings schemes that are flexible and allow for both early and late access to funds without prejudice. Companies are increasingly accepting that Xers and Millennials want freedom and flexibility. In the future many of them will encourage those Millennials who don't want to be constrained by prescribed company-managed pension schemes.

20

Finances

Attitude to money:

GIs:	Save it to leave to my children.
Silents:	Save it for a rainy day.
Boomers:	Something I'll always owe the bank.
Xers:	A means to an end – not an end in itself.
Millennials:	Use it to change the world.

Financial advice for your current lifestage:

GIs

Those of you who have been wise enough to live frugal, careful lives will have few worries. You are into your eighties and nineties so most of you are no longer working. You will need to save every cent you have and invest it wisely. Only let people you feel you can fully trust handle your precious retirement nest egg. This particularly applies to women. They vastly outnumber male old age pensioners and are extremely vulnerable to charlatans and crooks with flashy smiles at this stage of their lives. Unfortunately, this sometimes includes your children, who are only too willing to accept the inheritance you are unwisely offering them while you still need it. The tendency to live much longer lives and rapidly rising medical costs are just two cogent reasons why you need to hold on to your money. SKI (Spend Kid's Inheritance) most certainly applies to you unless you are a Getty, Rothschild, Vanderbilt or have famous movie or soccer star children.

Silents

You are the youngest, richest, healthiest generation ever to retire. You need to resist the urge to splash out one more time on a last ditch attempt to make money. Your generation often uses its hard earned pension or savings to buy a coffee shop or a failing company when you have little or no knowledge of the business you're buying. It's the fast route to financial ruin, don't go there. Take your savings, invest them wisely, and try to live off the interest, as far as possible, digging into capital only if there's an emergency. If you have a bit extra, enjoy it with your children and grandchildren. Do it together. That way you know your money is well spent. The stories of profligate Boomer children, now in their forties and fifties, spending their parents' inheritances are legion and sad. Many of you in your sixties and seventies are still working. Well done. There's a worldwide skills shortage and a growing number of companies are happy to keep on older and experienced staff. You need all the money you can save, so go for it.

Boomers

There's one dictum for you and that is: get out of debt. Do it now. You are the conspicuous consumption, the wear-the-label-on-the-outside, the keeping up with the Joneses, generation. And it shows ... in your unhealthy bank balance. Your parents spoilt you and you've never got over it, continuing the spending splurge on yourselves into midlife. The fast car, the holiday house, the yacht and even your home, probably don't belong to you because you're still paying them off. Furthermore, they are not the assets you so fondly assume them to be for the simple reason that they are not generating any income for you. Something is only an asset when it creates money for you. The chances are you are actually spending money on the items listed above. Get rid of them and start earning, instead of spending money in order to turn the colour of your bank balance into black instead of red. Only when you can pay cash can you afford those luxuries.

Xers

Think, and plan, long term. You're going to live longer than anybody before you ever has. Extreme sports and fancy cars won't last for ever. Realise that most people live just two months away from bankruptcy, with few accessible savings, and if that includes you, then the flexibility and freedom you value so highly might vanish virtually overnight. Ensure that you have at least six months' salary available in a call account. Put aside at least 15 per cent of your salary every month as long-term savings. This is of vital importance because your generation will be the first to fully experience the present pensions crisis (see chapter 19 Re-tyreing). Be 'boring' and safe with your money. Accept there just are not any 'get rich quick' schemes.

Millennials

Realise now that the label, the brand, the pop star's name on your expensive sunglasses or shirt will not buy you happiness, love or ensure success in life. Only feeling good about yourself from the inside out will do that. Your best investment is in self-education and self-growth. If you feel good about you, if you have a healthy self-esteem, then you will walk into companies where others find closed doors. You will set up and run your own businesses, make your own money, and own your homes because you've invested in the most important person in your life – you. Once you've done that, as a civic minded Millennial, you'll soon be helping your community, and the world.

For more details on generations and money read *Mind Over Money*, Penguin, 2002, written by Graeme Codrington, Sue Grant-Marshall and Louis Fourie.

21

The Generations @ home

Decor:

GIs:	Conformist – same as everyone else.
Silents:	Smart entrance hall but 30-year-old chairs inside (cost conscious).
Boomers:	Hire a well-known decor expert.
Xers:	Comfy couch.
Millennials:	Too young to own homes yet but will follow trendy designs.

Food:

GIs:	Served by the butler.
Silents:	Roast and three vegetables.
Boomers:	How many calories?
Xers:	Microwave culture.
Millennials:	Takeaway organic foods.

Fashion:

GIs:	Conformist (men). Flapper (women).
Silents:	Suit and tie (men). Twinset and pearls (women).
Boomers:	Designer labels. Too tight. Too small.
Xers:	Baggy, layered, grungy. Jeans halfway down their backsides.
Millennials:	Brand fanatical. Board shorts. Androgynous.

Music:

GIs:	Classical. Opera. Sing-along.
Silents:	Big Band era. Glenn Miller. Frank Sinatra.

Boomers:	Rock 'n' Roll. Elvis. The Beatles. Rolling Stones.
Xers:	Grunge, dark. Kurt Cobain. Sheryl Crowe. Alanis Morissette.
Millennials:	Tuneful: Jennifer Lopez. Britney Spears. Shania Twain. Christina Aguilera.

Music should be:

GIs:	Soothing or militaristic (bands).
Silents:	Melodic, harmonious, ballroom.
Boomers:	Loud, brash, fast. Irritate parents.
Xers:	Dark, sombre, intuitive, moody. Irritate parents.
Millennials:	Fun, lively, vibrant. It's irritating that our parents love it too.

Fun and leisure time:

GIs:	With family, around the piano or open fireplace.
Silents:	Tennis, birdwatching, fishing, listening to the wireless.
Boomers:	Must be in control, so horse riding, go-carting, motorbikes, fast cars.
Xers:	Could die doing it. Canyoning, bungee jumping, white river rafting.
Millennials:	Computer games, surfing the Internet.

Toilets:

GIs:	Away from the home, in a little outhouse that is beloved by snakes and spiders in hot countries.
Silents:	Moved into homes as suburban bliss arrived with improved plumbing. Only one per home.
Boomers:	Up to three in a home and main bedroom en suite. Bathrooms became high fashion items.

Xers:	In Ally McBeal, men and women shared toilets, and horrified GIs and Silents.
Millennials:	Watch this generation create some sort of biotechnology that turns waste into energy @ home.
Fact	In the late 1990s, research showed that 98.5 per cent of American homes had a TV set whereas only 96 per cent had flushing toilets. Some quipped, 'There's more junk going into, instead of out of, American homes.'

22

Travelling with the Generations

GIs (born 1900s to 1920s)

It is quite extraordinary to realise that there are people alive today who were born before airplanes were built, and who, in their young years, could not have conceived of people flying. Birds flew. And insects. That was it. Most GIs had childhoods without tarred roads. They hopped out of cars to shoo cattle off dirt tracks and to open gates between farms. There were no national roads and cars had to make their way carefully along roads that were dominated by horses and carriages. It was during the GI's youth that Henry Ford famously perfected the production line and churned out the Model T Ford, the first car to be mass-produced. At the height of production, a Model T was being rolled off the line every ninety seconds. The GIs were young adults when the next legendary mass-produced car arrived, commissioned by Adolf Hitler. It was the VW Beetle or Volkswagen, 'the people's car', and it has lasted their entire lifetime. It was only decommissioned in 2003 with the last one rolling off the line in South America.

This generation's early concept of travel was a trip to the next town or not much further than the border of their own state or province. Steam trains were what you boarded for a long journey and they chugged their way across continents under massive plumes of white smoke. GIs crossed the seas on ships and doing so was an adventure. Many a GI who set sail from Great Britain to one of the colonies would do so on a mail ship which enabled travellers to obtain cheaper fares than the more luxurious passenger liners.

An overseas trip, by its very nature, inferred an extended period of time away, either on a tour of duty (work) or to a new job. If GIs went on a cricket or rugby tour or to the Olympics, it meant being away from home for months.

Silents (born 1920s to 1940s)

They grew up in a similar environment to the GIs and they, too, have memories of crossing the ocean on mail ships in order to get to foreign lands. During their young adulthood, cars became more accessible to the middle classes. Trams and buses were introduced for mass transportation and cities like London, Paris and New York built underground train systems. As youngsters, the concept of air travel being eventually available to all was discussed, but at that stage it was still mainly for the rich and famous. Many a Silent can remember the first time a plane flew overhead or landed in a nearby village, field or town. Air passengers who flew great distances, for example, from London to Johannesburg, spent three days en route, stopping frequently to refuel and to overnight in grand hotels with white linen tablecloths and butlers.

Boomers (born 1940s to 1960s)

This generation experienced a massive change in transport. During the 1960s and 70s at a local and regional level the first massive highways were built. The interstate system was built in America. In Britain, Australia and South Africa, highways, freeways and motorways were built to open up the interior and to move many people in the rapidly growing car population. America had already moved to the two-car family but the rest of the world was content with one. Tar roads became the norm as suburbs were built to accommodate the booming Boomers with great tracts of land laid out with tar strips and electricity poles. Cars became an expression of personality, colours other than black were introduced, and American family cars featured massive interiors and huge gas tanks that guzzled petrol at 10 cents a gallon.

Cars became status symbols for the middle class. During the 1960s and 70s, as soon as young Boomers acquired a driver's licence they wanted a car of their own. Middle-aged Boomers are now driving massive SUVs and 4X4s that guzzle fuel but seldom get dirt on their tyres, requiring 'designer dust' to lend the necessary air of authenticity.

Internationally, Boomers were the first generation to have the opportunity and the potential to take a holiday anywhere in the world. They can stick a pin just about anywhere on a map of the world, and, if they've saved enough money, they can make their way at a reasonable price to that spot.

Business travel has enabled Boomers to fulfil their desire to have face to face meetings, the latter forming a huge component of the international airline industry's turnover.

Boomers saw the first astronauts in space and have recently become the first space tourists. Their travel horizons are limitless.

Xers (born 1960s to 1980s)

As they have grown up, so the price of international air travel has plummeted, especially as they hit their twenties in the 1990s and the no-frills discount airlines began to take off. The latter used out of date planes from national carrier's fleets, refurbished them and, taking off at odd hours from small airports situated some distance from big towns and cities, were able to make flying accessible to just about anybody. In Britain, some fares to the continent are as low as one pound. Some Xers fly from London to Rome to do shopping and return the same day. In fact, airlines have turned into buses in the sky, transforming what used to be a really glamorous industry with beautiful young air hostesses and uniformed pilots, into a utilitarian mode of travel.

Teenage Xers most definitely expect to have a car the moment they get their licence with the result that many of the world's great cities are gridlocked by traffic. Many are introducing tolls to try and force people to use public transport and to carry more than one person in a car. Clogged roads and high death tolls are by-products of the car generation.

Xers are the first generation to grow up with consistent childhood memories of hopping into a car in the morning, driving to the beach for the day and returning home at night. They are also the first to regard a summer holiday far away from home as normal. Boomers regarded it as a privilege. And although many a Boomer spent a year or two overseas after completing their education, it is Xers who have coined the term 'overseas experience' or 'OE' and now regard it as standard practice. Easy, cheap travel and working overseas are taken for granted by them.

Xer businesspeople have taken travel for work purposes to new lengths, working on their laptops as they fly, and walking straight into business meetings on arrival.

Millennials (born 1980s to 2000s)

They will be the most travelled generation of all time. They regard taking a boat or train trip as something you do purely for fun and romance, or they wouldn't use them, and they are becoming expensive compared with air travel. In London you pay four pounds for a day ticket on the underground whereas you can fly from Gatwick to Prague for one pound.

Millennials regard it as odd if there is only one family car and fully expect to have their own the moment they reach driving age.

International travel has become commonplace for some, with kids as young as ten rattling off the names of five continents they have visited to their class teacher. Unlike GIs or Silents, who probably kept a record of every trip they took, Millennials are so accustomed to flying that they can recognise different planes from the age of five years.

Millennials will probably see seriously new forms of travel in their lifetime with supersonic airplanes arriving at any airport in the world, no matter the distance, within a few hours of take-off. It won't be too long before aircraft will have onboard shops, massage lounges and gyms in an effort to get away from the 'cattle truck' syndrome.

New developments in airlines and tourism will be the growing increase in space travel as governments open up their space agencies to take tourists in order to make themselves some money to fund their space programmes. But private companies will also finally develop the technology to put people into space, even if it is only a low orbit, and space travel will become something that's not just reserved for astronauts.

In the process, the generations come full circle. As the GIs regarded planes with wonderment and saw only the rich and famous using them, so Millennials now assume that spaceships, rockets and shuttles will only be used by the wealthy and high profile personalities. But as life changed rapidly for the GIs so it will for the Millennials too. American president, Boomer George W Bush, intends to have a manned space station on the moon and astronauts heading off to Mars. These are likely to be Millennial astronauts. It's perhaps not too far-fetched to imagine that Millennials will regard space travel and a holiday on the moon or on Mars as standard practice.

Future generations

They will be able to do virtual travelling by putting a virtual reality helmet on and experiencing the sights, sounds and smells of exotic locations. Travel agents will develop virtual tours in their efforts to entice people to do the real thing.

Maybe, too, one day, we will be able to transfer people at a sub-atomic level. Today, nothing seems impossible and it's not inconceivable that the Boomers' iconic *Star Trek*, with Beam-me-up-Scotty's machine that can transfer you atom by atom from one place to another in a nanosecond, might become reality.

Flight:

GIs: First generation to accept that people could fly. Had the same view of it we reserve for astronauts today – it was only for the rich and daring.

Silents: Mainly for the military, the rich and famous. The 'romance' died as the Hindenburg airship came crashing down in flames. Gradually accepted airplanes as a viable means of passenger transportation.

Boomers: Travel by air became accessible to virtually everybody and jets became normal passenger planes. Flying, initially, was romantic and air hostesses had to be pretty. Concorde was a dream come true. Boomers watched the first space flights as children and regard them almost as commonplace now.

Xers: The 'romance' of space flight died when Challenger blew up off Cape Canaveral. Airplane hijackings also robbed flight of its gilt. 'No frills' airlines have confirmed what they all knew – planes are glorified cattle trucks.

Millennials: The first generation for whom space travel will be available to the rich and famous. Maybe in their lifetime they will see 'no frills' space flights to the moon.

The lesson of the generations, as we have shown here, is that what one generation only dreams about, and often scoffs at the possibility of it ever happening, does indeed happen *and* in their lifetime.

What Next?

The Next generation:

The purpose of this book is not to predict the future. But if generation theory is cyclical, as Strauss and Howe have suggested, and as our view of the GIs and Millennials suggests, then the next generation, to be born during the next twenty years, will probably strongly resemble the Silent generation. The generations cycle is driven by an underlying historical cycle of a crisis, followed by an 'outer driven' era, followed by an unravelling of the idealistic dreams of that era, followed by an 'inner driven' era, which results in another crisis.

This theory predicts that a global crisis that will make society 'stop' and deal with the issue, and then put itself back together in a different way, is due between 2010 and 2015. There is no shortage of crises from which to choose. They range from the financial meltdown of world markets to the ecological collapse of the planet and ozone layer, to another world war that might even involve nuclear weapons. It could be a nuclear or biological accident. Maybe it could be acceptance of the first human clone. Any one of these could constitute a global crisis that changes the way people live.

Children born during a crisis look for stability and predictability. They grow up in a chaotic world where chaos is bad, and order, structure, predictability and security are all seen as good. Like the Silent generation before them, these children will grow up to be reactive, instead of proactive. They'll be cautious and withdrawn, patient and conservative. Howe and Strauss have labelled them the Adaptive generation.

We'll have to wait and see...

23

Concluding the Generations

... so what?

You're probably asking yourself, so where do I go from here? I know which generation I am from and those of some of my friends and family. Even some of my work colleagues. But, so what! We'll answer that in a moment. Let's first address the concerns of those who feel that they've had no blinding flashes of revelation into what makes them tick as a generation. We've not captured your tough aunt or your dizzy cousin. It's possible you've arrived here thinking that generational theory is a facile concept. That it is too simplistic.

Well, we warned you upfront that it is a generalisation that would not apply to every person, in every country in the world. There are, after all, six billion people on the planet, each one of whom is a complex individual with special needs and dreams.

But, we repeat, the world is divided into only two sexes. Yet the generalisations and stereotypes, like men are from Mars and women are from Venus, have created millions of jokes, songs, books and poems down the generations.

Increasingly, there are generational songs and we end this book with one. Books on the different generations are starting to jostle for space on American bookshelves. We predict that bookshops will soon be adding a 'generations' section to 'food, health, business' etc.

Most of us will agree that there have been pivotal moments in our lives that we will never forget. They remain scorched into the fabric of our lives and those of the people with whom we shared them. The moment you realised that daddy was Father Christmas. The day you got your pet puppy and the night your dog died. Your little boy's first day at big school. That scary, joyous second in which the keys to your own home were pressed into your hand. The week your mother died and the dear friends who came to help you get through it. Your daughter's wedding day.

You have a bond with those who shared the moments with you. And so it is with generations who are, in a way, like extended families because they experience moments and times with you. Maybe you don't remember where you were and who you were with when Princess Diana or John F Kennedy died, or Neil Armstrong walked on the moon or midnight at the new millennium when we thought the world's computers would crash.

But many others do. And, because they grew up together being taught, parented, fed, medicated, in the same way, that common experience has bonded them. It has done so on a community, local, regional, national and, now, international level as the world continues to shrink into a global village.

We're the first to point out that we need to be wary of lumping everybody together just because they share a generation. Xers have grown up in the era of fast food but it doesn't mean they eat exclusively at McDonald's or Kentucky Fried Chicken or pizza parlours. You'd need your head read if you took your Xers to McDonald's for the Christmas party. Many of them only eat at the best restaurants in town.

Sue's Silent husband and Millennial daughter share a passion for Meat Loaf's music. That's quite some generation spanning. But get them on the topic of how best to study, or which movie to see, and they're generations apart again.

Those differences are particularly stark in the workplace because it's a more structured environment. There we rely on organisation and rules to make the place run smoothly. Only it's Boomers who are calling most of the shots right now and the 'hang loose' Xers want you to 'cut me some slack' and be more flexible. Soon the confident Millennials who can speak their minds, politely but firmly, will arrive at work and not be scared to tell you what they think. They know that you know that they know more than you do about technology and are therefore closer to the future than are Boomers.

Listen to them. They don't mean to be cheeky. They only want to share their knowledge.

You could learn to understand them by discussing generational issues at work. Try creating cross generational groups and give them the space and the time to discuss their passions, ambitions and preferred way of working.

Use our book to generate topics.

It's been impossible for us to apply generational thinking to everything. Life's too complex for that. What we've tried to do in the book is give you the broadest outline of generational thinking that we could by using examples from different life stages. We don't suggest you turn to just one section or chapter and blindly apply the few bulleted tips we've included.

We'd prefer you to understand, more broadly, why the generational cycle exists, how it has developed and what effect it has on the way people react in different situations, ranging from your family to global issues.

You could start by chatting as a family or to close friends about what life was like when you were young. Listen to the stories and use the categories that we have used in this book to guide your discussions and storytelling. As you listen, try to gain an understanding of the forces that shaped each person in the group and then trace how those forces still have an effect on them today.

Do the same in schools, churches and at work.

You will be surprised at how much better you understand why your family, friends and colleagues behave the way they do.

In the middle of writing this book, Sue returned to her mother's home, in London, England. A stroke has deprived her mother of speech and, as she shares the Silent generation's characteristic of being 'silent' and not talking about the sad, tough times, Sue realised she would have to sift through the dust of many decades herself.

She is learning about the events that shaped her mother's Blitz-torn childhood. She's understanding the forces that shaped her own.

The generational forces.

The generation gap.

Mind the gap!

Every generation
Blames the one before
And all of their frustrations
Come beating on your door

I know that I'm a prisoner
To all my Father held so dear
I know that I'm a hostage
To all his hopes and fears
I just wish I could have told him in the living years

Crumpled bits of paper
Filled with imperfect thought
Stilted conversations
I'm afraid that's all we've got

You say you just don't see it
He says it's perfect sense
You just can't get agreement
In this present tense
We all talk a different language
Talking in defence

Say it loud, say it clear
You can listen as well as you hear
It's too late when we die
To admit we don't see eye to eye

So we open up a quarrel
Between the present and the past
We only sacrifice the future
It's the bitterness that lasts

So don't yield to the fortunes
You sometimes see as fate
It may have a new perspective
On a different day
And if you don't give up, and don't give in
You may just be OK.

Say it loud, say it clear
You can listen as well as you hear
It's too late when we die
To admit we don't see eye to eye

I wasn't there that morning
When my Father passed away
I didn't get to tell him
All the things I had to say

I think I caught his spirit
Later that same year
I'm sure I heard his echo
In my baby's new born tears
I just wish I could have told him in the living years

Say it loud, say it clear
You can listen as well as you hear
It's too late when we die
To admit we don't see eye to eye

The Living Years
By Mike and the Mechanics

24

Bibliography and further reading

Books

Ackoff, Russell. *Re-Creating the Corporation*. Oxford University Press 1999.

Armour, Michael C and Don Browning. *Systems-Sensitive Leadership*. Joplin: College Press Publishing Company 1995.

Badaracco, Joseph, Jr. *Leading Quietly*. Harvard Business School Press 2002.

Barker, Joel Arthur. *Paradigms*. HarperBusiness Edition, New York: HarperBusiness 1993.

Barna, George. *Baby Busters*. Revised Edition. Chicago: Northfield Publishing 1994.

Barna, George. *Generation Next*. Ventura: Regal Books 1995.

Barna, George and Mark Hatch. *Boiling Point, It Only Takes One Degree. Monitoring Cultural Shifts in the 21st century*. Ventura: Regal Books 2001.

Bennis, Warren G and Robert J Thomas. *Geeks & Geezers: How Era, Values and Defining Moments Shape Leaders*. Harvard Business School Press 2002.

Brown, Stephen. *Free Gift Inside: Forget the Customer. Develop Marketease*. Chichester: Capstone 2003.

Brudney, Jeffery L. *Fostering Volunteer Programs in the Public Sector*. Jossey-Bass 1990.

Celek, Tim and Dieter Zander. *Inside the Soul of a New Generation*. Grand Rapids: Zondervan 1996.

Chernow, Fred. *The Sharper Mind: Mental Games for a Keen Mind and a Foolproof Memory*. Reissue edition. Prentice Hall 2001.

Chester, Eric. *Employing Generation Why?* Colorado: Tucker House Books 2002.

Chowdhury, Subir (editor). *Organisation 21C*. Financial Times/ Prentice Hall 2003.

Christian, Jeffrey. *The Most Important Thing You'll Ever Do: Finding and keeping the best people for the job*. London: Piatkus 2002.

Collins, James and Jerry Porras. *Built to Last*. Random House 2000.

Coupland, Douglas. *Generation X*. British Edition. London: Abacus 1992.

Covey, Stephen. *Principle-Centered Leadership*. Simon & Schuster 1991.

Drucker, Peter. *Managing the Nonprofit Organization: Practices and Principles*. Harper Collins 1990.

Davidson, James Dale and William Rees-Mogg. *The Sovereign Individual*. London: Pan Books 1998.

Dixon, Patrick. *Futurewise: six faces of global change*. Second edition. London: Harper Collins 2000.

Drucker, Peter. *The Five Most Important Questions You Will Ever Ask About Your Nonprofit Organization*. The Drucker Foundation. Jossey-Bass Publishers 1993.

Drucker, Peter F. *Managing in a Time of Great Change*. New York: Truman Talley Books/Plume 1995.

Drucker, Peter. *Excellence in Non-Profit Leadership*. Jossey-Bass Publishers 1998.

Drucker, Peter. *Management Challenges for the 21st Century*. HarperBusiness 1999.

Drucker, Peter. *Managing in the Next Society*. Butterworth/ Heineman 2002.

Dychtwald, Ken. *Age Power*. New York: Putnam 1999.

Easum, Bill. *Leadership on the Other Side: No Rules, Just Clues*. Abingdon Press 2000.

Elkind, David. *All Grown Up and No Place To Go – Teenagers In Crisis*. Reading: Addison-Wesley 1984.

Ezzo, Gary and Robert Buckham. *On Becoming Childwise: Parenting Your Child from 3 to 7 Years*. Hawks Flight & Association 2001.

Ford, Kevin. *Jesus for a New Generation*. London: Hodder & Stoughton 1996.

Fourie, Louis, Graeme Codrington and Sue Grant-Marshall. *Mind Over Money*. Johannesburg: Penguin 2002.

Friedman, Barbara M. *Connecting Generations*. Boston: Allen and Bacon 1999.

Gladwell, Malcolm. *The Tipping Point: How Little Things Can Make a Big Difference*. Boston: Little, Brown and Company 2002.

Goldsmith, Russell. *Viral Marketing: Make People Your Willing Advocates*. London: FT Prentice Hall 2002.

Greenfield, Susan. *Tomorrow's People: How 21st Century Technology Is Changing the Way We Think and Feel*. Allen Lane 2003.

Handy, Charles. *The Empty Raincoat*. Hutchinson Radius 1994.

Handy, Charles. *Beyond Certainty*. Harvard Business School Press 1998.

Handy, Charles. *The Hungry Spirit*. Broadway Books 1999.

Handy, Charles. *The Elephant and the Flea*. London: Hutchinson 2001.

Heifetz, Ronald A. *Leadership Without Easy Answers*. Harvard University Press 1994.

Hesselbein, Frances, Marshall Goldsmith and Richard Beckhard (editors). *The Leader of the Future*. The Drucker Foundation. Jossey-Bass Publishers 1996.

Hesselbein, Frances, Marshall Goldsmith and Richard Beckhard (editors). *The Organization of the Future*. The Drucker Foundation. Jossey-Bass Publishers 1997.

Hicks, Dr Rick and Kathy Hicks. *Boomers, Xers and Other Strangers: Understanding the Generational Differences that Divide Us*. Wheaton: Tyndale 1999.

Himanen, Pekka. *The H@cker Ethic*. New York: Random House 2001.

Humphreys, Tony. *Work and Worth*. Dublin: Newleaf 2000.

Hutchcraft, Ron and Lisa Hutchcraft Whitmer. *The Battle for a Generation*. Chicago: Moody Press 1996.

Jensen, Rolf. *The Dream Society*. McGraw-Hill, 1999.

Karp, Hank, Connie Fuller and Danilo Sirias. *Bridging the Boomer Xer Gap*. Palo Alto: Davies Black Publishing 2002.

Kaye, Beverly and Sharon Jordan-Evans. *Love 'Em or Lose 'Em: Getting Good People to Stay*. San Francisco: Berrett-Koehler Publishers 1999.

Kingson, Eric R, Barbara A Hishorn and John M Cornham. *Ties that Bind: The Interdependence of Generations*. Washington: Seven Locks Press 1986.

Lancaster, Lynne C and David Stillman. *When Generations Collide*. New York: HarperBusiness 2002.

Leifer, Loring and Michael McLarney. *Younger Voices, Stronger Choices*. Kansas City: Kansas City Consensus 1997.

Lindstrom, Martin. *Brandchild*. London: Kogan Page 2003.

Marías, Julían. *Generations: A Historical Method*. Trans. Harold Raley. Alabama: Alabama University Press 1970.

Martin, Carolyn A and Bruce Tulgan. *Managing Generation Y*. Amherst: HRD Press 2001.

Martin, Carolyn A and Bruce Tulgan. *Managing the Generation Mix: From Collision to Collaboration*. Amherst: HRD Press 2002.

Martz, Sandra and Shirley Coe. *Generation to Generation*. Watsonville: Papier-Mache Press 1998.

McAllister, Dawson. *Saving the Millennial Generation*. Nashville: Thomas Nelson 1999.

McIntosh, Gary L. *Three Generations*. Grand Rapids: Fleming H Revell 1995.

McIntosh, Gary L. *Make Room for the Boom... or Bust*. Grand Rapids: Baker 1997.

Mead, Margaret. *Culture and Commitment*. New York: Doubleday/Natural History Press 1970.

Muchnick, Marc. *Naked Management: Bare Essentials for Motivating the X-Generation at Work*. Boca Raton: St Lucie Press 1996.

Mueller, Walt. *Understanding Today's Youth Culture*. Wheaton: Tyndale House 1994.

Newman, Sally, et al. *Intergenerational Programs: Past, Present, and Future*. Washington: Taylor and Francis 1997.

Norris, Joan E and Joseph A Tindale. *Among Generations*. New York: W. H. Freeman and Company 1994.

Petzinger, Thomas, Jr. *The New Pioneers: The men and women who are transforming the workplace and marketplace*. New York: Touchstone 2000.

Popcorn, Faith and Lys Marigold. *Clicking*. New York: HarperCollins 1997.

Rabey, Steve. *In Search of Authentic Faith: How the Emerging Generations are Reshaping the Church*. Waterbrook Press 2001.

Rainer, Thom S. *The Bridger Generation*. Nashville: Broadman & Holman 1998.

Raines, Claire. *Beyond Generation X*. Menlo Park: Crisp Publications 1997.

Raines, Claire and Jim Hunt. *The Xers and the Boomers*. Crisp Publications 2000.

Regele, Mike and Mark Schulz. *Death of the Church*. Grand Rapids: Zondervan 1995.

Ridderstråle, Jonas and Kjelle Nordström. *Funky Business*. Second edition. London: FT Prentice Hall 2002.

Ritchie, Karen. *Marketing to Generation X*. New York: The Free Press 1995.

Robbins, SP, A Odendaal and G Roodt. *Organisational Behaviour: Global and Southern African Perspectives*. Pearson Education, South Africa, Cape Town 2003.

Rushkoff, Douglas. *Playing the Future*. (Also known as *Children of Chaos*). New York: Harper Collins 1996.

Seefeldt, Carol and Barbara Warman, et al. *Young and Old Together*. Washington: National Association for the Education of Young Children 1990.

Semler, Ricardo. *The Seven-Day Weekend*. London: Century 2003.

Senter, Mark, III. *The Coming Revolution in Youth Ministry and its Radical Impact on the Church*. USA: Victor Books 1992.

Sheleff, Leon. *Generations Apart*. New York: McGraw-Hill 1981.

Smith, J Walker and Ann Clurman. *Rocking the Ages: The Yankelovich Report on Generational Marketing*. New York: HarperBusiness 1997.

Stillman, David and Lynne C Lancaster. *When Generations Collide*. HarperBusiness 2002.

Strauss, William and Neil Howe. *Generations*. New York: William Morrow 1991.

Strauss, William and Neil Howe. *13th Gen: Abort, Retry, Ignore, Fail?* New York: Vintage Books 1993.

Strauss, William and Neil Howe. *The Fourth Turning*. New York: Broadway Books 1997.

Strauss, William and Neil Howe. *Millennials Rising*. New York: Vintage Books 2000.

Tapscott, Don. *Growing Up Digital*. New York: McGraw-Hill 1998.

Thau, Richard D and Jay S Heflin. *Generations Apart*. Amherst: Prometheus 1997.

Toffler, Alvin. *Future Shock*. London: Bantam Books 1970.

Toffler, Alvin. *Power Shift*. London: Bantam Books 1991.

Tulgan, Bruce. *Managing Generation X*. Santa Monica: Merritt Publishing 1995.

Tulgan, Bruce. *Work This Way*. New York: Hyperion 1998.

Tulgan, Bruce. *Winning the Talent Wars*. New York: W. W. Norton & Company 2002.

Van Zyl Slabbert, F, et al (editors). *Youth in the New South Africa*. Pretoria: HSRC 1994.

Wacker, Watts and Jim Taylor, with Howard Means. *The 500 Delta: What Happens After What Comes Next*. Paperback Edition. New York: HarperCollins 1998.

Wheatley, Margaret J. *Leadership and the New Science*. San Francisco: Berrett-Koehler Publishers 1999.

Zemke, Ron and Claire Raines. *Generations at Work: Managing the Clash of Veterans, Boomers, Xers, and Nexters in Your Workplace*. AMACOM 2000.

Articles

Aeschliman, Gordon. 'Generation X: Will the Church be in their future?' In *Prism*, May 1994, pp. 12-16.

Brinkley, Douglas. "Educating the Generation Called 'X.'" [Online] At: http://www.tomorrowtoday.biz/generations/xpaper2009.htm

Cobb, Nathan. 'Generations 2000: Meet Tomorrow's Teens.' In *The Boston Globe*, 28 April 1998. [Online] At: http://home.pix.za/gc/gc12/papers/p2020.htm

Codrington, Graeme and Kathryn Robinson. 'Generations and Advertising Literacy.' SAMRA Convention, 2002.

Available: http://www.tomorrowtoday.biz/generations/samra

Heskett, James L and Leonard A Schlesinger. 'Leading the high-capability organization: Challenges for the twenty-first century.' In *Human Resource Management*, Spring 97, Vol. 36 Issue 1, p105.

Mueller, Walt. 'Generation X Marks Its Spot.' In *Center For Parent/Youth Understanding Newsletter*, Fall, 1996. [Online] At: http://www.cpyu.org/news/96falll.html

Neuborne, Ellen. 'Generation Y.' In *Businessweek Online*, February 15, 1999. [Online] At: http://www.businessweek.com/1999/99_07/b3616001.htm

Payne, Stephen L. and Barbara Holmes. 'Communication Challenges for Management Faculty involving younger "Generation X" students in their classes.' In *Journal of Management Education*, June 1998. [Online] At: http://www.epnet.com

Popiel, Stephen and Paul Fairlie. 'Generation X: The Social Values of Canadian Youth.' In *Canadian Journal of Marketing Research*. Vol. 15, 1996, pp. 11-22.

Ward, Arian. 'Getting strategic value from constellations of communities.' In *Strategy & Leadership*, Vol. 28 Issue 2, 2000, p. 4.

Zimmerman, John C. 'Leadership Across the Gaps Between Generations.' In *Crux*. Vol. 31, No. 2, June 1995, pp. 42-54.

Zoba, Wendy Murray. 'The Class of "00." ' In *Christianity Today*, Vol. 41, No. 2, February 3, 1997, p. 18. [Online] At: http://www.christianity.net/ct/7T2/7T218a.html

Published articles in the popular media

'A billion boomers.' *The Economist*, 11 October 2003

Boyle, Matthew. 'thirtynothing.' *Fortune*, 18 February 2002

Cochrane, Kira. 'With a single lifestyle leap I was free.' *The Sunday Times*, London, 23 Febuary 2003

Colvin, Geoffrey. 'Worrying about jobs isn't productive.' *Fortune*, 10 November 2003. 'Over 60 and overlooked.' *The Economist*, 10 August, 2002

Craig, Olga. 'Silicon Valley up for sale.' *The Telegraph*, London, 4 August 2002

Cunningham, Tessa. 'Why my son does not need a father.' *UK Mail*. (undated)

Dai, Limin. 'Back to school the international way.' *Financial Times*, London, 21 September 2002

David, Grainger. 'Aren't you boomers ever going away?' *Fortune*, 7 January 2001

Docx, Edward. 'Small wonder politics bores young cynics of Spin Generation.' *International Express*, 6 October 1998

Dodd, Alex. 'A new family of friends.' *Cosmopolitan* (SA), December 1997

Etherington, Jan. 'Why the baby boomers are throwing their cash around.' 6 August 2002

'Families without kids.' *The Economist*, 27 November 1999

'Fathers of the Revolution.' *The Telegraph*, London, 24 March 2002

Geary, James. 'Childhood's end?' *Time*, 2 August 1999

Gerrard, Nicci. 'The Tyranny of thin.' *Sunday Times* (SA), 19 January 2003

'Going up in Smoke.' *Daily Mail*, London, 30 January 2003

Grimston, Jack. 'Hidden ills of the snack pack.' *The Sunday Times*, London, 4 May 2003

Groskop, Viv. 'Girls who dared strip nudity of its scandal.' *International Express*, 21 October 2003

Harris, Sarah. 'What's happened to the age of innocence?' *The Star* (SA,) 31 July 2003

Heathcote, Elizabeth. 'Fat of the land will rule 100 years from now.' *Sunday Independent* (SA), 10 November 2002

Iritani, Evelyn. 'Single-child policy creating a strong but ego-centred generation.' *Los Angeles Times*, 10 August 2003

Jones, Dylan. 'Myth of super dad.' *The Sunday Times*, London, 13 April 2003

Knight, India. 'And baby makes 1.64.' *The Sunday Times*, London, 15 December 2002

Knight, India. 'Be honest with us, Daddy.' *The Sunday Times*, London, 19 January 2003

Knight, India. 'Keep on working, mum.' *The Sunday Times*, London, 9 March 2003

Knight, India. 'Leave the money and run.' *The Sunday Times*, London, 30 March 2003

Lancaster, David. 'Hell's Angels seen off by Harley's Baby Boomers.' *International Express*, 8 May 2001

Martin, Jurek. 'Behind the Second Bush.' *Financial Mail* (SA), 28 March 2003

Matthews, Charlotte. 'Bornfrees hold purse strings.' *Sunday Times* (SA), 3 November 2003

Morlarty, Richard. 'Homework ruins family life.' *International Express*, 14 October 2003

Mlangeni, Bongiwe. 'SA kids want it all – and they want it now.' *Sunday Times* (SA), 5 October 2003

Naude, C. 'The Virtual classroom is a reality.' *Finance Week*, 25 January 2002

Ntshingila, Futhi. 'Teens today are a world apart from those of 1976. *Sunday Times* (SA), 15 June 2003

Overell, Stephen. 'Who cares what the customer wants?' *Financial Times*, London, 16 October 2003

Peachey, Paul. 'Pay someone else to hire the plumber.' *The Independent*, London, 8 October 2002

Pullman, Philip. 'They're reading like robots.' *Sunday Times*, London, 6 April 2003

'Retirement Ages and Pension Ages – a Complex History,' *Social Security Journal*, Australia, June 1996

Revell, Janice. 'Beware the Pension Monster.' *Fortune*, 9 December 2002

Revell, Janice. 'Bye-Bye Pension.' *Fortune*, 17 March 2003

Russel, Cecilia. 'Celebrities demand fee to endorse youth campaign.' *The Star* (SA), 25 January 1999

Schoonakker, Bonny. 'Video game junkie gets an early fix.' *Sunday Times* (SA), 31 January 1999

Shevel, Adele. 'Global grooming.' *Sunday Times* (SA), 13 July 2003

Smith, David. 'Life just got better.' *Sunday Times*, London, 8 December 2002

'The Boomer stats.' Baby Boomer HeadQuarters: www.bbhq.com

'The Crumbling pillars of old age.' *The Economist*, 27 September 2003

'The Future of Work.' *The Economist*, 29 January 2000

'The hot spot.' *The Telegraph*, London, 22 June 2003

Theil, Stefan. 'Young at heart.' *Newsweek*, 16 September 2002

Tozer, James. 'A snapshot of the millennium baby.' *Daily Mail*, London, 17 July 2003

Usher, Rod. 'Revels without a cause.' *Time*, 19 August 1999

Wendleton, Kate. 'The old gray mares. They're better than they used to be.' The 5 O'Clock Club.

Zamichov, Nora. 'Jogging your memory.' *Los Angeles Times*, 20 June 2003

Websites

TomorrowToday.biz's Generations Website. http://www.tomorrowtoday.biz/generations

Amman, Keith. *The Shadowrun Generations*. http://www.interware.it/users/paolo/sr2/society/srsoc.html

Brett, Jim. *The Silent Generation*. http://www.csulb.edu/~wwwing/Silents/

Fishman, Ann A. *Generational-Targeted Marketing: How to Grow Bigger by Thinking Smaller*. http://home.gnofn.org/chamber/fishman/menu.html

Harris, Louis. *Generation 2001: A Survey of the First College Graduating Class of the New Millennium*. http://www.northwesternmutual.com/2001/

Howe, Neil. *The New Generation Gap*. http://xroads.virginia.edu/~DRBR/generation.txt

Huitt, William G. *Maslow's Hierarchy of Needs*. http://chiron.valdosta.edu/whuitt/col/regsys/maslow.html

Jogensen, Lawrence C and Kirt Sechooler. *The Millennial Files* http://www.mmmfiles.com/

Maier, Jieranai T. *Boomers International*. http://boomersint.org/bindex.html

Manolis, Chris and Aron Levin. 'A Generation X Scale: Creation and Validation' In *Educational and Psychological Measurement*, August 1997. http://www.epnet.com

Margaret Mead. http://www.amnh.org/Exhibition/Expedition/Treasures/Margaret_Mead/mead.html

Newsweek and Kaplan. *Careers 2000*. http://www.kaplan.com/newsweek

Murray, Bill. *The Time Page*. http://www.timepage.org/.

Pritchett, Price. *New Work Habits for a Radically Changing World*. http://www.pritchettnet.com/

Strauss, William and Neil Howe. *The Fourth Turning: Website*. http://www.fourthturning.com

The Longwave and Social Cycles Resource Centre. http://web.1-888.com/longwave/

The Nintendo Generation. http://www.nap.edu/readingroom/books/techgap/nintendo.html

The World Future Society. http://www.wfs.org/

X . . . The Next Generation. http://www.hrlive.com/reports/genx.html

Leadership Development Planning. http://www.mapnp.org/library/ldr_dev/ldr_dev.htm

Overview of Leadership in Organizations. http://www.mapnp.org/library/ldrship/ldrship.htm

Retaining Volunteers (CASANet). http://www.casanet.org/program-management/volunteer-manage/retentn.htm

Volunteer Recruitment, Tips from Field: Keep Them Coming Back. http://www.txserve.org/mgmt/volrec/tips.html

Cooper, David EK. *Nonprofit Leadership – The Leader of the Future.* http://www.thepaf.org/palc/ldrship.htm

The Internet Movie Database. http://www.imdb.com

Other

Massey, Morris. *What You Are Is Where You Were When.* Video, Magnetic Video Corporation. http://www.nfb.ca/FMT/E/MSN/15/15568.html (1976).